ACQUAINTED
WITH GRIEF

By the same author

THAT AWFUL MESS ON VIA MERULANA

ACQUAINTED WITH GRIEF

CARLO EMILIO GADDA

TRANSLATED FROM THE ITALIAN BY WILLIAM WEAVER

GEORGE BRAZILLER *NEW YORK*

AN INTRODUCTORY NOTE BY THE TRANSLATOR

*C*ivil engineer Carlo Emilio Gadda, at some point between the two World Wars, worked for a time in South America, in Argentina. But readers of *Acquainted with Grief* (*La cognizione del dolore*) would be mistaken if they considered the book—set in an imaginary South American and Southern Hemispheric country—a realistic chronicle based in any way on Gadda's experiences during that period. As the author himself makes clear in many hints, veiled and less veiled, the country of Maradagàl is Italy and the Néa Keltiké province is Lombardy. From this equation, others can be derived: Lukones is the town of Longone, where Gadda spent much of his childhood and young manhood; Pastrufazio is Milan; the national poet Caçoncellos whose toothbrush patriotic literary societies are so anxious to preserve for posterity surely has many points in common with d'Annunzio; General Pastrufazio is Garibaldi; Maradagàl's smelly cheese, croconsuelo, is Gorgonzola; the Serruchón mountains are Lombardy's Resegone, celebrated by Manzoni. And so on.

Naturally, these equivalents are not of any great

importance. As the distinguished Italian critic Gianfranco Contini says of this novel, "If it is a *roman à clef*, the key is a skeleton-key." Still, one door—the important one—opened by that key must be identified, especially for the foreign reader not familiar with Gadda's other work or with the principal facts of his life. *La cognizione del dolore* is, to a great extent, autobiographical. In fact, as another Gadda authority, Giancarlo Roscioni, says, "Gadda never invents anything." And, to appreciate fully the profound humanity, the many subtleties of *La cognizione del dolore*, the reader must realize at once that Gonzalo, the son, the central figure, is the author's self-portrait.

Self-portrait, not photograph. Gadda's description of Gonzalo (at the end of the second chapter of the book) is a lacerating, biting caricature of the sober, fastidiously neat, tall, stooping Gadda who is occasionally—and reluctantly—seen at Roman literary gatherings. Like Gonzalo, the Lombard scene, the bourgeois villas of the Brianza region, and the peasants are scrutinized through the same penetrating, but sometimes deforming, lens.

Again it would be a mistake to underline too much the satirical aspect of the novel. With characteristic shyness or slyness, Gadda introduces his protagonist only after a long wait. And immediately the mood, the hue of the book change. As if, after a sprightly prelude, the tempo suddenly shifted to andante. The opening chapter is purposely misleading: we are in a comic-opera land, where even something as bitterly hated as fascism is reduced to the satirically presented Nistitúo (whose sinister capacities are, however, also suggested as the book proceeds). For a moment, it looks as if Gonzalo, too, will be a figure of fun, a greedy misanthrope and *malade imaginaire*. But even before he finally does appear on the scene, with the conversation between the doctor and the maid Battistina, the son of the Pirobutirro household becomes a darker, fuller character. And, at his entrance, the mood of the book loses its gaiety, which returns, later, only in brief flashes.

Readers of Gadda's *Pasticciaccio* (written a few years after *La cognizione del dolore*) will recall the author's fine, digressive rages. Several are present here, though it is Gonzalo, rather than the author directly, who is seized by these accesses of fury: against church bells, personal pronouns (symbolically), *nouveau riche* vulgarity, advertising. The rage also is directed against himself and, especially, against his mother.

In some of his nonfiction works Gadda hints at the profoundly tormented and tormenting relationship between himself and his mother, who—like the Señora in this book—was of German origin, a cultivated woman, a schoolteacher, widowed young and with little money to support her family, yet with social and educational ambitions for them. The social ambitions were summed up in the tenacious possession of the anti-economical villa in the country, one of the leading motives of the *Cognizione*. Other facts of Gadda's background may also be helpful to the reader unfamiliar with the rest of his work. His father came from a distinguished Italian family, of some means, which the older Gadda lost in a series of industrial speculations, so that the author was brought up in an atmosphere of genteel poverty, exacerbated by the typically Italian middle-class mania for keeping up appearances, for making a *bella figura*. The author's brother, who haunts *La cognizione del dolore* like an omnipresent ghost, was killed in the First World War. Gadda's War Journal, recently published in Italy more or less in its entirety, indicates the author's almost pathological attachment to his brother, an attachment

vii

tinged also with jealousy because of the mother's preference for this older son.

The lasting scars of the relationship explain, in part, why the *Cognizione* was never finished. For the same reason, the incomplete third section (translated here) has never been published in the original Italian, by explicit veto of the author, who has referred to it as a self-inflicted wound. In fact, it is virtually unrevised and, perhaps even in translation, it will be seen to have less Gaddian involution. It is considerably less baroque than the preceding chapters.

Baroque is an adjective often applied to Gadda, and it is one he dislikes. He has written an answer to the critical slogan "Gadda is baroque." "The world is baroque," he replies, "and Gadda has perceived and portrayed its baroqueness." And he gives the same response to accusations of being grotesque. In any case, the style of *La cognizione del dolore* is considerably different from that of *Quer pasticciaccio brutto de via Merulana*. The latter, Gadda's "Roman" novel, is a dazzling linguistic display, with many passages written in Roman dialect, with liberal admixtures of Milanese, Venetian, and Neapolitan. *La cognizione* is linguistically (though not stylistically) simpler. An Italian scholar has made an extended study of the language of *La cognizione*, and he concludes that, in it, dialect accounts for only three percent of the words. Here, classical influences are much more frequently at work, not only in the direct quotations from Horace and Virgil, but in numerous echoes from other Latin writers. One must, by the way, take Gadda's Spanish with a grain of salt; as he does frequently with Italian, he has not hesitated to invent Spanish words when he requires them. Proper names, too, often have connotative echoes, and even Maradagàl's humble maize, or banzavóis, probably derives its name from pancia vuota (empty belly, in Italian).

Written between 1938 and 1941, *La cognizione del dolore* first came out—like Gadda's *Pasticciaccio*—in installments, in the Florentine literary review *Letteratura*. The fact that the novel appeared under fascism explains the indirectness of Gadda's references to the regime; his anti-fascism is much more explicit in the *Pasticciaccio*. The novel was first published, by the firm of Giulio Einaudi of Turin, in 1963. The third part, as indicated elsewhere, was translated from the manuscript. Apparently only a few pages remain unwritten, in which it would have been made clear that the mother's aggression was the work of the Nistitúo guard, while she could not help but suspect the intervention, too, of her unhappy son.

Again, the translator would like to thank the author for his kind help. For many explanations of particularly obscure passages, he has benefited again from the assistance of Giancarlo Roscioni and, for the preparation of the footnotes, of Ariodante Marianni, a dauntless fellow translator. A final tribute must be paid to Signora Molly Schacherl for her patient and rapid typing of the manuscript.

—WILLIAM WEAVER

Monte San Savino, May 1968

ACQUAINTED WITH GRIEF

PART   I

I

*I*n those years, between 1925 and 1933, the laws of Maradagàl, which is a country of few resources, made it optional for landowners to join, or not join, the night watchmen's organizations of the various provinces (Nistitúos provinciales de vigilancia para la noche); this alternative was accorded in consideration of the fact that these same owners were already subject to levies and to numerous taxes whose total, in certain cases, equaled and even exceeded the cash value of the few ears of banzavóis that the rural property managed to produce, Ceres and Pales willing, every leap year: or rather, in that one year out of four when there was no drought, or no persistent rain at sowing or harvesting time, and when the caravan of diseases hadn't passed that way. Feared above all others was the ineluctable "Peronospera banzavoisi" mentioned by Cattaneo: it causes, in the hapless plant, a drying and crumbling of the little roots and stem in the very months of development: and for the desperate and the hungry, it leaves, instead of corn, a powder similar to that left behind by the termite, or a gimlet, in an oak beam. In certain regions hail also had to be taken into consideration. This

3

last scourge, to tell the truth, doesn't have a great effect on the wrapped ear of the banzavóis, which is a kind of sweetish maize proper to that climate. Climate or sky, in certain regions, as hail-bearing as the sky that hangs over certain half-acres of our own unforgettable Brianza: a land, if ever there was one, carefully acred out.

As is well known, Maradagàl in 1924 emerged from a bitter war with Parapagàl, a bordering state with a population of the same ethnic origin that had gradually immigrated there from Europe, beginning in the first decades of the seventeenth century. This too is known. The few Indios who survived the Reconquest and lasted into the century and the clamor of the radio live in tribes and almost in herds in the distant "Territorios," blessed with a special tuberculosis of their own and a special syphilis, and happy also in their distance from the *gendarmerie:* drawn, some of them, and with great effort, by the obstinacy of a few Piedmontese missionaries, into the fold of the Faith of Christ; from whence nevertheless they still take leave on occasion for one of their deplorable orgies of caña-drinking, which leave them for a few days lying on the ground, along some path, like stones. Each of the two nations insists it has won the war and lays the terrible burden of responsibility on the other. In the years after 1924, therefore, both in Maradagàl and in Parapagàl, there were war veterans, some of whom belonged and still belong to the worthy category of the disabled: and they limped, or had scars on their faces, or a stiffened limb, or they lacked a foot or an eye. It is not unusual, in the more squalid cafés of Maradagàl or Parapagàl, to be stared at by a glass eye. Of other veterans it was known they had been wounded, though this wasn't evident; the scars, hidden by clothing, were thus cheated of the meed of

4

admiration to which they were entitled. There were also some deaf from the war.

The use of the noun "war" as an adjective expressing cause or origin, followed by a hyphen and a second adjective such as "invalid," "disabled," "blind," "deaf," "lame," and so on, had given rise to a certain jest: of questionable taste, to be sure, though not forbidden by the law, since it was innocent. It sometimes happens that life, which is loquacious, unfortunately oversteps the bounds of deference and composure. And so at Terepàttola, on the lower slopes of the Cordillera, the Terepattolese girls would shout "war-fool!" at some swain whose hand was a bit too bold, though after ten minutes of sulking, he would be forgiven and peace would be made, as the envoys of Maradagàl had made it with the envoys of Parapagàl.

"Fool" in Maradagalese is "mocoso," and the precise expression therefore is: "¡Mocoso de guerra!"

Now in fact, when it came to signing up the watchmen for the Nistitúos de vigilancia para la noche, it was decreed that preference should be shown to war veterans, without excluding from their ranks the glorious wounded, provided of course that they seemed suited to the job: which meant still able-bodied—sufficiently robust, indeed, to be able to carry out an assignment of that sort, which can require intervention *manu armata* and presupposes in any case a certain degree of strength and consequent authority in the watchman, so that he can effectively persuade the outlaw to follow him to the nearest police station. Follow him or, to be more specific, precede him, since with certain characters it's better to have them before than behind.

It's true that in Maradagàl there are guards who are no taller than a portion of cheese; but this, in addi-

5

tion to being a nice Tuscan idiom, is also more the exception than the rule. And moreover one suspects that, small though they are, they reveal, when necessary, an unsuspected strength. In any case dwarfs, properly speaking, and humpbacks are severely excluded from guard service day or night and from conscription in general. Another perquisite of the night guard is that of perceiving alertly all suspicious noises, which might be, to give an example, the shuffle of the cloth shoes of a couple of thieves on the ground floor of a villa, or the clink of a silver fork falling into a sack at night—inside the same villa, naturally. In theory the night watchman, the ideal guard, should be equipped with very special ears and have all five senses in perfect condition: a bloodhound's scent and a cat's retina, which can glimpse mice on the run, they say, in the darkness of basements. A deaf guard or a half-deaf one is scarcely conceivable: and even in Maradagàl, in fact even in the postwar period, such a guard was conceived with difficulty. But the tissue of collectivity, more or less everywhere in the world perhaps, and in Maradagàl more than elsewhere, has a happy tendency to forget, at least from time to time, the imperative end aimed at by the daily work of the single cells. And then, in the tissue's compact warp, the charitable rents of exception are unraveled. Ethical purpose and carnal benevolence toward the human creature emit contradictory calls. If the former wins, a new series of events is initiated, burgeoning like a bud, and then a branch, from the teleological pole.

As far as hiring war-deaf in the Nistitúos de vigilancia was concerned uncertainty therefore reigned: and certain appeals through which the concerned and the rejected felt it was opportune to apply to the law, as having been discriminated against, in the end received, from the law itself, ambivalent replies. In

6

Terepàttola yes, and in Pastrufazio no. Even the two Courts, to which the appeal had been made in some cases where scrupulous distinctions could most easily be defined, had occasion to make contrasting statements, in the elaborate sentences laid down by their more elucubrative magistrates—who felt called upon to issue, from case to case, divergent decisions: or rather indecisions. From these came further appeals and petitions to the Supreme Court and postponements for further scrutiny, to last for all eternity: a stroke of luck! for the tobacconist who sold the official forms at his shop on the corner. Then some very odd situations developed—imputable perhaps to the mechanism of electoral favor, which becomes the province of the incapable and the worthless but vote-bearing: and this must be counted among the least confessable and most persistent characteristics of democratic and republican mores in virtually all South America. In the province of Zigo-Zago, for example, in 1926 a guard with bicycle was hired who was to keep under surveillance an area two kilometers long: only slightly frequented, true enough, by thieves, who had nothing there they could rob except stubble. The poor guard had a stiff leg: and he had managed to pass it off as a war disability, whereas it was really a case of ankylosis of the knee, of probable though remote syphilitic origin. He used a bicycle with a single pedal, on the right, for his good leg; and on the other side, larboard, he let his left leg hang rigidly, like a gangway over the side of the ship. In local myth and lore, after a while the stiff and nonpedaling leg was transformed into a leg of aluminum. When chicken thefts occurred, they all said: "Oh, well, for a mere chicken theft!" And when something more serious took place, they all said: "Poor man, after all, he has to keep an eye on half the province! And with that aluminum leg!" Others said: "He has a wife and children!" Others, with a shrug: "Live and let live!" They're kindly people, in Maradagàl.

Then there was the little rural scandal in Lukones, in the arrondimiento of the Serruchón, which is in the province of Novokomi. Lukones: a village with an oficina de correos (post office), a telephone, a midwife, a tobacconist, a doctor, the Lion d'or Hotel, public wash basins, and of course a parish church; with a few curves, it is crossed by the provincial highway that from the station and poplar woods of Prado leads windingly to Iglesia. Prado is connected by ferrocarril both with Novokomi and Pastrufazio: the track continues as far as Cabeza (a single line), where a red cap on the head of a man of forty awaits the gasp of the train. Pastrufazio, the most dynamic city of the country, spatters its suburbs—rather sticky and rather filthy—to west and south, a hundred kilometers or so beyond the morainic ranges that encircle Prado, in the green plain.

The Serruchón, which gives its name, as the most outstanding feature, to the arrondimiento, is a long, steep mountain all triangles and peaks, like the withersthreat of the dinosaur: rising almost horizontally except for the up and down of those cusps and relative dips, bulkheads for the wind. A very high gray wall lowers suddenly over the idyll, with grim cliffs: and broad passages along the towers where cold shadows lurk at dawn and persist, with their cold, for the whole first cycle of the morning. Beyond black peaks the sun suddenly shines: its rays break against the ragged line of the mountain and are spread beyond toward Prado, descending to gild the earth's mists, from which hills emerge among the shrouded lakes. Something similar, in name and even more in appearance, to Manzoni's Resegone. There some bolder tower (with matutinal bells) rips the gilded veil of the fogs; the mist, a white tufting, stretches

8

out in a thread, is lost, whistles through distant echoes among the hills, and twists: it bears the crammed, black crowd of poor men, who spill from it toward the factories and the plants or, on the scant river, the smith's drop hammer.

The scandal wasn't much: it was really a poor excuse for a scandal, and it came out, when the September Madonna was already near, thanks to an unknown cloth merchant and the Lukones doctor, who then herborized more exact data from a medical colonel on his summer holiday.

One fine day, all of a sudden, it was universally learned that a certain Pedro Mahagones, namely the bicycle guard of that zone, whom all knew as Manganones or Pedro, wasn't Manganones at all, still less was he Pedro: those were instead the surname and Christian name of a maternal great-uncle and the guard's real name was, instead, Gaetano Palumbo. In those two years of guardship he had lengthily commemorated, more or less with everyone, the kindness of his uncle and godfather, carrying about the world—to honor him the more—his first and last names; and he would drain a glass from time to time, moved, and perhaps with the gleam of a half-tear behind his virile smile, to the uncle's health, which meant and could only mean the health of his soul, that is to say the true, definitive, and eternal health, the only kind that really matters; since his dear uncle's mortal remains had already been in the earth for eight years.

But his uncle had brought him up, Pietruccio who then became Pedro: and had cared for, loved, guarded, nursed (with a bottle), protected, educated, advised, and beaten him—oh! for his own good, and he truly deserved a beating sometimes—and even made him wee-wee and do "number two," and then washed his little behind, a child's of course, like a wet nurse. As if the child were his own son.

Therefore tears and a drop of bitter to his memory, but mostly scrounged cigarettes, from all the tobacconists in the area.

The new name aroused a certain surprise, both in the villagers and in the vacationers, some of the latter having occasion to find "There was something about his face. . . ." It was, above the imposing corpulence of his person, and resting on the buttoned collar of the uniform, a broad and paternal face with a clipped red brush of a moustache, and a short, straight nose: the eyes were sunken, tiny, glistening, darting, with the bright sparks of a blade's flash in his gaze, attenuated by his visor, which however couldn't extinguish it entirely. When he took off his cap, as if to let his cabeza steam, his forehead then appeared, high but narrower than the cheekbones, and receding with some modulations of hue into the dome of the white, bald cranium, which was, truth to tell, very clean, that is without freckles of dust and grease kneaded together. Then, visorless, the eyes remained alone in command; they wounded the interlocutor with an expression of demand and expectation; one had the sensation of absolutely having to pay something, a sort of virtual fine, by law—because this is what the law required—receiving in return for it a pink or pale-blue chit, as a receipt, detached from a little book with counter chits which he could draw from a side-pocket of his tunic with extraordinary naturalness. Everyone, or at least almost everyone, in the Lukones area had tried hard and with all the will in the world, since they had paid up, to form an idea of those perilous rounds in the dark: and they also had finally swallowed the importance and the delicacy of the assignment that weighed on his shoulders, through all the length and

10

darkness of the night, and everybody now believed in it, in this importance: since a man's good name, in South America, or an official's notoriety doesn't always derive from the uselessness of his duties.

Mahagones-Palumbo—this information also spread rapidly and was the kernel of the scandal—had in due time, in 1925, been granted a pension, sixth degree, fifth category, namely almost the maximum of his rank, because it was found he had been deafened in both ears by the "penetrating and lacerating" explosion of a grenade. In the action on Hill 131.

He had thought up the two adjectives himself on the spot, as he was recasting the event for the consumption of the Lukonesi, when finally he felt himself called to account by the winks and the hints of the peasants. And he proffered these adjectives with such a firm and authoritative tone, supported also by his uniform, that he froze the smiles, every time, as they grazed the lips of his listeners. It really seemed to everyone that there existed, in a war, common, ordinary grenades (which in fact had killed their brothers or sons), not penetrating and still less lacerating; whereas Palumbo's grenade had been instead a special one, of a high class: and coming from a distinguished cannon, far more frightful than the usual ones, good enough no doubt on weekdays, for killing peasants haphazardly.

So they were forced to indicate the grenade in that way. Those two adjectives were taken very seriously and I would say appreciated in a very special degree by the girls and women of the village, and by the ladies in the villas who daydreamed about the matter for weeks, having nothing better to do in that period, despite the undeniable and multivarious resources of their brains.

The action on Hill 131, the action on Hill 131.

The whole Serruchón arrondimiento, for quite a

long time, knew no other hill save Hill 131. Palumbo's narrative was given credence. Whatever may have been incompatible between deafness and guarding was probably annulled by the religion of memories. Valor has a true cult of its own, of true spirits. Everyone repeated "the action on Hill 131, the action on Hill 131," as if it were a universally known event. Waterloo, Aboukir, Porta Tosa.[1] And this, apart from the idea that Hill 131, lost and recaptured a couple of times per week during a whole six-month period, had known, by itself, more than ninety-two actions, each more murderous than the last.

Pedro smoked a great deal, perhaps more for looks and vanity than out of need or habit. Smoking helped him greatly with the women, who like smoke, and who consider it, perhaps rightly, a pleasant foretaste of fire. The action—at which the Lukonesi wanted to smile, but which they finally had to have Pedro narrate despite himself, a very detailed, endless report, overcoming his extreme reluctance to talk about himself—the action, it emerged, had been an attack, preceded by a suitable barrage from the Maradagalese artillery and followed by a "bombardment" (so he said, very wretchedly) from the Parapagalese, which then led to a counterattack. Then there was a "counterbombardment" and a second counterattack, this one Maradagalese, and finally a thunderstorm, which looked like a downright cloudburst, hailed as savior by both sides. In the narrative, which gathered attentive listeners in every tobacconist's in the area, and which was finally stereotyped in a report without too many contradictions and even fairly polished, though watered down in that way, various military locutions were introduced, virile ones, without any bombast, such as "slaughter," "risk our necks," "we'd just about had it," and others of that sort: they gave the Lukonesi and the Serruchonesi, al-

12

ready half-persuaded by the sultriness of the tardy new moon, an idea of what seriousness is, and simplicity, and true valor, which, when it's authentic, and not dragged in with pulleys, is also blended with modesty and avoids big words. Pedro wasn't a gentleman from a villa, like those whose villas he guarded, at night; nor was he, God forbid! a writer: a baroque and labyrinthine writer, like Jean Paul, or Carlo Gozzi, or Carlo Dossi, or some other Carlo even worse than these two, already so sorry in themselves;[2] good perhaps at making use of war, and the sorrows of war, in order to fiddle about with them and split hairs and produce sterile witticisms, with a light pen. No, Pedro was simple, pure in heart; and so one had to believe in his bare, effective word, his "slice his guts out," tossed casually on the zinc bar of the tobacconist's amid the rinsing of the glasses, like a counterdrink or a counterpacket; "his" war was to be believed in completely. He had a leather belt with holster and pistol; it was immediately clear that he knew how to use weapons.

In reality, in the Maradagàl-Parapagàl war, Hills 131—or 151 or 171—has existed by the handful, thanks to the contradictory resolutions of the opposing strategists, who scraped over them, over those hills, their massacred battalions, as if they had been safety matches: and any veteran, however slightly imaginative, or perhaps even an Indio deserter, had a wide choice.

The first rumors concerning the true identity and the pension and thence also the heroism of Pedro now again Gaetano and his ex-deafness or rather his recovered hearing spread in the Lukones area, as said before, thanks to a "merchant" with a rather loose tongue who traveled third class to Prado and came up, then, on foot, with a kind of cousin or aide after him and with a cubical and heavy sack on his shoulder, filled

13

(as was revealed a short time later) with bargain lengths of stuff—a cloth that was very soft to the touch and extremely hairy. The wondrous news spread then in the tree of the collectivity by the natural process of absorption, made possible by an active endosmosis: the fresh and stinging greed of the uncorrupt, the vital toiling of the cells who have no better epos to elaborate.

And a hand was lent, right willingly and happily, more or less by all, men and women. Among the first was Peppa, the washerwoman, she of the basket heaped high with wrung sheets: a man-woman harder and tougher than ever stevedore was, with her lopsided burden on her arm and therefore the axis of the person hanging from the other side; tenacious and poor, and yellow in the face along the painful rockery of the little roads climbing toward the towered villas with lightning rods and sometimes, in the wind, a flag; stopping, every now and then—basket on the ground—to rest and catch her breath, but not to catch it too much, not so much as to prevent proper use of her tongue in the event that her halt was shared by some goodwife coming down the road.

After the now-remote death of her Mama she had brought up, besides herself, her seven brothers and sisters, whom she had taught in the fine season to do without shoes and therefore without stockings, and some of whom, in the past few years, were already working in the factories or on the land; and for one indeed, the oldest, she already had nicely prepared in mothballs the black wedding suit, given her by the Señora's son, who had inherited from his forebears that suit at the age of five but at forty-five still hadn't found a bride.

In those days her cow had taken sick, and she had even purged her: but the animal was a constant worry to her.

14

Second, or among the seconds, was the barefoot fishwife Beppina, famous in all the territory of Lukones and in the neighboring villas, not so much for her trade in whitefish as for her brisk and rather Amazonic way of pissing (time is money): and she directed her pee to a nobly agronomical end, as will be specified below. This second Giuseppa or Beppa was brisk also in her speech, hammer-like indeed, or even monosyllabic, and yet she was no less effective than other women. And then—things come in threes—Pina, also known as Pinina del Gôepp, in the registry Giuseppina Citterio née Voldehagos, who was the dwarf wife of the chief gravedigger and always dressed in black, either out of respect for her husband's profession or because she was the inheritress of mourning left off by some of her shameless benefactresses.

These three had promptly taken on the job, with other women and husbands and priests and tavern keepers and coachmen and the Lukones postman, of spreading in their way that mess which had been carried up there by the "merchant," mixing it up even further, if that were possible; and Peppa had been the first to bring it to the ear of the Señora, in Villa Pirobutirro. Beyond whose wall, along the rocky little road, bold corn cockles, like whips, put forth swollen drupes pale blue against the September azure sky, plums, to be sure, wall plums: forbidden to the passerby.

The cloth merchant (we might as well exhaust this stupid story and be rid of it once and for all) was not, obviously, a merchant from that area; he came from very far away and he had to return afar, precisely because of his trade. He managed to sell a few bolts of hairy cloth to the more clever Lukonesi and after a few hours he vanished.

Thus all merchants of his nature and class vanish.

They spread out cloths and calls of invitation, ladies! gentlemen! in the churchyard on a fine September morning, they discuss and syllogize at length, unwearying, with sudden summons to coresponsibility directed at the dazed observers in the front row, and so throughout the whole morning, as long as it lasts, until, sack crammed again, toward the hour when the stomach is a cave, they vanish—as an apparition of the Madonna would vanish —and from that moment on not a word is heard of them again, of them or of their cousin.

That morning Pedro was late. He had lingered in certain villas to produce the bills and had had to wait for his money, argue over a slight increase, and then sign two or three times on two or three bluish papers, one per villa—an operation, this business of signing, a bit less easy for him than taking the receipt book from his pocket.

Eight o'clock had struck. And so he had come down slowly, pushing his bicycle, sleepy after his night of guarding, taking care to avoid with his soles and his tires the greenish and muddy pats plopped by the cows along the little road, all stones, that leads into the village agora, at the tobacconist's corner. There, at the very door of the shop, he bumped into the merchant, who, breathless and exhausted, had left his cousin-helper a bit to one side to guard the sack, and was about to go in and ask for a "tamarisk and water" to be served him, after a long inner struggle. He had also taken off his starched collar, which he was now holding in his hand and which was visibly soaked with sweat and dyed by the aniline green necktie.

The two looked at each other and, it seems, recognized each other immediately as neighbors (so they said in the Trecento), that is to say, fellow villagers or countrymen, as they say today. There was a moment's hesita-

16

tion, in both; then a sudden and common cry; the first interjections were followed by a whole confetti of wonderments, joys, demands for news, which summoned a number of women to their windows, including Peppa, in the alleyway, just before the mouth of the street. She looked out, all ears and eyes, hanging up her stockings to dry, and she seemed to drink in every word. After which the two men, that is when they had recovered from their surprise, reached a more relaxed jabbering, quite jovial, though Mahagones maintained a bit more reserve; and they decided also to embrace. Then there came fresh news, memories, nostalgia, but in a tone by now more restrained: and Josés, Pedros, Gonzalos, and Fernandos in abundance (as if one were to say, in Italy, Pasquales and Peppinos), all and each with his question mark, who had married, who had shot himself; and the conjuring up of girls, the Ineses, Mercedeses, Doloreses, Carmelitas—¡niñas queridas! ¡y que guapas!—young things a moment ago and now already grandmothers at twenty-six; and finally the two men ended by going into the tiny and filthy shop where they sell tallow candles and pieces of washing soap, as well as certain tobaccos with Greek names, or Macedonian, or Tuscan, for use of the Turk-Celtic population of the Serruchón. They greeted, beyond the dirty panes, the limpid morning sun that had only then appeared in the valley, with a cherry squash and a shot of grappa, raised high in a toast from the puddle of the zinc trough. Neither of the two paid, each supposing, out of delicacy, that his friend would pay.

Then they said good-bye. The tobacconist, who still had to wash his face and remove again his pants in order to slip on the drawers he had omitted, said nothing.

Though a natural and I would say a necessary conspiracy of silence tends inevitably to be established

17

among countrymen, or fellow villagers, or neighbors, as you choose to call them, the desire to appear informed and to seem important and the lack of any solid share or interest in the "societas bonorum vinorum" defeats, on occasion, the wink of natural, silent conspiracy.

The merchant, a short time later, in selling his bargain cloths in the little square and in unrolling the cloth —oh! certainly not English, nor even from Biella—before the yellow of the faces and the jeweled curiosity of the glances, as he whirled his tongue for whole half-hours till you couldn't understand where the devil he got the needed saliva, and after having mixed witticisms and gibes of public domain but extremely rare for the gaping Lukonesi, with erroneous war memories and stereotyped jokes of the time of the Reconquest, and false memories with sighs, and sighs with pyropes, some perhaps well found and poured into an ear with a searing tremolo of passion, of the odorous peasant girls of the Keltiké (they didn't grasp the meaning, these squat girls, but they blushed *quand même* and nudged each other, twisting their necks and hiding their faces in both hands, as if in shame; but the hands were slightly parted; beyond that fissure and the fingers there were lips, eyes)— after having allowed his soul-tongue to pirouette in that way for almost the duration of a Solemn High Mass—he began to drop, in Pedro's direction, a remark here, a word there, an extra half-sentence, as he continued croaking, gesticulating, rushing, recovering himself, and waving his cloths like flags. Pedro had gone off, then had come back through the square, but he had stopped a bit to one side, with his bicycle, and he gazed upon the scene from the distance, able to hear only the cries of "Ladies! Gentlemen!" but not the remarks and the half-whispered proposals that the man clickety-clack slipped swiftly between one chapter and the next of his

18

trade. Some people, from time to time, as he proceeded with the swiftly interpolated tale of "the activity of our firm whose sole aim is to satisfy people's needs," turned to look at Pedro, seeming to perceive him, gradually, in a new aspect—even though the uniform persisted, that is, the boots, the belt and holster, and the visored cap with metal badge—and then the peddler smiled at him, at Pedro, and Pedro smiled back, from the distance, paternally, with a blade's flash in his gaze, at the friendly smile.

When it was barely past eleven, the merchant managed to fascinate some Celtic peasants, and to persuade them to purchase: a surely unaccustomed triumph. Having trapped them in the circle of "my special and highly secret information," he succeeded in palming off on the more advanced a few half-lengths of the best, the most brown, and the most green, from which to make up a sack of a jacket, or a "pantalón," however hairy. But those half-sentences and that half-information hadn't fallen there without sequel: spun properly and woven together, they already formed almost a logical sequence. And they were enriched and complemented at the tavern toward noon where, in exchange for a more extended discourse, privately, in the little room with the green rugs when the cousin had been sent away on some pretext, the host Manoel Torre offered, to the merchant, a few glasses of wine—and two magnificent portions of croconsuelo. (This is a kind of Maradagàl Roquefort, but a bit fresher: fat, sharp, smelly enough to make an Aztec vomit, with rich mold of a dark green in the ignominy of its crevasses, very tasty to spread with the knife on the water-lily tongue and to chew over for quarter-hours in a foul mush; red wine was drunk over it to restore the trade-used tongue and recover saliva.)

And so it was that Mahagones became again Palumbo also for his night-guarded Serruchonesi, as he had always been, for that matter, at the Central Registry of the Republic and on his birth certificate. And this wasn't all: it was learned that, in addition to having obtained the maximum pension in his category, in 1925, he had lost it immediately thereafter; whereas after having lost his hearing on Hill 131, it was instead miraculously regained. His uncle, little by little, also died out in the veneration of the people of the Serruchón. Physically, in 1933, he had already been dead for eight years.

Villas, villas! Villettas—eight rooms—two baths; princely villas—forty rooms—spacious terrace overlooking lake and view of the Serruchón—garden, orchard, garage, porter's lodge, tennis court, drinking water, septic tank with seven-hundred-hectoliter capacity;—southern exposure, or western, or eastern, or southeastern, or southwestern, guarded by elms and antique shadows of the beeches against the winds from the mountains or the plain, but not against the monsoons of mortgages, which blow full blast also over the morainic amphitheatre of the Serruchón and along the poplar groves of Prado. With villas, villettas, villinas, with crammed ones and isolated ones, double villas and villa-homes, homely villas, the Pastrufazian architects had gradually bejeweled all the lovely and placid hills of the pre-Andean slopes, which, needless to say, "descend gently"[3] to the mild basins of their lakes. One was commissioned by an enriched manufacturer of motorcycle seats, another by a bankrupt dealer in silkworms, and another by a repainted count or a faded marquis; the first hadn't been able to grow tapering fingers and the second built his villa neither to become rich nor unfortunately to fail, since his nobility of spirit had been able to support him in the land of cocoons all at sea and motorcycles up in the air. Speaking of many of those villas, when they emerged more "cute" than ever from the locust trees or from the superabundant foliage of the banzavóis as if from a banana grove in the Canary Islands, one could have affirmed, in case of necessity and if one were a writer of talent, that they "flowered among the green cauls of the hills." Inasmuch as cauliflowers aren't our forte, we'll be content to point out how some of the most obvious of those polytechnic products, with the roofs all eaves and the eaves all spikes, with northern and glacial ugly triangles, had pretensions of being Swiss chalets, though continuing to roast in the immensity of the American mid-August: but the Oberland wood was, however, only painted (over the Serruchonese whitewash) and was a bit too faded from the downpours and the monsoons. Other little villas, where the eaves jutted out a bit more, rose, nice and pretty, with a pseudo-Sienese little tower or in Pastrufazian Norman, with a long and black pole on top, for lightning rod and flag. Still others were decked with little domes and various pinnacles, Russian style or almost so, a bit like radishes or upside-down onions, tile-covered and often polychrome, that is with the scales of a carnivalesque reptile, half yellow and half pale blue. So they had something of the pagoda and something of the spinning mill, and they were also a compromise between the Alhambra and the Kremlin.

Because everything, everything! had crossed the mind of the Pastrufazian architects, except perhaps the features of Good Taste. Umberto had appeared and Wilhelm and neoclassical and neo-neoclassical and the Empire and the Second Empire; art nouveau, Liberty, Corinthian, Pompeian, Angevin, Sommaruga's Egyptian, and Alessio Coppedé; and the caramelized-plaster casinos of Biarritz and Ostend, the Paris-Lyon-Méditerranée and the Fagnano-Olona,[4] Montecarlo, Indianapolis, the Middle Ages, that is, a Filippo Maria goodnaturedly arm-in-arm with the Caliph; and also Queen Victoria (of England), though sprawled on a Turkish ottoman (sic). And the functional twentieth century was also at work there, with its highly functional, leg-breaking stairs of pink marble, and endless porthole-windows, true quarterdeck scuttled, for the ironing room and the kitchen, and with a larder known as *office* (a foreign word that exercised an unimaginable fascination for the new Vignolas of Terepàttola). With latrines where the user had to be built in, they were so rational, fifty-five by forty-five; or, once inside, would be unable to call up even a suspicion of how one could ever abandon oneself: that is to any manifestation of one's free will. For, however free, they are however sometimes impelling and demand, in any case, a certain amount of elbow room. With gymnasium for the children, if they chose to indulge the whim, not seeming sufficiently supple and loose-limbed between one term's failure and the next, between the July examinations and the make-up exams in October. With terraced rooftops for sunbaths for the lady of the house, and the master also, who had longed for such a time, though in vain (both she and he), for the permanent bronze (of the meninges) so fashionable nowadays. With guillotine glass walls a meter-sixty wide in cement frames to summon inside the mountain and the lake, that is into the foyer, to which they give a delicious temperature—that of hardboiled eggs.

But this must suffice, as a list of these functional excogitations.

Among the villas on the San Juan hill, along the main road to Prado (they shot the red reflections of their panes against the taciturn twilight), there was also,

22

somewhat run-down, and at the same time strangely gangling, the Villa Maria Giuseppina, the Bertolonis' property. The twilight, and its melancholy and distant brow, seemed streaked, at times, with long horizontal wrinkles, of ash and blood. The villa had two towers and two lightning rods at the two extremities of a long, low central structure; so they suggested Siamese-twin giraffes, or giraffes incorporated, one into the other, after an ass-to-ass meeting followed by unification of the behinds. Of the two lightning rods one seemed to be pondering a special mischief of its own toward the northwest, oh! a real discovery, but diabolically functional— and the other, the same thing exactly toward the southeast—to pass on the thunderbolt, the minute it came within reach, to the "adjoining neighbor" on the right— and the other, instead, to the one on the left—respectively Villa Enrichetta and Villa Antonietta. Huddled there below, in a truly modest posture, and a bit subaltern with respect to the two appendages of Villa Giuseppina, and painted brightly, they had that meek, lymphatic air that most excites, or so it seems, the cruel sadism of the element.

This suspicion of our fanciful tension had become release of reality on July 21, 1931, during the persistence of a hailstorm without precedent in this century, which enriched with pesos papel all the plate-glass dealers in the arrondimiento.

To describe the fright and the shards of that untoward lightning is not even thinkable. But the buck-passing behavior of the two lightning rods had judiciary consequences—immediately directed along the road toward eternity—both in the civil courts, with claims for damages and interest, technical expertises, counter-expertises from the parties involved, and expertises of arbitration, never accepted contemporaneously by both

23

parties, however; and in the penal courts, for culpable neglect and damaging the property of others. And this is because the suit appeared, from its very beginning, of the most controversial nature. "What you expect from me," old Bertoloni, an immigrant from Lombardy, protested, "if that bastard didn't know himself which way to go?" The lightning bolt, in fact, when it realized it could no longer resist the call of nature, fell upon the little rod; but since that pole didn't seem sufficiently distinguished for him he sprang back at once like a demoniacal ball and crashed on the other, slightly longer, on the higher tower—and that is, definitively speaking, moving away from the earth, something absolutely incredible. There, on the silvered and gilded curl, he had blinded for a moment the terror of the chestnut trees, under the new guise of an oval ball—mad fire balanced on the tip—as if seized by a grim fury in his impotence, but in reality unraveling and tangling a skein and counterskein of elliptical orbits in alternating directions a couple of million times per second—all around the false gold of the metal curl, which in fact had melted, along with the silver-plate and also the iron, dripping down the pole like candle wax.

Then he flapped more or less everywhere on the roof, this hellish butterfly, and acted like an acrobat and sleepwalked along the roof ridge and the drainpipe, from which he overflowed into the cellar through the kind offices of the drainpipe itself, rising thence like a serpent, twisting in the copper cord of the little lightning rod, whose task instead was to get rid of him below, the fool. And in that new, raving resurrection he gave his all to the metal fence of the chicken yard behind the house of Maria Giuseppina (imagine the chickens!), which fence could hardly wait to redirect it *ipso facto* to the spiky gate, dividing the two adjoining properties, namely

24

Giuseppina and Antonietta: which introduced him in turn, wasting no time, into the latrine under repair from being clogged in the garage of Antonietta, whence, no one quite knew how, he immediately fell upon Enrichetta, skipping completely Giuseppina, in the middle. There, with a remarkable shot, and after the annihilation of a grand piano, he plunged into the dry tub of the maidservant. This time he flattened forever into the mysterious nullity of the earth's potential.

It was the various expertises that gradually allowed the sketching, with successive adjustments, in an atlas of official papers, this catastrophic *itinéraire*. That was at the beginning. In a second stage it was the expertises themselves that muddied the waters, or rather shuffled the cards, to such a degree that any outline of the route became unthinkable. The mason of Villa Enrichetta, with the common sense of all villagers, advanced a hypothesis of his own, for that matter highly plausible: that the final withdrawal of the yellow beast, so he called it, was due to his finding the latrine's pipes clogged, whereupon he couldn't make use of the passage necessary to such a lightning bolt. But the electrologues wouldn't hear of such a hypothesis, and they flourished differential equations, which also succeeded in complementing the rest, one can imagine to what joy on Captain Bertoloni's part.

Parallel to this, in the myth and lore of the Serruchón, the idea took shape that the pianoforte is a very dangerous instrument, to be carted out into the garden without wasting a moment as soon as a thunderstorm is seen approaching.

The mishap, for Captain Bertoloni, would still have been bearable but, just as the experts' reports were being drawn up by both parties and a first attempt at a procedure of arbitration was being celebrated, then—to cut short all hope of accord—a second lightning bolt fell on the three villas, now made brothers by the celestial "lubido"; that is, two years after the discharge of the washtub, in June of '33. The most bespectacled electro-technical engineers of Pastrufazio, having been summoned to yet another expertise, arrived *in locum* one splendid morning in mid-August with every sort of boxed instrument, very delicate ones, and ohmmeters and portable Wheatstone bridges of extreme fragility; but on that day in Terepàttola the obsequies of Carlos Caçoncellos were being performed—the great Maradagàl epic poet had died two days before, plunging the literary world into consternation and, to a special degree, all epic poets. So the engineers, in the deserted villa without even its watchman, were unable to achieve anything. For several years the Grand Old Man had rented the villa, where he was in the habit of spending the greater part of the summer tended by his faithful Giuseppina, training roses and amaranths and tomatoes in the "parterre" to the west of the terrace but refusing to bestow any care on the chicken coop—since he considered it, that coop, a banality unworthy of the sweet singer of Santa Rosa—and whose cockadoodledoos would surely have upset him in the polishing of his heroic alexandrines and certain iambic tetrameters, which were even more difficult. Only the maidservant, inside that rusty and lightning-struck enclosure, raised for him in secret a few melancholy louse-ridden chickens, which turned out, in practice, to be absolutely inedible.

Carlos Caçoncellos, as everyone knows, was the *aedo* of the Reconquest and of the Battle of Santa Rosa (May 14, 1817—a Sunday), the singer of the exploits of the Maradagalese cycle of the libertador. The whole Maradagalese epic of the nineteenth century is enlivened by the figure and the name of the libertador, General Juan Muceno Pastrufazio, the victor of Santa Rosa, terror of the "gringos," scatterer of the Indios, reconstructor of the city that bears his name; exalted in stupendous verses as the Belgrano and also the Moreno of Maradagàl, though on other poetic occasions they have also compared him to George Washington, Tamburlaine, Garibaldi, and Mazepa.

Sobre ese mismo—caballo hasta el Domingo
¡Vuela Usted! dando—nos el grito de guerra:
Como allá cuando—despavorido esta tierra
Dejó, en la sangre—y volvió espalda el gringo.[5]

That is, when the day of battle came, Sunday the fourteenth of May, 1817, in the plain of Santa Rosa, Nepomuceno Pastrufazio defeated the "ancient" conquistadores and immediately before the hordes of Indios in full revolt—it isn't clear whether against him or against those others.

Highly embarrassed after the Bard's decease, the Bertolonis didn't know what to do in order to keep body and soul together. Their need was immediate, to extract a few pennies from the ribs of the gangling and bechickened Giuseppina, to be able to pay the taxes, the experts, the lawyers, the interest on the mortgages—and to make the most urgent repairs.

They were highly embarrassed and dismayed, poor things, so many and so great were the troubles sown all around them and so many and so great the storm clouds that had been piling up over that Serruchonese treasure of theirs.

On the one hand, the public's idolatry of the Departed (who, it was said, had written about two hundred thousand Alexandrines and twenty-three thousand iambic tetrameters) forbade them in the most peremptory way to "remove even a pin" from the various rooms of Giuseppina—to disturb the way he himself, the Departed, had left them before he moved to the San José clinic, in Terepàttola; still, in the meanwhile, his slippers were mysteriously missing, as were a rubber douche and his toothbrush, and this even before the trental: certainly spirited away by some admirer and some fanatic collector of relics, so at least it was supposed. Which, in the press de izquierda, was immediately attributed to the "bourgeois ignorance of the owners" and to their "materialistic ignorance of the highest spiritual values."

On the other hand the republican papers were already conducting a great campaign, insisting that Villa Giuseppina should become the Poet's shrine, the temple of his memories, and that all his relics should be collected there, including his fishing line and, what was more important, his manuscripts, of which about fifty volumes had been published but the greater part lay, unpublished, in the various publishing houses of Maradagàl, which had a hard time, they say (and are having a hard time even now), in finding an outlet for them on the literary market, despite the high cultural level of Maradagalese society. According to some, the Villa Giuseppina should even, and without delay, be declared a national monument, after legal expropriation at the state's expense; and it should then be maintained by the state as well. But the state was already overburdened with monuments, ancient and modern, and the archeological society for pre-Columbian studies gave it no peace, managing to procure for it as many as twelve or fifteen monoliths a week, and tombs of Inca kings, which were received by the moustaches of the Minister of Instruction with the same joy as orphans are received in an asylum without funds.

So the law for the restoration of the toothbrush to its pristine splendor, with marble plaque and Gregorian inscription—*in dignitatem pristinam redactus, anno domini,* and so on—threatened to remain only a project. The tax collector, in the meantime, a very fine man for that matter and truly a man with an incisive pen, wasn't joking.

To exacerbate the situation, already terribly complicated for Bertoloni and his wife, who both suffered from myocarditis and were in the hands of physicians, engineers, bookkeepers, and lawyers, a third lightning bolt fell "unexpectedly" on the villa, unexpected also in the way it fell, namely, assisted by the lightning rods; and a strange rumor spread through all the lands and villas from Lukones to Prado and to Iglesia and as far as Terepàttola and to Novokomi (and this, truly, was the final blow for the hapless couple), according to which, it was said, at night the Villa Giuseppina was *hantée.* The rumors spoke of mysterious luminosities, of ghastly, or ghostly, nocturnal wings, and of spectral apparitions; some asserted that it was a single ghost, a monstrous figure of the Grand Old Man, and every time the same, especially on moonless nights and on Tuesdays and Fridays. The owl at midnight emitted three times its malicious and ominous cry and a bluish form, senile, was suddenly present. The horrible sunken cheeks denoted a sepulchral dwelling place, as did the two arcs of teeth which, lips withered, at times were revealed, shut, to deny any assent, and the flowing translucence of the beard, and the white, shapeless chlamys, like a shroud; and the head and hair haloed by an incorporeal horror: everything was cause to make him, with an inexpiable presence, blanch the tenebrous abandonment of the place.

From the chicken yard, where he appeared all of a sudden in his terrifying immobility when the excited insistence of the owl was not yet spent, in the funereal echo the specter moved without a footstep, as if passing in a vapor through the metal fence, to make the whole tour of the building: and having reentered into the chicken yard, he stayed at length in that enclosure of zinc-covered wire in the attitude of cursing with a broad and yet terrible gesture some few beings of very tiny stature—who however weren't there, and it could absolutely not be seen where they were. Then, passing through doors and bolts as if they were fog, saturated with horror and silence, he took to wandering through the house from cellar to attic, without, however, touching or uttering anything—only before the wash basin he lingered for hours, exalting or attenuating his own luminous intensity like a thermionic bulb and staring uninterruptedly at the soap dishes, the soap dishes!

In a pose full of majesty and wrath.

"This was all we needed!" exclaimed old Bertoloni when they reported those apparitions in the villa to him, describing in addition the character precisely as he presented himself in the chicken yard at midnight at the ominous and invisible summons of the owl. He, Bertoloni, was a Lombard immigrant who had become rich in a negocio of ironmongering; now, however, he was on the brink of ruin.

So, putting aside all thought of lucre, he pondered instead a solution on a smaller scale that would operate at least temporarily as amulet and double anti-evil-eyes to break that accumulation of absurdities that had been piling up, mountain-like, on the basic absurdity of the villa. And since it was also vacant, he thought, instead of the villa, to rent the porter's lodge, "at least that!" which was in itself a nice little house, which had five rooms, basement, attic, electricity, well, and separate septic tank and was thoroughly suitable to a respectable little family, such as, for example, that of a state official (whether he was of the customs or land registry or was a civil engineer or of the battle of wheat,[6] it was indifferent to him).

In this he was assisted not only by the direct intervention of heaven, which at the right moment never failed to rain down in his aid, as we have seen, but also by the three following circumstances: first, the lodge was quite a few paces distant from the villa proper and was excluded from the itineraries of the phantom, who, given the distance and the tenderness of his feet, was forced to ignore it. It was situated on the Prado high road, in a clump with other little houses and villas of the rank of lodge also and near a pleasant little tavern with a bough over the tables,[7] whence, that is, from the kitchen, a good aroma of stew every evening toward seven used to put superstitions to flight, of whatever nature they might be; and Bertoloni, though old and myocardical, understood this at once. Second, the medical colonel Di Pascuale, with a c—to whom he managed to rent it—at that time, namely, in the summer of '34, had already found wives or husbands for all his sons and daughters, and he kept only, with himself "and lady," a little maid about four feet tall (with two premature half-melons at wash-basin level) and, in turn, some grandson or granddaughter, no more than one at a time, as well as a certain reserve of underpants for both sexes. Third, this same Di Pascuale, brought up in a positivist atmosphere in the Maradagàl of President Uguirre, of Carlos Venturini, of Luis Coñara, of José Barrieto, and of others of that ilk, but above all in the Facultad Médica of Pastrufazio, and made still more skeptical by the exercise of his profession, as you will have occasion to read, had very little belief in the Madonna—this, alas, is true—but even less in ghosts. On the subject of the lightning bolts he limited himself to saying, "That was a crazy one" or "That was a bastard," according to his mood: in the first case with a shrug, in the other with a characteristic stubborn, vindictive expression, as if he were planning to avenge himself at the first encounter. He saw that the rental was to his advantage, the proprietor being screwed simultaneously both by the phantom and the glory of the Bard, by the democratic press and the republican—and by the true thunderbolt—and he signed the contract without hesitation. His lady wife approved.

Already during the first month in the villa he had won the affection of the local doctor by abstaining from causing him unseemly competition and from examining below cost the neighbors, namely the noisy and cousin-bearing families crammed four to a room in the little houses around the villa-lodge. Only once, summoned urgently to Villa Antonietta for young master Pepito who had broken his leg at tennis, did he hurry; and he arrived (his lungs all embers) when the doctor had also arrived, summoned also, by telephone, and provided with the necessary; and, both together, they were able to repair the damage. It was in that encounter that they got to know each other and, in setting the leg, "came to respect each other." From that time on they cultivated the little garden of a certain friendliness and mutual deference, watered by the fact that the attentive doctor, every time the colonel's wife asked him over the telephone, took it upon himself to furnish her with canned peas in Prado or Iglesia: the most exquisite and the most indispensable of the Serruchonese vegetables. When the whispers about Pedro's identity began to assume the form of a scandal, the good doctor had ample opportunity to entertain the colonel's lady and she, after a while, her husband, who at first paid no attention to the story, concerned as he was with the arduous task of succeeding (for once!) in if not digesting at least in directing to the exit those musket pellets, the peas, which had escorted down to his colon a guanako stew worthy of the Borgias. (It was a kind of humped veal of Maradagàl, exquisite, but without horns, somewhere between a calf and a dromedary. Cut into small pieces with the "cuchillo," and with a pinch of ginger and red pepper added, a delicacy is created.) But the doctor didn't give up: the next day, though his head continued to wag like a sage's over the mysteries of the World, he nicely reiterated the information and completed it with the distinguishing marks and biographical data of Palumbo, and then, following the thread of that name, the colonel plunged into the labyrinth of memory and turned up a whole pitiful postwar episode, dating that is from a few years back, which had kept him on his toes for two months in a row in his office of the Second Reexamination Commission of the Central Military Hospital of Pastrufazio. "Palumbo? Palumbo?" he asked himself, his lower lip jutting out, as was usual when he reminisced. Why, of course, Palumbo! Ah! He remembered very well! Palumbo Gaetano! Born '90, the wounded veteran of Hill 131, tall, heavy . . . all the endless calvary of his liquidation procedure . . . that is . . . yes . . . they had liquidated him.

"Liquidated!" he repeated, moving his head up and down as if to close the case. Those were the days, toward the end of August, after the cloth merchant's passage, when everyone at Lukones came to know the story of the name and the pension and to enrich their lexicon with the two adjectives "penetrating" and "lacerating"—even the peon of Villa Pirobutirro, José, who hung around the tavern of the Alegre Corazón, even Don Giuseppe, the good pastor, and the coachmen who drove hacks to Prado. José Inrumador, Fernando el Gordo, Mingo Ruiz,

33

Carlos La Torre, Miguel Chico, old Batta, Carmelo De Peppe; and the nonegenarian Indio Huitzilopótli known as Pablo and also as Repeppe; and the women too, the girls, Peppa, Beppa, Pina, Carmencita, the murmuradora, the bullinosa, the mariposa. The doctor, already informed of the "asunto" by popular whisper, in order to inform the colonel's lady of it, and the colonel himself, received from his colleague, the superior officer, that surplus of clarifications and medical appendices that from then on made him lord and master of the news item of the day, in victorious advantage of four or five lengths over popular whisper. So, in those days, he no longer seemed himself.

He forgot his thermometer at home, and another time his stethoscope. Once, tapping with his fingers, he kept making a man take a deep breath, another deep breath, another deep breath, when the man really only needed to take a dose of oil. The veiled interest, renewed every time, with which he heard the narrative from everyone, who served it up to him again, only then to toss out as if it were nothing, on his own, those three or four sharp words, the words of a man of science who knows his business and enunciates facts in impeccable terms, swaying his head in a gesture of compassionate diagnosis as an economist might do over the dying law of Ricardo—all that unapparent but extremely excited curiosity, and the eucharistic ardor of divulging the latest news—had been the reason, at that time, for his postponing for two more days his shaving, which was a Thursday and Saturday liturgy, neglected already for six days at that juncture (in addition to the first day, which doesn't count), and hence he was more and more fearsome and sharp in his prognosis and predisposing toward anguish. He achieved then a ten-day beard, an accomplishment for that matter not infrequent in his

34

biography, mirror of a very busy life all devoted to the good, or rather to the ills, of his fellow man.

On the tenth day, August 28, toward eleven in the morning as he was returning from his first round of visits on his bicycle, having removed his trouser clips and shaken off a bit of dust, the good doctor was about to find no further excuse for postponing any longer a good lathering, developable in a victorious crescendo between chin and ears, which would have been followed, the job done, by certain reasonable blood-colored stripes, laid out a bit in all directions over the virile region of his cheeks and also under his chin, and these, however, were such as to suggest the Battle of the Metaurus. He was just about to succumb to the evidence, before the mirror of the wash basin, when José (the José of Villa Piro-butirro) came to say that the Señora's son would like him to come for an examination at his convenience. "What's wrong with him?" he asked. The peon shrugged. "No me entere," he said.

The doctor, happy to be able to exempt himself from that nuisance of shaving, started washing his hands gaily.

He was completely at peace again. "Anda, anda," he answered, "pero ligero, otra vez acabo yo de llegar antes. . . . And tell him I'll be there at once. . . ."

"Very well, I'll say good morning," the peasant said, and he went out. He hadn't even taken off his hat or removed his hands from his pockets.

"This is it!" the good doctor thought; the call had unnerved him slightly.

The Señora's son was expecting him! Probably for nothing, for one of his usual worries—such as the fear of dying. Why, he lived like a king! The doctor chuckled. He had thermometer and stethoscope in his pocket; he took the trouser clips from the bicycle, but then changed his mind and decided to go on foot instead; he put the two clips back on the iron bar of the frame, where they sit astride, took a little walking stick, and went out.

And he thought, as he went along, what an unsavory reputation surrounded that son, so apart, so remote from everyone at Lukones that he could have been called a misanthrope, or, worse, an enemy of the people, if not a downright police suspect.

Besides, he was married and the father of children, was the good doctor—children that the Military Service Bureau of Prado had systematically overlooked, since they were female—five of them, each more spinster than the next. And the Señora's son, however misanthropic, might well not be a misogynist. A bachelor he was certainly, like Beethoven, and even more so, if that were imaginable; but he seemed still to have time to amend that fear of a wife, if he dared a bit, and knew how to master himself. Come now! A dash of courage, ¡por Dios!, the doctor thought, as he went on his way.

A man—like that! A hundred and seventy pounds at the very least! A man . . .

Concerning him, also in Pastrufazio, the most extraordinary rumors circulated. At Lukones, however, they knew him better, having seen him at times mail a letter or buy stamps at the window of the correo, where he had aroused the curiosity of the postmistress. An enemy of the people? That he had no sympathy for the humble could be sensed from his walk, his bearing: not haughty, no, but he seemed to exclude from his gaze, and perhaps from the gaze of his soul, the wretchedness and the yellowishness of povertydom.

José, the peon, insisted that he had in him, all seven, in his belly, the seven deadly sins—locked in his belly like seven serpents; that they bit and devoured him from within, from morning to evening—and even at night, in his sleep. He slept in the morning until eight or even eight-thirty, and he had coffee brought to him in bed, by the Señora, who was always going up and down steps for that son, poor old woman! And the newspapers too; he would read them afterwards and slowly absorb both coffee and papers, stretched out in bed like a cow (so the peon said): and he also kept some books on the chiffonier, to read them also from time to time in bed, as if the papers weren't enough. Whereas the peasants, at eight, have already been sweating for three hours and have to stop and sharpen their scythes. So he said, and so it was repeated afterwards by other people. The doctor, thanks to his merciful ministry, had had the opportunity of listening to all more or less, including Battistina, Batta's cousin, the maid at the Villa Pirobutirro, daily and seasonal for the summer and for the very early hours of the morning, which are golden, and suffering from goiter.

And then he hadn't wanted to take a wife, in order to be freer—that much was positive—to do anything that came into his head. On the score of this indignity, as it happened, the good doctor and good father couldn't manage to be scornful with the virulence the situation demanded. "The present state obstructs a potential change," he argued, "and potentiality and act are mother and son, in our Aristotelian world." And he had such a desire not to take a wife that he had hastened to pass on to Peppa the black wedding suit for Peppa's brother, Peppino, and the suit had been left him as a sacred souvenir, on their deathbed, in the old days by his uncles Giuseppe and Nepomuceno, who had been ambassadors to Portugal. Others, however, mitigated this accusation: he hadn't hastened at all, and in fact he had preserved it religiously in mothballs for forty years, from the age of five to the age of forty-five, and had sent money orders

37

home, when he was most worn from crawling over stony ground,[8] and his wretched skin wasn't worth a centavo, money orders to provide for mothballs for the wedding suit and above all peppercorns, peppercorns so necessary to the conservation of whatever cloth. The good doctor, as he walked, felt obliged to concur with this second opinion.

Recently other rumors had spread, all very sad, or downright disgusting: that he was wrathful as well as idle. So much had long been known. Now the report went that, wrathfully, in bestial accesses of rage, he was accustomed to maltreat his aged mother: this was denied for that matter by Peppa, the washwoman, who was in special intimacy with the Señora, and who received from her the most tender and human confidences—and therefore also that reiterated denial, from charity and maternal love. Poor Señora . . . He arrived unexpectedly. He left when they all thought he was reading. They said he was voracious, greedy for food and wine; and cruel —this already as a boy: with lizards, which he clubbed treacherously, with the chickens belonging to José (the first José, predecessor of the present one), which he pursued fiercely with a mad whip of his, sometimes even making them, such was their fear, rise from the ground and almost fly, just think! Think! Fly! As if they were falcons, those chickens!

Since a Jewish doctor, in reading mathematics at Pastrufazio, and with the help of calculus, had demonstrated to him how the cat (from whatever drainpipe it falls) can safely reach the ground on all four paws, which is a marvelous gymnastic application of the theorem of impulse, he at various times hurled a handsome cat from the third floor of the villa, having become curious to test the theorem. And the poor animal, landing, in fact furnished him each time with the desired confirmation, each time! Each time! Like a thought that, through every vicissitude, never ceases being eternal; but, as cat, it died shortly thereafter, its eyes veiled with irrevocable melancholy, saddened by that outrage. Because all outrage is death.

He was voracious, and greedy for food and for wine, cruel, and very miserly—so miserly that he would go on foot to the Prado station; whereas all real gentlemen went there in a carriage, Batta's or Miguel Chico's, or in their own automobile, or at least in the bus. And it was through miserliness that he wanted to discharge the women—laundresses, maids, and others—who assisted the old lady in the management of the house, saving a few pennies or a few morsels of bread, that is from the leftovers of his crapulous banquets.

José, the peon, at the Alegre Corazón tavern, specifically confirmed this vice of avarice, one of the worst and one that the Church most severely condemns; and he lamented the scarce quantity of wine produced and the great amount he had constantly to pour out into the big bottle of the master, drawing it from the barrel. Moreover Peppa, Battistina, the tavern keeper Manoel Torre, and his scullery boy and messenger Pepito, distributor of flasks, all agreed in testifying that the Pirobutirros, mother and son, consumed only white wines of Resqueta or of the Sierra Encantadora, with which Torre himself supplied them punctually—and it was wine of good quality, like that with which he supplied the monks at the monastery to say Mass—or at most those light and pale wines of the Nevado or the Zanamuño. The other landowners and sausage makers of the place were praiseworthily abstemious, thought the doctor as he went on, lashing his right calf (which was full and sturdy, and cyclistical) with his little cherry cane. All that could explain that scoundrel Manoel Torre's evident indul-

39

gence and even partiality toward Pirobutirro the son; obviously as far as tavern keepers are concerned, a man who doesn't drink wine should be sent to jail. Some people had observed, with much humanity and a certain boasting, that in Lukones the air is especially sharp and hungry-making, or at least stimulating of a good appetite for those who come up, wan, from Pastrufazio, poisoned by urbanity and urbanism and by that rationalizing flatness that constitutes its climate.

And the son, in his rapid apparitions, must have arrived hungry: and perhaps the appearance of serenity, unaccustomed in him but native to those hills, in them so diffused and sweet and in the trembling drops of the countryside, invited him to a Dionysian celebration, and the drowsiness which in Elysian clemency was accustomed to rise, misty there, below the lofty snows. They crowned the peaks, gelid diadem of eternity. Perhaps he sought the ephemeral oblivion of the cup and a faint gastric stimulus—to elude the day, the Pastrufazian day! and to reach, as best he could, the vespertine star of the ocean.

But the majority added that these were fancies, these notions about the fine air—whims pure and simple —and that poor people, too, in that case, after having worked out their day, should have dined on stew, if it was the good air that made the rules. No, no. He was pink and white: and the sunset's melancholy didn't prevent him from polishing off certain chunks, down into his stomach, of prime beef, oh yes indeed, with little onions in sweet-and-sour sauce.

The doctor snickered, thinking of it, that the Pirobutirro son spent too much time brooding over his ailments, shut up in himself—ailments now rusted by time —and thoughts poisoned his soul, like rancid garbage. To be sure, around this patient of his, so far outside every standard, the strangest opinions had been formed in Lukones and, for some time now, rumors of every sort had been circulating. His greed for food, for example, had become legendary. Unanimous, the poor, the undernourished, the beggars execrated that vice of the palate, which is so vile in a man, and that barbarous habit, after having eaten, of drinking some Nevado on top of it, or some Cerro; almost as if he, the voracious son, were banqueting with the shades of his Vikings. None of the landowners of the area, abstemious for the most part, and some even vegetarians, could think of such a thing without being overcome with disgust.

"We all eat too much!" the doctor proclaimed, to himself. "Half an apple, a slice of whole wheat bread, which is so tasty on the tongue and contains all the vitamins, from A to H, none excluded—there's the ideal meal for the just man! What am I saying? For the normal man . . . more than that is only a burden for the stomach. And for the organism. An enemy introduced wrongfully into the organism, like the Danai into the citadel of Troy"—these were his very thoughts—"which the gastroenteric system is then condemned to grind up, knead, expel . . . the peptonization of the albuminoids! And the liver! And the pancreas! The amidification of fats! The saccharification of the starches and the glucoses! Easier said than done! I'd like to see them try. . . . At most, in the critical seasons, a few fresh vegetables might be allowed, as an addition . . . raw, or cooked . . . beans . . . peas. . . ."

He went on, absorbed in these considerations: "And then they don't want stories to get about! as in '28!" He alluded to the Pirobutirro son.

In 1928 people had said, the gentlemen and ladies of Pastrufazio among the first, that he had been on the point of death in Babylon[9] after having swallowed a sea urchin; others said it was a crab, a kind of sea scorpion colored a scarlet color rather than black, with four moustaches—also scarlet, and very long, like four ladies hatpins, two on either side—in addition to the mandibles, in the form of steering oars, and also highly dangerous; some mythologized also about a swordfish or a brooch fish—oh yes! tiny, barely born—which he must have swallowed whole (having boiled it the bare minimum, but others said raw), head first, or rather sword, or brooch. They said the tail then flapped for a long time outside his mouth, like a second tongue he could no longer retract, and came close to suffocating him.

Cultivated people refused to credit such baroque tales: having dismissed unquestionably both the ichthyoid and the echinoderm, they believed they could identify the horrendous crustacean as a lobster of Fuerte del Rey, an Atlantic resort well known throughout the country precisely for its lobster beds. Por suerte some inkling of the Aristotelian system had reached their ears. The almost fatal lobster assumed the proportions of a human infant: and he, with a nutcracker, and pressing hard—harder!—both elbows on the table, had fiercely crushed its claws, coral-colored as they were, and had removed from them the best part, his eyes supergleaming with concupiscence and then squinting more and more inwardly, since aimed on the prey to which he neared, his nostrils flaring desirously, the obscene sucker of that mouth!—foul entrail which he had in anticipation extruded to approach the longed-for voluptuousness. Such an animal, in Babylon, according to the legend, they hadn't seen before or since. And he had had the nerve, the sin vergüenza, to dip them in tartar sauce, one by one—that is, those appetizing and quite innocent strands or shreds (of a white or pink mother-of-pearl color like a marine dawn) which he had been gradually extracting,

42

also with his fingernails, from the inner void of the two claws, crushed! shattered! And, having also used his hands, and his fingers, he brought them to his greasy and sinful lips with an extraordinary greed.

Then, sated, having set down the nutcracker, he had drunk.

His snout and his porcine aspect were also adduced by the legend to support the above, as if in the course of a whole interminable summer he had dined on nothing but lobsters in tartar sauce, cod in white wine with spurts of mayonnaise, or two or three times on peje-rey; and roast pigeons in casserole with rosemary and little new potatoes, sweet but not too sweet, and tiny, but already a bit overcooked, stewed in the very gravy derived from those very pigeons: stuffed in turn, according to an Andalusian recipe, with oregano, sage, basil, thyme, rosemary, horsemint, and pimiento, raisins, pork lard, chicken brains, ginger, red pepper, cloves, and still more potatoes, inside, as if those others set around weren't enough—that is, those outside the behind of the pigeon; which had almost become a second pulp, they had become so incorporated with that behind: as if the bird, once roasted, had acquired entrails more suited to his new position as roast chicken, but smaller and fatter than the chicken, because he was instead a pigeon.

And they were, these potatoes within, for that matter like those without, extremely mealy to a first touch of the tongue, on which as soon as they were spooned, since the spoon had to be adopted by the glutton, they deliquesced at once into a single paste with their meaty envelope, that is the evacuated and restuffed animal, of a general flavor of rosemary or, if attention were paid, of basil, which soon ceded and then gave way entirely, to that hellfire of the red pepper. He chewed everything at once—pigeons and potatoes and brains and lard and pepper and cloves—the pig, washing them afterwards before they had even gotten to the bottom with choice wines of the pre-Andean region, and the fish instead, and the lobster, my God! with those dry whites, crystalline, costing twenty-two and even twenty-eight centavos, of the Nevado or the Cerro Pequeño.

And he wanted, between his lips, the subtle, ground lip of an icy goblet, the vitreousness destitute of all thickness, the frigid and bodiless purity, sheer crystal. And in those moments of contempt he abhorred, wrathfully, the cheap glasses against the red carpet, squat and crooked as at Manoel Torre's, faceted crudely up to the middle and paltry with their air bubbles and cracks. But for want of anything better he wouldn't have rejected them; not even them! Oh! he wasn't, according to legend, the "transeat a me!" sort.

Suffice it to say that these vandalous nutcrackers and African pepper he used, to his own gluttonous capacity, in a very tenebrous den on the Riachuelo, where gypsies came and other people with guitars and nothing to do, and cats male and female of free love among the shoes of the feeders, in constant hostility over the chicken bones and the fish skeletons, however fleshless, that those supernal eaters throw down to them, after their every lofty defleshing is perpetrated, to the catty ground. And after all this licking and lapping he had the nerve, the sin vergüenza, to argue every time with the innkeeper, saying that the latter charged for similar portions too much more than an ordinary dish of puchero. The host, though he had apron in hand and not a knife (he wiped usually, with that dishwater-colored apron, his sweaty neck, all around the fat), one fine day told him where to go, and exhorted him to find some other place to eat, where he could stuff himself better, and for nothing; and then he, el hidalgo, instead of breaking a gravy boat

44

over the man's head, that wretch's head, shrank and shrank from vergüenza in the face of all the other tabled feeders who cropped and gnawed with such decorous benignity, some gurgling down a drop or two; so that as soon as he had the chance he slipped out of the little street door: because he also saw clearly, hidalgo though he was, that there was no other pigsty on earth where he could nourish himself on crusts of lobster with spoonfuls of mayonnaise in that way, and at such bargain prices. Sometimes even a marquess of Néa Keltiké manages to understand a thing or two.

In that season of crustaceans and rosemaries, much bathed (also because of the searing sun, which led, after the unusual drying up of the major rivers, to a summertime desiccation of the lands), the vindictive Powers of Heaven chose that there should follow, for him, thanks to their rightful intervention, a long and very costly disease. And it was this that prevented him, once and for all, from continuing to double his stomach with soft potatoes kneaded with wines of the Pequeño: for it forced him to eternal fastings, and it reduced him to powdering the mucous membrane of the gastric system with powdered kaolin, or discipline of bismuth (subnitrate of bismuth), as it willed. Which the more honest among the druggists of Pastrufazio supplied to him, this bismuth, at twenty times its cost, with the excuse that it came from Europe—from Darmstadt, to be precise.

He sniggered, the good doctor, in picturing that mad avarice, mingled with such clumsiness that he would have liked to limit the pharmacists to a profit of one hundred percent.

He, the son, claimed that he had translated into bismuth the savings from ten years of work—that is to tell the truth, ten years of miserliness. In local myth and lore, and despite the repeated denials of men of science, first among them himself, the doctor, and immediately afterwards the tax collector, third the librarian who headed the association of pear growers, and so on through the fourth, fifth, and many others, all went on believing and insisting, in Lukones, that it had been the sword of the swordfish to perforate the wall of his duodenum, coming to a dangerous curve, which the anatomists passed off, as they are used to, as duodenal loop or duodenal lobe of the gastric tract, or Hanseatic bottleneck of the perigurdium, to use the most recent terminology.

"Poor human entrails!" the good doctor thought, whipping his calf with his little cane. "And even those of marquesses, who have coats of arms on their turrets." From arms to arms, entrails to entrails, tripes to tripes! And, parallel-wise, from thought to thought and, perhaps, from soul to soul. But there is no discipline for mistaken souls—their wounds know no powder. He tried, the good doctor, the first pebbles of the last rocky stretch: a little road sunk between two walls y por suerte in the shadows of the locusts and some elms, for the final patience of his heroic feet.

Oh! along the road of the generations, the light! which recedes, recedes . . . opaque . . . of the unchanged becoming. But in days, in souls, what elaborating hope! and abstract faith, pertinacious charity. Every practice is an image—sendal, device, flag in the wind. The light, the light receded—and the device summoned forward, forward, its quartered descendants: to gain the fugitive Occident. And the breath of the generations suffered, de semine in semen, from arms to arms. Up to the incredible landing.

In his villa without lightning rods, surrounded by pear trees, and consequently by pears, the last hidalgo was reading the *Groundwork of the Metaphysic of Morals.*

Ha! Ha!

He descended in the direct male line from Gonzalo Pirobutirro de Eltino, who had once been Spanish governor of Néa Keltiké and had made himself all too famous, in history, through his thirst for justice, his high cultivation, the thinness of his face, his punitive spirit, and his inexorable and predatory government. In collecting tolls from the ferries, where the stream bathed the boundary of his possession, or at the gates, where the fortifications of the cities opened, he had chosen not to observe the least mitigating precaution, any moderating or opposing entreaty, any humane or political distinctions. "¡Buscador de plata!" the populace had hailed him. What are the people croaking about? There should be no unraveling, in the stuff of his idea; in that net, no fishy rent of condonement. But he would not allow a hair of a person's head to be harmed, nor a penny taken, never! unless it occurred in carrying out a decree of Don Felipe, el Rey Católico (and then Don Fernando), or, lacking that, of his own; and the centavo must be joined, by sail, to the glorious Exchequer of the Crown of Castilla, thanks to that same decree, royal or his. For himself he hadn't extracted a peso, nor subtracted a doblón; he had not shorn a merino, nor sniffed a pinch of snuff. He had died poor, without an ear, and blind in one eye —he had lost the eye in war. "¡A los Reyes salud! Y levántenos a los cansados ¡Dios caballero, en Su luz! ... con los demás caballeros. ...."

Having exhaled these words he had ceased to live, stone dead, much hated by all, on April 14, 1695. The Realm where the sun never reached its Occident had raised him to the dignity of a salary; had sent him several patents, covered with sealing wax and royal congratulations; had conferred on him the title of Marquess of Eltino, inheritable, many ribbons, y algunas brazas de tierra below the new bastions of Pastrufazio (then called San Juan), where his bones could be laid—which were, in spite of everything, the longest in the Realm. On the subject of honor and duty, what they meant, how to observe them, though still cultivating his fingernails, he had never hesitated, never flinched, never despaired; since, high over the flood, in turning the wheel of the helm, he had stared only and always at his star. Shame, for him, and incurable regret in all the sidereal course of the years, not having arrived in time to have hanged on the public gallows a certain Filarenzo Calzamaglia or, as all said, Enzo, who had eluded the grip of his just justice; which had put the cuffs around his wrists during certain disorders in San Juan, in November '88. This man, from one fire to the next, and after having listened to other fools' chattering, had played the fool himself, beyond any conceivable provision of pardon from the Governor, or remission from the Sovereign Clemency.

It was believed by some, especially by a learned genealogist of Pastrufazio, whom others, however, considered a visionary, and others an impostor and a bribe taker, and a fabricator of Dukes without Duchy, that the Pirobutirros must have retained the nobility and blood of the Borgias, and that in honor of Saint Francisco Borgia and of Don Pedro Ribera, known as Spagnoletto, they received not infrequently, at the font, the baptismal names of Pedro or of Francisco. The librarian and head of the association of pear growers (headquarters in Pastrufazio) who, needless to say, had his villa and his pears in the Lukones region, in the November, 1930, number of the association's periodical, entitled *The*

Pear, developed instead a curious philological thesis, one doesn't quite know whether in honor of the Pirobutirro or the Butter-Pear, and that is to say that "hacer una pera," to "make a pear," in the idiom of Castilla la Vieja, meant to carry out a great feat.

The cicada, on the shadeless elm, was chirping full blast toward noon; it expanded the bright immensity of the summer. The good doctor, having consumed the worst of the stones, was about to arrive at the gate; in his lively mind, full of curiosity and of memory, these memorable figures of the illustrious house became unraveled with the swiftness of a dream: the image of his patient came back to him, after that of his ancestor, in an absurd light.

On his maternal side his patient was of barbarian blood, Germanic and Hun, as well as Longobard; but the Hungaricity and the Germanism hadn't ended up in white stockings, double soles, nor even in the knees, which suggested very slightly those of Siegfried; and also in the role of Magyar lion who wakes, he seemed to come off very little. Although . . . although . . . you never can tell. . . .

Germanic he was in certain manias for order and silence, and in his hatred for greasy paper, eggshells, and lingering at the door in formalities. In a certain inner torment in wanting to swim against the current of meanings and causes, in a certain disdain for superficial veneer, in a certain slowness and dullness of judgment, which seemed in him more like an inhalation before a sneeze, and in turbid and tardy synthesis, never with flashing ray of parrot-gold color. Germanic, above all, was a certain pedantry more obstinate than the tapeworm, and for him disastrous, both at the barber's and at the printer's. "You must pull yourself together!" they said to him. "Live and let live," they added. He had no

49

talent for pulling himself together and for living and letting live, in which he found himself more awkward than a seal frying pancakes. Irked by the noises of the radio, he would have liked an investiture from God, not to govern Néa Keltiké for the stipend of Don Felipe, el Rey Católico, but rather to write a gloss on the *Timaeus*, in silence, salaried by no one.

And there was, for him, the problem of ill: the fable of disease, the strange fable spread by the conquistadores, who were enabled to note down the dying words of the Incas. According to them death comes for nothing, suffused in silence, like a tacit, final combination of thought.

It is the "invisible ill," of which Saverio Lopez narrates in the last chapter of his *Mirabilia Maragdagali*.[10]

II

At the passing of the cloud, the hornbeam fell silent. It is companion to the elm, and in Néa Keltiké they prune it unceasingly until it has grown as many turbaned stakes, along the paths and the dust: rough-barked, and stripped thus of boughs, it has wretched, worn, almost tattered leaves, which fling out those knots at the crown. The locust was silent, without nobility of song, unknown to the fugitive fear of the dryads, as to the syrinx of the ancient, two-horned one: utilitarian and propagative root introduced into that countryside from Australasia and immediately thick-leaved and pungent in the guardianship of enclosures, in supporting slopes. It was thanks to the attentions of an agronome who speculated on Progress and gave its presage as certain, predicting an end to oaks, to elms, and, inside the lime kilns, to the ancient dreaming of the beeches. Which nonfabulous giants, toward the end still of the eighteenth century, were gold and purple under the autumn skies over all the flank beyond the dolomites of Terepàttola, which on this side drops sheer, spreading, on the turquoise flattening of the valley bed, which we know to be a lake. The lime, it goes without saying, was to build the villas, and the garden walls of the villas—with espaliered pear trees.

51

That little road the doctor had to climb up proceeded for a long time in the shade, not of the pruned
hornbeams, but of the endless locusts. From the little
branches the leaves spread out, numberless, laudably
green but nevertheless full of sound judgment, animated
by the determination to serve man as example and to
make happy the reborn city halls, with that idea of order and of money well spent constantly suggested by
symmetrical arrangement. The little elliptical leaves,
equal as all creatures of the Standard and of Australasia,
seemed rationed out to the stems by a sharp-eyed Administration and were worthy surely of a Station Boule-
vard with equestrian monument to General Pastrufazio,
the victor of Santa Rosa. And each peduncle, on each
of those branches, two long pinnacles like two tiepins,
one on each side—which did not prevent their being
tasted, when opportunity arrived, by the optimistic
tongue of the jackass. And so, around the villa and the
pear trees, all was locust, as well as banzavóis. That
white parallelepiped, thrown open to the winds and to
the clogs of the Peppas, was gripped by the locust in its
greening siege. During the georgic siesta of the Pirobutirros, the locust triumphed over all other images. Its
mediocre stink made it considered useful by many; like
all useful and faintly stinking products it became indispensable, one fine day, to the collective economy, in
the improved hopes of Maradagalese life toward the
end of the nineteenth century. And so also in Lukones.

A quadrupeddaling among the pebbles stirred the
doctor from his thoughts; he raised his head, saw himself watched by Battistina descending. The woman had
a little package under her right arm, and with both
hands she was holding a deep dish, covered by another
dish, overturned; her face was addressed to the left, so
it seemed that they had been mistaken when they fastened
it to her bust, like a dignified puppet facing west—in re-

ality, to make room for her goiter, three or four hecto-
grams. Her manner was a bit suspicious and shy, with
that dinner that occupied her hands—she was like an
animal whose food might be taken from him; and the
goiter seemed an animal on its own which, after having
clawed at her trachea, was now drinking forth half her
breath, hiding however under her skin like the photogra-
pher under his cloth. So its proprietress panted slightly,
though she was coming downhill, with a barely percepti-
ble gurgle that was like a thread of catarrh. The doctor
seemed ready to stop: and both stopped then. From the
woman's goiter bubbled forth a "Good day, Doctor," so
subdued and damp that it seemed the cooking of a cab-
bage with carrots in a pot from which for a moment the
lid has been removed.

"What's wrong with him?" the doctor asked, looking at the ground, his eyes heavy, swollen as if with
sleep; meanwhile, using his little cane, he was removing
some of the less bastardly pebbles from the ground. The
brambles of his beard gave him the face of the bad thief
of Golgotha, but retired. "I'm late today, noon will be
here any minute." The word "here," in the sense of
"place to which," is denoted by the word "scià" in the
dialect of Keltiké.

"I mean Señor Gonzalo."

"I wouldn't know; he roams around the house like
a madman, those few hours he's there; there's no living
in that house any longer."

"Living . . . living . . ."

"The Señora went to the cemetery with the flowers,
and with Pinina along, who had the key. Poor woman!
After all she's been through . . . reduced to such a state;
to be afraid of her son."

"Afraid! It must be disagreement, differences in
character—"

"No, no, Doctor . . . it's a fear. When he starts

wandering around the house like a ghost, the Señora is sick with fear. Believe me, Doctor, I've known her for a long time. Poor woman! After all her troubles!"

"But fear of whom? Of what?"

"Fear of being alone in the house when he's there . . . I'll tell you . . . she always wants me to stay there, to be there; she cooks dinner for me herself . . . provided I stay, and she never lets me go home . . . like today . . . when it's already almost noon. But I can't, you understand; I have my own things to attend to . . . and all my chores . . . I still have to make the bran for the hens, and here it is almost noon."

"True," the doctor reflected, "the house is in a rather remote spot, a bit lonely . . . with all these woods around"; he gave the foliage a lash.

"Oh! The lonely part wouldn't matter," the goitered woman gutturalized. "It's the fact that she's afraid of her son . . . she, his own mother! When he starts roaming around the house with his hands in his pockets . . . There, Doctor, that's what it is—I ask you now—"

"God, get along with you. You women are always having ideas! What could she be afraid of? Why, he's a man like anyone else! He may shout a bit, every now and then, because he got up on the wrong side of the bed . . . because the soup's overcooked . . . the way all men do—"

"If it was just the shouting . . . but when he says anything to her it's worse still! And to an old woman seventy-three years old! His mother! When I see her going down to the cemetery, with flowers, with Pina after her, I have the feeling she's going there to reserve her place. The last time she even said, to Pina, 'When I'm here too, you'll come, won't you? Now and then, to say an Ave Maria for me, too. . . .'"

"Oh, well, poor woman, people say these things. . . ."

"And when he starts roaming, and goes from one room to another . . . and looks at her . . . that's when she's afraid the most . . . and he seems to be looking at her earrings."

"Why, you're mad! What should he care about her earrings?"

"I don't know, Doctor; what can I say? But this morning, too, I saw he was looking at her diamonds . . . because for a while now he's been keeping his eye on her diamonds."

"What diamonds!"

"On the earrings, which the Señora can't be without for a minute . . . you know. . . . And he went on watching, watching . . . I . . . but I'm afraid too, sometimes . . . I'm a poor old woman same as her—and with this misfortune here, you understand." She meant the goiter. "Now I'm getting on toward sixty-eight myself."

"Sixty-eight, eighty-eight . . . it's the same thing after all"; he shrugged and gave the locusts another flick with his cane.

"That's true enough, too, Doctor . . . we poor folk have nothing to lose . . . that's certain. . . . And he wouldn't take his eyes off the diamonds . . . the Señora moved about the house and he followed her . . . and kept staring at one ear . . . and then at the other . . . and she went into the drawing room, and he went after her into the drawing room. And she went into the kitchen to clean the coffee pot, the whistling one, which she won't even let me touch, oh no, not on your life . . . and he, after her, into the kitchen. . . . Ah! What a life! What a life! With all that fear in her heart, all day long . . . not able to live in peace for a minute! And every time he tells her not to lose them, to be careful . . . and he clenches his teeth and says to her: '¡Anda, anda! Those diamonds won't save you!' Save her from what? I ask you. She surely has a right to wear her earrings, the poor old soul, that were given to her by her husband . . . and after all the work she's done!"

The doctor remained silent, looking at the ground; he had discovered, with the tip of his cane, a stone that was more stupid than the others, fixed in the earth like a stone diamond; and he had to use both hands to prize it out.

"And sometimes, all of a sudden, he shouts in her face that the diamonds cost five thousand pieces, five thousand! And that they've suffered cold and hunger for the pears. He doesn't know himself what he says: for the pears? Cold? Hunger? And then he bursts out in a noise that only he can make, like it was the devil laughing at the feet of a dead man he's just sniffed and is about to snap up: and he says that women are animals with five thousand pieces worth of diamonds on them, and nothing but animals, he says, filthy . . . and that meanwhile the dead have filled up the cemeteries, so nobody will make up his mind to die any more, not even the animals.

"Then you should see her, Doctor! that poor old woman, how she cries! Crying in secret . . . maybe with the windows banging"—so she said—"because the wind blows right through that house. And then she has to call José, but she comes after me, because she's afraid to stay there alone with her son, I tell you!

"And he says they're like the blacks in Africa . . . like the Arabs, he says, with pearls in their noses, the women, with rings hanging from their noses, in the middle"—she raised the two dishes slightly—"between the holes, you see . . . because he says that's how the blacks are . . . that is to say, their women, the black women. . . ."

"What nonsense!" the doctor grumbled, shrugging one shoulder; and he started swinging one leg. "Why, he's a good devil! Who can say what you women start thinking . . . what you dream up. . . ."

"I swear to you, Doctor! I tell you that woman, in that house, suffers more than she lives. . . ."

"Why, it's probably the matter of a moment . . . a burst of anger." He was about to move on. "Like the wind, when you hear all the doors slam, all of a sudden . . . and then it goes off, and it's nothing. Living alone like that . . . barred into his room . . . reading . . . day-dreaming . . . that's what happens to a misanthrope. . . ."

The cicadas, reawakened, speckled with noise the green motes beneath the abundance of light; all the summer sky crackled with that endless noise, in the unison of a deafening vacation. The doctor had an idea. His diagnosis was in the process of ripening: or, perhaps, considering the five daughters that Doña Carlotta had presented him with, it had been ripe already for some time. "Vae soli!"

"Ah, Doctor! You know more than I do, surely . . . but there are times, believe me, when Don Gonzalo has a look on his face, a look! You'd think that his mother, for him, is in this world only to keep those diamonds, like a tree bears cherries." The woman's breath had become shorter, drier: that big onion that boiled in her throat seemed, thanks to the cooking, to have lost its gravy. From that goiter, enormous, the death rattle strained the sadness of her speaking. "And poor woman, if she spends a peso on one thing, or gives away a centavo for another . . . or if she buys whitefish from Beppina . . . or if she gives something for the cemetery . . . he says he's already given . . . that what he gives is enough. And he doesn't give anything! 'Give them some old shoes,' he shouts, 'those wretched beggars!' But he wants her to save all the money for him, and nothing for the poor . . . nothing! Let them die, he says. . . ."

57

"Come, come!" the doctor protested again, "what a pack of stories!"

"She has to give me my money secretly, or on the days when he's away," the old woman went on, paying no attention, "because it wouldn't do for him to see! He's the only one who's to spend anything; he's the only one who should eat! And his Mama has to jump at his least whim! A man who's already over forty-four . . . I ask you . . . and bring him his coffee . . . and go up and down steps . . . because in the morning he wants it in bed, with the newspapers. And he wants this, and then he wants that: and all the servants are to be chased out of the house. If a woman comes to wash, or to iron . . . or if it's the carpenter, come to fix the door . . . out with them! Out! Out with them all!"

The rattle was dying away; still a few brief gurgles of that catarrh remained. Then she said, but as if in a whisper, in an opaque fashion: "And now that the little boy comes to do his homework, and the Señora is so patient! You know, the colonel's grandson. But the day he finds the boy in the house! That's the day he'll strangle him. The Señora tells him first, the boy, when he must come, when the other's away."

"And how are things with you?" the doctor asked her paternally.

"Me?" the woman was amazed. "Oh! blessed Madonna! Can't you see me walking along the roads?" She tried to move her head to accompany that hoarse moan, composed of poverty and sadness; but the shaking, hindered by the goiter, came out with reduced elongation, almost imperceptible. "What do you expect, Doctor? So long as we're here! We must still thank the Lord!"

The wick of the report gave a sudden spurt. Her

eyes, filled with a wicked epos, harpooned the swollen and red eyes of the doctor. "When he's in a rage, and has lost his Lord, he himself doesn't know what comes out of his mouth. He doesn't know what he's doing! Don't go and repeat this, but the Señora, helping me dry the dishes, told me that last winter, down at Pastrufazio, he went and crushed a watch under his heel, like a grape . . . and it was a family heirloom: and then, right after that, he took the portrait of his poor Papà, which was hanging in the dining room . . . and he walked over it, with his feet . . . to trample on it." She made the Sign of the Cross. She displayed a great respect for the dining room. The cadence of that speech was oxytone, as the words for "detach" and "hang," in the Serruchón dialect, are "destacagiò" and "takasú." And also, "trample" is "pestalgiò." "And he broke the glass into a thousand little pieces like this"—she stretched her chin forward a millimeter, her hands being taken up—"like crumbs, under the soles of his shoes—oh! the beast!—for his father was a real man; you never knew him, but I can tell you all right . . . for a man like that nowadays you can't even find the seed, for men of his sort . . ."

"Nowadays, nowadays," the doctor retorted, and shrugged. "What do you women know?"

"Oh! Madonna! I was just talking, Doctor. Nowadays life is different, I understand that . . . and it isn't the way it was once, after there's been a war. Not even the silkworms are what they were once. Forty centavos a kilo! I had to sell them: less than cherries! Forty centavos? For a kilo of silkworms! What are forty centavos? Not even a hectogram of croconsuelo—that comes to forty-five, and this morning fifty . . . because every day there's something new . . .

"But him! To smash a gold watch under his foot

. . . what nerve! Mean as he is: to threaten to kill his mother! Lucky there was the glass on the portrait, so it could be saved."

The doctor began to lash his calf, with the air of someone who hasn't a minute to waste.

"Ah! That war," Battistina concluded, and the thread of a sigh was cut off by the goiter. "And sometimes, instead, when the moon is right for him, he's capable of being generous, even with the first person who comes along; as if he were drunk. Oh! my goodness! Then you can be lucky. He goes according to moments, moods. That's enough now; I'll say good morning to you."

The two separated at the striking of half-past eleven from the tower, monstrous metal over the creaking of all the trees; it was almost as if the hour counter on its rounds had caught them in sin. After a few more stones and boulders another turn led the doctor to the open space: there stood the main gate to the villa, of decaying wood.

Through the wooden bars, half-rotten, of that mild assertion of private possession there was, as every time when he arrived there, in a glance the resplendence of the summer. The infinite chirping of the earth seemed consubstantial with the light; and the hill sloped down, quite green, and there, after the brief leisure of the lakes, there were other hills in the light, and on, and on. The dazzled eye wanted to pursue there a new fable, tenuous, very sweet, among distant scenes, in the deceit of the prospect of flight, wandering about as if for a theft of love in the pale blue of those leveled basins. He saw, vanishing with a black tail and a white wisp, the steam of the Railway of the South, as every time, having passed Ranchito station, fleeing toward the plain and the city. The city . . . the city . . . full of good matches for every girl, even the most foolish, where there were doctors of renown, with people standing in the waiting room—specialists who cost seventy-five and perhaps even a hundred.

As for the gold watch, he thought he had heard once before—from Peppa of the laundry, or was he mistaken?—that it was silver; or rather, no, that it was instead an alarm clock, a table clock; and one day it had rung on his table, Señor Gonzalo's, unexpectedly, just as he was deep in reading, or writing, or perhaps was furiously distilling from his memory one of those difficult words of his that nobody understood, with which he enjoyed decorating his prose (stiff, gluey, which nobody read); and it had also started dancing about on the table, the clock that is, so that it had made a whole turn on its own, and what was worse for it, without its owner's permission. In pieces, to be sure, it had met its end: with certain little geared wheels that were found months later, brass, in the sweeping up . . . as you notice a little ladybug, shy . . . with seven dots on its elytra . . . lingering in the desolate hearth of a drawing room . . . memory, desert . . . to forgive. . . .

And besides, either Peppa or Beppa, one of the two in any case, had told him the same thing also about a pen, which had ended up under a heel—a sharp blow, determined—and immediately thereafter under the other, crunch and crunch, a Waterman. Urged in vain to eject, after stubborn attempts lasting several minutes, it had presented him, plop, on the sheet, with a nice big drop of pale blue ink: and then it had had its deserts, on the spot, under both heels. These things happen to a man who lives alone, the doctor opined, without the virile concerns that the burden of a family give us, together with the most lofty, the purest joys—the hearth, to be sure! He omitted the adjective domestic, but he

61

understood himself that he referred to that . . . that family, in fact, that Señor Gonzalo . . . had never conceived of making up his mind to. And meanwhile away with pictures from the walls, and down, at once, under his shoes . . .

The Señora, they had told him (seventy-four!), her eyes veiled with sorrow (because she had understood immediately), had come in; had bent one knee to the floor, trembling; had bent over in despair. So the women had reported to him, and they had heard it from the woman in Pastrufazio, who had run in after her mistress.

She had forced herself to overcome her dismay, as a duty. Overcome the anguish . . . a duty toward the earth, bent down: with sparse, white hair, without caresses now . . . as if from her weakness were to be born the final devotion . . . whereas already, from the fading of all external appearances, she was prompted to utter weary, interior words . . . like caresses of shadow.

Lacking all succor, she summoned the last weariness to the devotion of a final fulfillment; she wanted to save that picture. She had bent over; she had taken it—with trembling hands, skeletal, where the blue veins conducted a weak pulsing over the bones, a memory perhaps. In her memory: only memory . . . In time were the images and the erased truth: and she had been daughter, bride, and mother.

So with her own hands she had gathered up the shards: they were sharp, sickle-shaped . . . they might hurt someone. She had raised that portrait, its frame miraculously saved, with all the gold embellishments, so delicate. The Pastrufazio maid had also run in. They had erased the disorder in the room as one would bind up a wound. A glory of crockery fragments haloed that fabulous gentleman of cowardice and laziness, sordid and greedy, capable only, in his best moments, of maltreating his bent mother and of insulting the memory of the deceased. According to some the watch had been neither gold nor silver, but silver-plated nickel.

The doctor climbed up to the little iron gate, a bit farther on and a bit higher—painted green—that served as normal introducer into the silence and light of the villa, from the north where the building seems lower, a storey less because of the uneven terrain. The idea of entering from behind, without any formality of calling out or solemnity of flinging open, gave the visitors a certain calm security, an ease, as if they were in their own home: and as if everything then would go as it should, and in the best possible way, as in the family. The "Beware of the dog!" had been replaced, for the Pirobutirros, by a blind faith in the honest passing of the wayfarers—few, given the pebbles!—and the dog by a smile of civil cordiality. From the fixed idea of a moral equity of bipeds, which is perhaps a consequence of moral clear-sightedness, there descended upon them a vestment of practiced love and grace: even if the bipeds, with those clogs, could be acoustically perceived as quadrupeds. The affability of Señora Pirobutirro, and of the lamented Señor Francisco, were downright proverbial. The collectors of contributions for the new bells in the spire, in 1903, were left faint at their sweetness, as soon as they read the sum marked down by Don Francisco's own hand on the sheet of signatures, and both husband and wife had subscribed with the most moved concern—and with complete fluency, since in that family all knew how to manage a pen.

A cork popped and a toast, Nevado of the past year, dry, and tongue cluckings and tastings, after the cork's flight, had closed the ceremony with a few tears. "Do, dedi, datum, dare," grumbled the doctor, as if on his patient's account. "Dono, donavi, donatum, donare.

Obfero, obtuli, oblatum, obferre." Another drop . . . enough, enough, Señor Francisco . . . but this can't do any harm.

He entered and descended the two steps. Crouching among the flowering onions, the peon, on hearing the gate creak, raised his head and took a look at the visitor, whom he expected. Without rising, touching two fingers to his ragged hat, he confirmed, from the distance, for the newcomer that his mistress had decided to go to the cemetery with flowers—which he himself had procured for her—and accompanied by Peppa. This he enounced in some clashes of a tenebrous phonation with *ü*'s and *ö*'s as the white globes of the onion flowers occupied to the left a limited stretch of that enclosure, planted with vegetables and vines; it was hard to say which was more vigorous. "Very well," the doctor said.

The son, in the meanwhile, came to meet him along the little alley of plum trees, flanking the outside wall. He was tall, a bit bent, round-chested, ripe-bellied, his face flushed like a Celt's; but the skin was somewhat sagging and the appearance weary, though it was a marvelous morning. Dressed barely decently, with high shoes of kidskin, very black, with black laces—the kind that were not very suited, in the country, to win the esteem of men tennis players, or the affection of girls playing the same game. He was extremely courteous. His person was not adorned with a pullover nor any other garment worthy of mention. A slight facial prognathism, like a child's desire that had been transmuted into the muzzle of a melancholy animal, usually gave his speech—though not always—that disagreeable tone of bewilderment and uncertainty, and seemed to explain the reason for a certain detachment from the living—detachment, the doctor opined, perhaps more suffered than desired. In some moments, some feature of the face

64

appeared actually babyish, and any question predestined to every sort of rejection. People, someone said on looking at him, have concerns and interests that keep them occupied, and every minute—they haven't time to converse with doll-babies.

His words were precise and poor, like his clothing —and far from impertinent. He didn't think of himself at all, and still less of playing a role, one would have surmised on observing him—for example, the role of ex-soldier. He had for the doctor, whom he hadn't seen for some time, cordial but brief words: and he showed him his esteem. With native tact he immediately dismissed as unnoticed the four millimeters of salt-colored beard that reduced his chin, the doctor's, to being that horse brush it was: and he seemed to consider it more than natural that he should allow himself, a short time later, to be pricked by that brush on the back, in the mammary region, in the epigastrium, in the abdomen.

His de Eltino, or Del Tino, agnates had no bearing on his behavior except as distant causes, with poor effect; these causes had long since been completely forgotten: as, on his last name, vanished, the old tombstones of the graveyard outside the wall. And the walls demolished. So it happens, in the back streets of the city, that one asks the motive for an unforeseen curbstone: and it is, among surviving walls, a relic of long-lost reasons. Perhaps that correctness, so human and useless and a bit sad, was a manner not of today, but one that came from afar.

III

Questioned by the doctor, he listed his recent sufferings, the usual ones. The doctor shook his head and
said he wanted to examine him. They went up to the
bedroom floor, he first. They entered a large room, the
walls covered with a yellowish wash, where two windows, one bright, opened over the locusts, the cicadas,
and two beds. The mountains of the north could be seen.
Almost black, with beams and planks, was the ceiling:
varnished with linseed oil in a smoky hue, as was the
custom in Spain once upon a time.

The son freed himself of his jacket, stretched out
on the near bed, his—very white of blanket, like the
other, and of solid walnut—so that the termite could
be heard creaking with difficulty, with a hard and brief
turn, like a corkscrew, after weary intervals. On that
monastic whiteness the long body and the eminence of
the belly created an image of chief engineer decently
deceased, except for the flush of the face, and also the
gaze and the breathing, which prevailed over the heavy
immobility of the head, which sank a little into the pillow, white and swollen, all flounces. Its neat coolness
immediately ennobled the forehead, the hair, the nose:

66

one would have thought of a mask, to be turned over to the plaster-cast museums of posterity. It was instead the face of the only living male Pirobutirro who looked at the beams of the ceiling—horizontals against white.

The two tapering shoes, shiny, very black, looked like two black peppers, though upside down and pointed. Moving his long, white hands in the buttonholes and the suspenders, the dead man prepared for auscultation. On the wall opposite, between the windows, from a walnut frame the coruscating gaze of General Pastrufazio, in a daguerreotype. He dominated, head and shoulders, the semidarkness, with his poncho and two tips of a South American kerchief on his left shoulder, and on his head that cap, somewhere between a homely head covering and a doge's hat, cylindrical; he was adorned all around with scrolls of gold thread in patterns of tendrils, rare acorns, filigree. The hero's blond hair, bleached many years before in the bath of fixative, flowed harmoniously to the shoulders and, once there, turned gently in a very noble roll, so that it seemed made by Andrea Mantegna or Giovanbellini: like a page of the Estes or of the Montefeltros come to the pampas, and to the years of flags and muskets. He was well past fifty; both cheeks and the nether lip were thickened with a male generosity of hair; he showed a plebeian and ancient vigor—hardened in the vastness of his wars and overflowing from the frames of his portraits.

The examination was "conscientious." The doctor touched the engineer at length, and even with both hands, as if to squeeze the guts out of him: he seemed a washerwoman enraged with her laundry, at the bank of a little pond; then, having let go of the tripes, he listened to him everywhere for a bit, jumping here and there with his head—that is, with one ear—pricking him and tickling him with his beard. Then he put the stethoscope to his heart and his apexes, the apexes both before and behind. He alternated his auscultation with digital percussion and digito-digital, both the bronchia and the lungs as well as, again, the belly. He said, "Turn over," and then, "Turn back again." In listening to him from the back when he was sitting on the bed and all bent forward, with the swell and the folds of his belly between his femurs, to split the stomach, and his face between his knees, his shirt thrown over his head as if by a gust of wind, or else stretched out prone, half-crooked, underdrawers and trousers with no nexus then, at times the doctor seemed to be communicating his desiderata to him by telephone: he made him take deep breath after deep breath. And the engineer lent himself to this exercise with good grace, his face between his knees.

With that, the examination came to an end.

From the open window, the light of the countryside, streaked by that infinite chirping.

The sick man regained his composure, having descended from the bed; his useless figure recovered itself from an outrage not motivated by the facts; the doctor, with a slightly mortified tone, confessed that he had discovered nothing to worry about—he shook his head —nothing, absolutely nothing. He prescribed some Sedobrol cubes, each dissolved in a cup of warm water, a couple of times a day, between meals. Warm water—yes, exactly. Water, water. He became impatient because the engineer asked him a couple of questions like an idiot, or was perhaps absentminded. In a teacup—why, yes, yes, of course, certainly, to make a nice little broth. The bismuth, if he liked, he could give up.

And the cicadas, populace of the immensity outside, masters of the light, chirped on.

The son thanked him for the suggestion. He took

the paper with the prescription from the doctor's hand, read in a glance the few words written there and the letterhead with the telephone number, and set it on the table that was beyond the beds, at the first window; he weighted it with a polished little polyhedron of ground crystal, all glints. He seemed to have attached no importance to the doctor's statement or, by now, to the ceremony that had preceded it—indeed, on buttoning his doublet, to have forgotten the sickness—"*le mal physique,*" in this case: the visible sickness.

There was, all the same, something else: his eyes became sad again; gradually his expression changed, as if at the rebirth of a painful thought that had for a moment been dulled; in all his face an alarm could be read, an anguish, which the doctor, privately, didn't hesitate for a moment to ascribe to "a new seizure of lack of faith in life": and also, of course, of course, to "the aftereffects of the gastric ailment that had so upset him last year." For some time, in any case, he had known the sudden changes of that appearance and of the whole behavior of his client. His eyes seemed to desire and at the same time to reject every word of comfort. An inscrutable opacity and, one would have said, a general sensory dullness added the note of quiescence in that undistinguished physiognomy: then, all of a sudden, there were distinctions and even unpleasant prominences. The gaze became kindled in a perspicacity tinged with shyness, in a kind of childish readiness; the speech became animated only to run aground shortly thereafter, as of a man promptly overwhelmed at the harangues of his fellow man. Sometimes the sternness of the inquisition assumed brief tones, sharp, stern, such as would be frightening if they had been supported by a pragmatic superiority of any kind, hatred, wealth, power, authority of office.

69

At that moment the eyes seemed to signify certainty of poverty, to look with desperate dignity at solitude. The doctor and father, nevertheless, persisted in the opinion that even a shipwrecked man, if one is really determined, can be fished from the waves, from the howling night: the social tissue then intervenes to help, and acts against the cyanosis of the single individual with the never-spent vigor of charity; it operates as artificial respiration, which restores to the prostrate man, after the blue breath of hope, the red warmth of life. The patient remained silent. The doctor thought, therefore, to meet him halfway by risking an invitation, and he did it with that slightly rough though still cordial manner of his: he praised, casually, sticking his head out of the window for a moment, the season and the village: "Days like this! Why, look! It's a crime to waste them—as you do." He praised again the mountains, some of which he mentioned by name. Then the bodies of water. Then the climate and the coolness of the Serruchón, zephyrs, and balms. Then from the salubriousness of the air he moved up, up, little by little, to the blue of the skies, to the renewed asphalting of the main roads, to the Romans of the past and the Chryslers of the present; until nonchalantly still, and as if by chance, as if speaking to himself, or to a cloud, he finally let himself go and suggested a little drive in the automobile the next day, with his Juana and his Pepa.

"My Pepa will do the driving. You should see her! Everybody says so, for that matter . . . why, that girl was born at the wheel! But then . . . you know Pepita well . . . a devil! A devil in skirts!"

The male descendant of Gonzalo Pirobutirro de Eltino didn't bat an eye: he looked beyond things, beyond the furniture; an inexplicable grief seized his face and, indeed, almost his whole person. He was like those who have a brother or a son: and they see the peaks of the Alp without return smoking, smoking, budding with cumuli, in a distant rumbling.[11] The corkscrew woodworm did not desist from his progress; after the accumulation of every interval he hastened to remind them of himself.

"All by yourself, reading—or, worse still, writing! But what the devil do you read, after all? What do you write? Your memoirs? Why, wait a while for them and write them when you're ninety! On days like this, in places like these! Enjoy the air, the light. Move about . . . walk . . . become drunk on air, too, like all the others. . . . Look at the others, how they know how to take things philosophically . . . Borella . . . Tabacchi . . . Pedroni. . . ."

These were some recent immigrants, highly expert cultivators of lettuce; of undoubted Aryan stock, if one were to judge by the names. The ecstasy of the villa, each his own, of course, had brought them to that state of unreversible anaesthesia, though rubicund and consoled with celery, which is one of the happiest offspring of a Serruchonese holiday.

From dusk to dawn an unmuzzled dog howled in the happiest of their sleep, while the night guard attended to his guarding outside.

"Can't you see? Days like this? This sunshine? Go, go! And learn to drive, too. Pepa can give you lessons— a devil like her. You'll see, you'll see."

"I believe you, Doctor, and I thank you," the character rebutted ceremoniously, "but tomorrow morning I have to be again . . . that is . . . I could leave at eleven." His voice died out halfway along its route, between the gullet and the lips. He adduced various engagements that would take him away the very next morning from the peace of the villa (immersed in that marinade of

71

cicadas and light), and deprive him, to his unspeakable regret, of such an auspicated excursion "with your young ladies." He said also, as if to complete the justification, that he felt truly mortified at not knowing how to drive. This was putting his foot in a hole. The stupidity of that assertion, after the paternal suggestion of driving lessons, would have appeared self-evident to anyone else, less distracted or less awkward than he.

"But as I said before, there's my Pepa . . . yes, yes . . . Pepita. You know her, don't you? Why, you've spoken to her many times!" The Pirobutirro son seemed to be navigating in vagueness; he easily confused the Juanas with the Pepitas, and also with the Teresitas; but more than anything, to terrorize him, there was the mixed salad of Marias and proclitic Marias, namely the Marys, the Mays, the Maria Pias, the Anne Maries, the Marisas, the Luisa Marias, and the Maria Teresas, especially when he discovered they were sisters, five in a bunch, and he had to distinguish them then and there in the hurly-burly of the refreshments, after schematic introductions. "Anyway, I tell you, it doesn't matter," the doctor continued. "You can sit there like a king; up front, perhaps, where there's less jolting, and look at the landscape . . . and drink it in with all its sweetness . . . And my Pepa will drive. Don't you trust my Pepa?"

Oh! Of course! He had complete faith in the "Señorita Pepita." (That onomastic abstraction gave him no way to find his bearings.) He expressed his thanks again, warmly. "But it's not possible." He emitted a sigh. He was very worried—almost annoyed. He was very polite. A sense of boredom, of irritation was in his blood: an ineffable anxiety about the turns of the gastric system, where the duodenum lies, like lead: an image of guilt, of fulfillment, in his mien. In his now-weary, hooded eye, painful things collected, remote things— too remote from that conversation.

Meanwhile, after twelve enormous strokes, the bells of noon had sent into the hills, beyond the tiles and the smoking of the chimneys, the full uproar of glory. Twelve drops, as if of monstrous bronze, celestial, had gone on falling, one after the other, inexorable, on the shiny leaves of the banzavóis—even if unperceived in the tangle of the asp, soft, tobacco-speckled terror. Overcoming locusts and cicadas, and hornbeams, and everything, the matrices of sound were flung into self-propaganda, all of a sudden: which burst forth in the infinite blindness of the light. The chirping of the animals of light was submerged in a propagation of bronze waves: they irradiated the sun's country, the desperate progress of the roads, the great green foliage, infinite laboratories of chlorophyll: five hundred lire of waves, of waves! Five hundred, five hundred! Enough, enough Señor Francisco, but this can't do any harm—of waves, waves! From the tower: from the stocking-colored spire, artificer of that Trentine din. Furious Sicinnis, they proffered their entrails and then turned them back against the mountain, in waves, tumult of the Lord made matter, androgynous bacchantes at the municipal lubido of every gray-haired offerer. Upturned in folly and shamelessness, they displayed alternately their clappers, like mad heavy pistils, or to the poor man's hunger, the obstinate inanity of the cervix; and the wheel, at each one's side, made the pattern more complex; and they were the morning glories of the Enormous Bronze, upset by stormy gusts of madness. Drunk with sound they swung for quite a while in evacuating their glory! glory! glory! with which they were glutted: to spread in every field that clamorous annunciation, of a bit of puchero and of chopped chiquoréa, seasoned with linseed oil.

The two men came out of the bedroom. The doctor seemed unwilling to give up: ". . . In any case, we'll wait for you"; he was counting on the extreme value of that statement, on the hypostasis of the *fait accompli*: "You can do as you wish then." And the tone this time was the meek tone of the just man, of the weakling who cannot oppose tyranny. "Tomorrow morning at seven, or quarter after . . . we're off!" But the hour that, according to folk wisdom, bears gold in its mouth finally exasperated that withdrawing patient, who seemed to be inexplicably alarmed by each more cordial announcement of happiness.

"Half-past seven at the latest . . . when the Seegrün is still in shadow—you should see! And you'll be able to discover for yourself, finally, whether or not Pepa can drive . . . yes or no . . . and how she drives! . . ."

They began to go down the steps, slowly, the doctor ahead. He stopped on each step, without turning around, as if conducting a monologue: "You might say that they all know her, on all the roads of the Serruchón! From Iglesia all the way down to Prado: from Novokomi to Terepàttola. A bolt of lightning! You only have to see her arrive. Or perhaps even from a distance, the way she takes a curve: so casual, so elegant! Everyone says immediately: 'It's her!' "

A few days before, on the Iglesia road, Señorita Pepina had barely begun (engine turned off) the curve at kilometer 9, when she found Recalcati under her headlights, not to say underfoot: a mountaineer from Iglesuela who was going down to the market with some cheeses and one who was considered a man of character, like all mountaineers in general. In fact, with the empty basket on his back, and at the arrival of a truck loaded with sacks of cement, he suddenly halved for her that easiest of slopes which should have set her down, without wasting a centavo, at the first houses of Prado.

Forced to find a makeshift solution, the girl, as usual, faced it with masterful lucidity. And after the sacrifice of the braking (and her heart clickety-clack

74

down to the heels of her stockings) she still had breath enough to give him yet another little push, Recalcati, with the help of her fender, but so gentle, so well gauged, that she simply deposited his character and his basket beyond the ditch, against the wall of Villa Giuseppina, precise as you please. The strong son of the mountain, after tasting the flavor of the wall, heard the doctor (a different one from Papà, naturally) and heard the magistrate; they immediately saw, all three, that there was no cause—no hubo elemento—to suggest "ni un centavo's worth of damages": neither from her, Higueróa Pepita di Felipe y Carlotta Morelli, nor from Señor Bertoloni, the responsible proprietor of the Villa Giuseppina.

"Muy bien, la muchacha . . . muy bien . . . muy bien. . . ." the son muttered to himself, teeth clenched, as he went over the event: as if he were chomping a toothpick. The doctor must have had some suspicion: "Last week . . . Thursday the twenty-second . . . you must surely have heard, too . . . because an hour afterward everybody knew. It must have been just about five, or five-thirty . . . after the milestone at the tavern, after the pergola, you know where I mean? It's the worst curve in the whole arrondimiento . . . at the Bertoloni's gate-lodge. Well, I tell you she saved Recalcati's life . . . you know, the cheese man." The son had to permit the cheeses to enter the painful circle of his apperception. This was the world's baggage, of the world of phenomena—the evolution of a sequence that unravels richly, from time: among the pomps of the subscribed large bell, the oblation (from obfer, obtuli). And the things narrated by time and by souls crumble in the evidence of the day, from their silly limbo: as, from a full cornucopia, a marvelous cataract of almonds, apples, dried figs.

He arranged them as best he could, those wheel-like

forms of cheese, in that outrageous field of nonforms: in that caravansary of impedimenta of every sort: cicadas onions clogs, hebephrenic bronzes, paleo-Celtic Josés, Battistinas faithful through the decades, goiter-cretin from birth: all the Acheron of mala suerte that had spilled down from the sense and prescience of his fathers, who could be read there, gay, joyous, in that river of tar, the dear normality of contingency, the healthful ingenuousness of country custom.

And he saw again in joyful relaxation the lovely rural scene of the basket and the fender, a lovely tapestry dream: a Louis Quinze somewhat modernized: *"Les quatre saisons. L'été."* All scythes, baskets, crops, cows, peasants: and Pepita coming down on him full-tilt. Oh! that measured and reasonable acceleration inflicted—via behinds—on the lagging step of stubbornness!

But everything, in time, became weariness to him, stupidity.

The chat didn't seem to coalesce. "Besides my girls could give you some driving lessons. Who doesn't know how to drive, nowadays? Even Manoel Torre's aunt has learned, that old woman! And how she races! I see her going down to Prado every Saturday, to the market, whenever she needs peas, tomatoes . . . I'm sure that after three or four lessons you would manage splendidly"—he shrugged—"don't you think so?" Then he lowered his voice, as if to share a secret with him: "With your intelligence—with all the mechanical knowledge you have in your head . . ."

The idea of lessons wasn't a bad one, poor doctor. "And believe me: you'd enjoy yourself. After all, dear Señor Gonzalo, at that age . . . they're full of beans." The beans, too, were received by the son with a smile: they were brief smiles, circumstantiated, which didn't carry the conversation a step forward. Reaching the

76

landing of the steps, which served also as vestibule, they started scraping their shoes on the bricks, both of them, as if to test the paving; the doctor picked up his cane again, which he had left in a corner.

They went out on the terrace from which you could look at the summer, to south and west. The bells were silent: the cicadas crammed the immensity, the light. A sense of puchero swallowed at the family table had followed the uniting metal of the liturgy. The terrace was on a level with the little garden behind the house, with which it communicated directly after the sole obstacle of a gneiss step. This triangular garden, flowers with a few vegetables, of minimum extension, with onions and vine, and the fig tree, all coolness and shadow in the morning, allowed anyone to enter the house from behind, pushing the little green-painted iron gate, through which the doctor had entered and was now about to leave. The house sat squarely, white, on the hill, indeed at the peak, facing south, corresponding to the last slope—which made a difference in level of 4.25 meters, the height of one storey. On the front, against the sun, there was an extra floor.

From the terrace the view extended as far as the eye could see, to the distant hills, and then farther perhaps, in the sun. It was extinguished at the distant horizons, and at the last smoke of the buildings, barely discernible in the haze; it rested on the villas and the parks, green clumps, ancient, all around the mild and familiar partnership of those little lakes.

They were pale blue, opaque levels, future peat bogs, among the rise of the thousand pleasant accidents of a serene orography, which had known the tread of the Graces. Earth dressed in August; the names, the villages, were scattered there. And it was a land of men and of a people, dressed by their labor.

Both the doctor and the son paused; they went to the railing, summoned by that evidence of life. Everything had to continue and develop, and be fulfilled: all works. The morrow from the ridges of the east peering forth with gilded brows would find things again: as the smith picks up again his hammer from where he left it in the forge. Huddled, intent on looking, the son had both hands on the wooden railing, his arms spread and open like tired wings. He looked sorrowingly. "My mother has aged," he said. Then, with violence: "It's been years now . . . I'm in despair." He uttered these last words as if in a dream: and the hour from a distant spire seemed to signify: "All has been fulfilled." An extraordinary forewarning like a cruel jest, plunged down on the extracommunal chicken yards that lie in sequence: but not much, not much! And the true hour would then strike, the serious truth: the decree of Lukones beyond appeal. He drew back. The doctor looked at him. Now he had clasped his hands below his belly, as monks keep them, fingers interlaced, as if praying—white, long, a bit thickened at the knuckles: unskilled, it was clear, for any mechanics, or motor, or pump, or dirty task. The face, sad, a bit childish, eyes veiled and filled with sadness, with the nose prominent and fleshy as of a strayed animal (something between the kangaroo and the tapir); he looked beyond the little boundary wall toward the mountain, and the ultramontane blue: perhaps, over there, were the skies and the hermitages, and nothing.

His mother, returning from the cemetery, should have appeared from behind the corner of the house, with the old umbrella that she used to lean on: Mama! After having gone down the steps to the little gate through which all entered, without asking, bent, perhaps she was supported by the maid, holding her arm so she wouldn't make a misstep and stumble. After having walked slowly along the little path by the wall, humbly, she would announce herself with the faint, crunching chirp of her slow footsteps. "I can't understand what came over me . . . I complained to her because there were no flowers on the grave . . . and then she was determined to go herself . . . with these roads!" He went to the corner of the house; he looked, in anguish, at the little road that came down from the higher villas, which his mother would have to cover, stone after stone, returning from the cemetery. He came back onto the terrace. "I had mentioned it to her so that she would speak to José, her beloved José, the peon—the adored fellow citizen whose taxes we pay . . . whom we pay." The doctor, head bowed, lashed his right calf with his cane. "Electricity . . . rent . . . wood . . . ink . . . as if by right . . . so that he will condescend to shuffle about the house in the filthiest trousers he can find to put on. A couple of geraniums, after all, on that grave! But she says they won't grow there . . . And Mama wanted to go herself, then, out of fear that I would start shouting."

An easy step, a light and carefree running, and the rapid crumble of the gravel after the gate's unexpected creak warned them that somebody was arriving, a boy certainly. From around the corner of the house a boy did come running, in a sweat; suddenly, glimpsing the two men, he broke off his running, in a somewhat vexed pose, as if he had seen his chocolates vanishing. With a coffee-colored jersey, a copybook in his hand; his legs quite bare. His knees, full of bruises and scratches, were the chief thing one noticed after the childishness of a round face, pearled with sweat. He was panting slightly, like a locomotive that goes on puffing even after it has stopped, despite the presence of cabinet ministers. He was a healthy child, with a coffee-colored chest, about twelve years old, his eyes empty of any judgment; all the world, for him, must have been a kind of unripe pear, into which he was unable to sink his teeth. His soul, without syllables, bore witness to its anamnesis. Now he was silent, looking—rigid and still, on those legs. "What do you want?" the son shouted at him rudely, as if irritated at his silence. The boy, without moving closer, stammered from the distance something like "Lesson . . . French . . . the Señora." "Clear out!" the son commanded, with an inconceivable severity, which made the boy disappear—and left the doctor dumbfounded.

"But isn't that Di Pascuale's grandson?" the latter asked.

"I don't know who he is, or whose grandson. What I do know is that my mother's in her second childhood . . . like all old people." He spoke in agitation. The doctor lashed his calf with his stick. "She has to drool kindness on the first calf that she comes across . . . on the first stray dog that comes in . . . even the grandsons of colonels on holiday, now . . . making them repeat *choux, bijoux, cailloux,* poor darlings. Because, in the end, everybody becomes good!" He shouted. He seemed to lose his mind. "Good! Good! Everybody . . . until some geraniums, or violets, reward us for our good conduct . . . for our definitive goodness."

"He's a first-rate physician," the doctor ventured with that somewhat grumbling speech of his, perennially uttered with bowed head, like a monologue, "and, I believe, an official of the highest integrity": poor man, he seemed to be taking "a part" in the aristocratic theatricals.

"That's no reason to drag into the house his whole litter of grandsons! Let them learn French in school . . . that's what it's for. And if they don't learn it"—he stared at the doctor—"if they don't learn it, thwack!"

He pretended to lash the legs of someone (a horse?)—
they were long ones, naked and straight. He lowered his
head horizontally to accompany the jerk of his shoulder,
the impetuous gesture of the arm, as if he really had a
whip in his hand. An incredible wrath transformed his
incoherent physiognomy. "And they don't learn it . . .
and they'll never learn it! Because calves haven't the
power of speech. They have a hard time writing two
simple sentences in Castilian. So thwack, thwack, thwack
then! on their bare legs. Here comes charity, goodness!"
He was shouting. "The French lessons are coming! On
the calves' necks . . . gratis. One foot in the grave . . .
for others! For the peon . . . for the grandson . . . anything, provided it's for others . . . for others!"

The doctor was silent, confused: embarrassed by
that half-centimeter of beard, one would have said—in
reality amazed, grieved. Without being able to justify
in any way what he was hearing, what he was seeing, he
nevertheless understood that something ghastly was
churning in that soul. He thought of guiding elsewhere
the sick man's ideas, if ideas they were.

The son regained his composure: he seemed to
wake from a hallucination; he looked at the doctor,
staring, as if he were asking of him, "What did I say?"
—as if he were imploring, "Tell me what I said! I was
ill! Couldn't you see? Couldn't you see that I was ill?
Why wouldn't you believe me, why wouldn't you assist
me? I had lost the thread of our talk—what were we
saying?" His eyes brightened again in an expression of
anguish. A footstep ran by outside, descending, the step
of a stupid imp; under it the pebbles of the road crum-
bled, after the creak of the gate, which was painted
green.

"I was a child myself," the son said. "Then I deserved perhaps a kindly thought . . . no, not a caress,

that was condescending too far, it was too much!" And wrath returned to his face, but died away again. Then he resumed, "Mama has aged frightfully . . . she's ill . . . perhaps it was I . . . I can't resign myself. But I had a frightful dream."

"A dream? And what harm does a dream do you? It's a bewilderment of the soul . . . a momentary ghost."

"I don't know, Doctor: mind you . . . perhaps it's forgetting, it's resolving! It's rejecting the sclerotic images of dialectics, the things seen according to force."

"According to force? What force?"

"The organizing force of character . . . this glorious kerosene lamp that smokes us up from inside . . . and makes a black wisp, and smudges us with lies, within . . . meritorious lies, greasy ones, lying ones . . . and has a good opinion of itself, and of itself alone. But to dream is a deep river, which rushes to a distant spring, bubbling up again in the morning of truth."

It seemed incredible to Doctor Higueróa that a man of normal height, rather tall in fact, and of such "lofty" social station, could let himself become anchored to foolishness of this sort. But alarm and sadness were all too evident in his gaze; the gaze of a person who fears, who has something that preoccupies him, some remorse —terror, hatred?—even in broad sunlight, in the song, in the sweet and relaxed fullness of the earth.

"A dream . . . wriggling toward my heart . . . like the treachery of a serpent. Black.

"It was night, late evening perhaps; but a frightful, eternal evening, in which it was no longer possible to recover the time of possible action, or erase despair . . . or remorse; or ask forgiveness for anything . . . anything! The years were past! When we could love our mother . . . caress her. Oh! help her. Every finality, every possibility, had turned to stone in the darkness.

82

All souls were distant like fragments of worlds; lost to love . . . in the night . . . lost . . . weighted down by the silence, aware of our former mockery . . . exiles without charity from us in the desperate night.

"And I was as I am now, here. On the terrace. Here, you see? In our deserted house, emptied of souls . . . and in the house there remained something of mine, of mine, something that had been saved . . . but it was an unspeakable shame for the souls . . . documents, receipts . . . I didn't remember for what. The law's delays had been concluded. Time had been consumed! Everything, in the darkness, was stony memory . . . definitive idea, beyond erasure. Receipts . . . that everything, everything was mine! Mine! Finally . . . like remorse.

"And the dream—a moment!—was resumed in a figure of shadow—there, there where I just went, you see? At the corner of the house. You see now? There . . . black, silent, very tall: as if she had come back from the cemetery. Perhaps, with her silence, she reached the eave: she seemed a funereal veil, falling from it. Perhaps she was beyond all dimension, all time.

"Not suffused with any meaning of love, of grief. But in silence. Under the sky of shadows. Veturia, perhaps, the motionless mother of Coriolanus, veiled. But she wasn't the mother of Coriolanus! Oh! the veil didn't dispel my obscure certainty: it didn't mask her from my grief.

"I knew her, I knew who it was. It could be no other —tall, motionless, veiled, black.

"She said nothing: as if a horrible and superhuman force were preventing her from any sign of love. She was immobile now. It was a thought . . . in the dark catalogue of eternity. And this black, ineluctable force . . . heavier than a tombstone . . . fell upon her! As the outrage falls, beyond all reparation. And it had risen in me, from me! And I remained alone. With the documents . . . scriptures of shadow . . . the receipts . . . in the house emptied of souls. Every delay had reached its time, time dissolved."

The cicadas collapsed in the even continuity of time; they spoke of persistence: they reached the boundaries of summer. Doctor Higueróa seemed to look for the birches, white commas in the oak trees to the west of Lukones.

He continued to cane his right calf; now with light touches, repeated as if following a rhythm, or as if to beat the dust from his trouser. His gaze, unusually horizontal, was anchored to the wall, and then wandered outside, toward the mountain, with heavy, swollen eyes, acting as brackets to his beholding. A slight reddening of the conjunctivae gave those two poor instruments of a country doctor the weary expression of toil—like that of a suffering dog, running about all day—a merciful and bewildered sweetness, the sadness of a man who had by now given up all whim of itinerary, of journeying, and who asked the weather and the clouds only to help him, along that bit of road left him. The prickling of the beard on his chin seemed to take the place of the bits of broken crockery, the triangles of bottle glass that were missing from the ridge of the wall. It was a Pirobutirro wall, without bits of bottle, or shards of crockery.

"I don't know what came over me," the son repeated. "I don't know what to do anymore. Why doesn't she come back, now? She's aged frightfully. Her face, her lips, you would think they hid a thought that isn't hers . . . that they silence unspeakable words . . . but distance is already in her—my mother! I hadn't seen her for several weeks; how can I help her now? Her hands are like a skeleton's." As no judge spoke, he began again to justify himself: "I shouted, true; but not because of her . . . because of that scoundrel whose taxes we pay—"

"But still you shouted," the doctor said sagely, "and you shouted with her! For that matter, if you think it right, we could examine her . . . even today . . . even now"—professionally, he used the royal plural. "An examination is not tiring."

"Ah! not tiring? For you, perhaps, Doctor, since you're used to it. But Mama! It's been years! I'm in despair . . . it's like hoisting a corpse to the top of the Eiffel Tower"—his voice became agitated again, then settled into gloominess—"a stubborn resistance . . . incurable." Then he was filled with wrath, with mockery: "Women's brains, if they barely manage to reach thirty . . . the brain becomes marble. Their soul doesn't move any further. The tables of old white-beard, the one with the two radioactive horns who shed light for the Hebrews . . . his tables . . . must have been made of oatmeal, in comparison—"

"We'll try to persuade her. What else can I say? If it's because, after all, she doesn't have confidence in . . . in yours truly, and wants to have someone else, why! of course! That wouldn't be the end of the world. Nothing wrong with that—we're here precisely to lend each other a hand. If we can't find one, there's another. We can take her to Novokomi to Doctor Balánzas, in the car. Pepa would be delighted. Poor Señora . . . or to Doctor Oliva, right . . . better still! Or even to Terepàttola, if you like, Professor Lodomez, the man who treated Caçoncellos." He looked at the wall, the low parapet.

The son had doubts, in his face: "Mama won't want to hear of it; I know her. There's nothing to be done with her. It's a mania, a real psychosis . . . from the time she gave birth to us . . . perhaps, who knows, as a little girl; when she couldn't stand the doctor's spectacles . . .

85

and they frightened her . . . with the beard of the bogey man. Perhaps because she's always been healthy.

"She says, 'Thank God for fresh water . . . the best medicine is to keep away from doctors.' She isn't completely wrong, after all.

"Very well, but today? Today? She says, 'I'm perfectly well. All I need is to be left in peace . . . leave me in peace a bit!'

"A fine way to take care of yourself! To say, 'There's nothing wrong with me. I've never needed anyone! The farther away the doctors stay from me, the better I feel. I can take care of myself; that way I'm sure not to make mistakes'—I, I, I!"

And again he allowed himself to be seized by an idea, and he raised his voice, angrily: "Ah! the world of ideas! What a fine world! Ah! this I, I . . . among the almond blossoms . . . then among the pears, and the Battistinas, and José. I, I . . . the foulest of all pronouns!"

The doctor smiled at this outburst; he didn't understand. Still he seized the chance to direct into more serene channels their words, if not the man's humor and thoughts.

"And why, for God's sake? What have they done wrong, pronouns? When a person thinks something or other, he still has to say, 'I think . . . I think that the sun is strolling on our cucurbit, from right to left.' " (In South America, in fact, and in the Song of Legnano.[12])

"*Je pense* true *mais j'en ai marre de penser*," the son murmured. "Pronouns! They're the lice of thought. When a thought has lice, it scratches, like everyone who has lice . . . and they get in the fingernails, then . . . you find pronouns, the personal pronouns."

The doctor burst out laughing in spite of himself, with half of his mouth; with the left cheek—as, even when you don't want to, you finally smile at a child; when in the most infernal of his misbehavior, in the raging of his anger, as he stamps his feet, amid pearls of tears and screams to the stars, he roars, "Go way, I hate you!" at anyone who wants to calm him with a caress, and he amuses everybody.

The aphorism, to decipher it, no, not at all; he never thought of that; a chess problem, and beyond his strength.

He drank a healthy, full draught of that warm air —so pure, the breath of life. Under his stringy tie he swelled the whole cage of ribs and sternum, to inhale; to let it burn his lungs. He turned toward Prado, on the right, which with its shiny darkness partially hid from him the foliage of the *olea*[13]: the distant houses seemed to smoke in that August fold; but already the lice, the lousy pronouns, even that he had to hear! He, who when he had to say "my wife" said "my lady"—in Castilian of course: mi señora.

"The mere fact that we go on proclaiming 'I, you' with our uncouth mouths . . . with our avarice of the constipated, predestined to putrescence, I, you—this very fact, I, you—reveals the baseness of common dialectics . . . and guarantees our impotence in preaching anything about anything . . . since we are ignorant of . . . of the subject of every possible proposition—"

"Which would be?"

"It's useless for me to take its name in vain. What just finished coming out of there"—with his face he indicated the tower—"from the matrix of those maenads hurled bellyfirst into the air . . . with clapper hanging out. Mad beasts! And I went hungry because of them, as a child, hungry! Five hundred pesos! Five hundred: Pirobutirro munificence: five hundred pesos! With my jersey patched . . . chilblains on my fingers . . . my feet wet inside my shoes. Punishment because my frozen fingers couldn't grasp the pen! With a sore throat over the Phaedrus . . . with six degrees centigrade of paternal love upon me . . . and enough smoke to make my gray cells turn green . . . so that the dear clapper would turn out well . . . good for anthems and glory . . . the clapper . . . to deafen the dear villa, with the dear potatoes, in dear Lukones . . . to break our eardrums for forty years! They destroy the peace of the living and the dead, believe me; they prevent me from writing, from reading; they even make me throw away the Gospels, because of the racket they raise, after two minutes! They give out such a pandemonium from morning to evening, from four to eleven . . . such chaos! Why it's enough to make you shoot yourself."

They started off around the corner of the house, slowly. They went down the service step: "I, you; the thieving butcher excludes the scoundrel butcher who has his shop opposite—all right, he's a worse thief still— but after all, since they're both thieves . . . Caçoncellos, the Camöens of Terepàttola, said that Virgil was a fool: because Palinurus is a lie, and the naval games a bombastic invention of parasites. Oh, yes . . . so he thinks! Eight years of a naval war that starved Rome seemed to him a glass of tamarisk and soda . . . and Sextus Pompey, a boatload of anchovies. Whereas his Terepattolese dimeters were the mystery, the future! I have given immortal expression to the most modern ideals of my people! I have descended into the depths of their souls . . . oh, yes . . . in Villa Giuseppina! I, I—he, too!— watered the flowers with a watering can that had a hole in it, pissing half the water over his shoes—and besides, if one idea is more modern than another, it means that they're not immortal, neither the one nor the other.

"I, you . . . When the immensity coagulates, when

truth becomes wrinkled in an overcoat—of a Deputy in
Congress—I, you . . . in a mean and shrunken person,
when righteous wrath becomes heavy in a belly . . . in
mine, for example . . . which has as its end and only
destiny, in the universe, the stuffing of tons of bismuth,
at five pesos the decagram . . . down, down into the duodenum . . . bismuth by the shovelful . . . waiting . . . one
day after the other, to the end of one's years . . . When
Being becomes separated into a sack of foul guts, whose
boundaries are more miserable and more foolish than
this foolish, taxpaying wall . . . which you can climb
over in one leap . . . when this fine business happens . . .
then . . . that's when the I is determined, with its fine
monad upon it, like the caper on the rolled-up anchovy
on the lemon slice over the Wiener schnitzel. Then, then!
That precisely is the very moment! That lousy, incom-
parable I . . . swaggering . . . erect . . . beplumed with
attributes of every sort . . . purplish, and feathered, and
taut, and turgid . . . like a turkey . . . in an open fantail
of engineering diplomas, of noble titles . . . saturated
with family glories . . . laden with bric-a-brac and mus-
sel shells like a Negro king . . . or else"—they had
reached the corner and he lowered his voice—"or else
saturnine and Alpine, with eyes hollowed in distrust,
with the sphincter blocked by avarice and red within the
shadow of his nits . . . a dark red . . . like a Celt who's
taken to the woods in the mountains . . . who fears the
pallor of Rome and is terrified by its dactyls . . . *mili-
tem, ordinem, cardinem, consulem* . . . the I of the shadows, the animalesque I of the forests . . . and a fine red,
a sweating red. I, with sweaty feet . . . with armpits even
sweatier than the feet . . . with plenty of good air in his
a—— among the onions and the espaliered pears . . .
claiming his rights . . . like that thief over there . . .
who's been all morning taking the seeds from the on-

89

ions!" With his chin—his hands in his pockets—he motioned toward the peon, who now, one knee in the grass, could be seen and heard scraping, with a little knife, the hollow of a pot. Certainly, at the striking of noon he had left off his labor to prepare his puchero. The doctor, silent, had allowed that angry hail to come down, without even hinting at opening his mouth: his eyes, sad, swollen, looked at the mountains.

"I, I, I! But I'll drive him out of the house! With his packet of rights tied to his tail . . . out, out! . . . to crawl on all fours beyond the wall . . . to clog it over the rocks, up and down from Iglesuela, from whence he dropped on us." The peon, finally, raised his head and his hat from the pot, but he couldn't take it in. He understood that the conversation didn't concern him: fine gentlemen, he knew, often talked metaphysics.

"The wall is humpbacked, you see, and even the souls of the dead could climb over it . . . the poor departed!—to come back and sleep in their bed . . . which is there, white . . . as they left it when they went away . . . and it seems to be waiting for them . . . after so much warfare! It's twisted, all humps, I know: but its symbol, its meaning remains, and for the honest it should have value, for people: it must have value, perforce. For it signifies possession: the sacrosanct private, most private mine, mine! My own personal possession—which is the possession of my fingernails, ten nails, of my right and true ten nails! He lifted his hands from his pockets and put them actually under the doctor's eyes, both equal, with hooked fingers, as if they were the talons of a vulture.

"And what about the toenails? Where do you put them?"

"Inside, I put them, in my house, with my mother: and all the Josés and the Battistinas and the Pep—— the

Beppas, all the jackass grandsons screwed in French or mathematics of all the colonels of Maradagàl . . . away, away with them! Out! Out with them all! This is, and must be, my house . . . in my silence . . . my poor house."

IV

*T*he doctor, with his little cane, swinging one leg—
that is, swinging first one for a bit and then for a
bit the other, in alternating filling of the void—had put
his left hand on the top of the little wall and now reiterated there some fleshy slaps, with the palm and the
opened fingers, the way you slap the hot, full withers of
a fine horse to estimate its worth or pat it; the withers of
the wall, in cement smoothed by the trowel, had shed the
damp of the morning shadow cast on it by the house and
with the day's cycle had appropriated a warmth of its
own like an animal's and in a short while, indeed, one
would have said like the warmth of a stove.

"This wall, to tell the truth, has never seemed much
of a wall to me," he grumbled softly, to deviate the
furies; and just to establish a more reasonable line of
conversation. The wall came up to the brim of his hat,
and to the son's nose; but it was a bastion for the lizards'
strollings, for their climbing darts, with a rough coat of
plaster, rustic and full of footholds under the smoothed
crown; above it, blue, the dragonfly darted, oblivious of
all—appearing who knows from where, exalting in the
sun, like a vain thought of summer's. Diaphanous and

theatrical, she enjoyed trespassing on Pirobutirro property without a passport, and without asking anyone's leave. She too! So it was. She had the air of a handsome woman out for a spin without itineraries, light of wing and of life, to say nothing of brain, allowing herself to be summoned here and there by a thousand vague diversions, gold, stuffs, flowers, trinkets, at summer's boundless bazaar.

"It's never seemed much of a wall to me," the doctor repeated. "You're right: with one jump a man's inside."

"Outside, however, it's two feet higher," the son said, as if he felt called upon to guarantee, to his own doubting anxiety, the inviolability of the enclosure. Now he spoke calmly, and decently, but still with apprehension. The doctor shrugged.

"Yes, with those curbstones . . . they look as if they were set there on purpose . . . to help one climb over. Like so many stools . . . you know, those short-legged riders . . . perhaps with their behinds a bit too developed . . . who need a stool in order to climb into the saddle."

That wall, in fact, was only for the view, like all walls, perhaps, of every earthly property. It was quite low, especially at that point, namely, the point corresponding to the northwest corner of the house. It sloped down from the iron gate, indulging as best it could the external cataract of the road and the internal course, gentler, of the little *allée* or path that followed it, with the espaliered plums. It ran obliquely to the northern wall of the house and came here to within five feet of the corner, so that you could only see a patch of grass at its foot, and a plum tree branching over it, right here, granting passage with the chirp of the gravel. The outer road was caving in, with big pebbles, or rather sharp splinters and stones; it lost altitude more rapidly, and whereas at the gate there were three steps to descend, only to enter, at this point the cataract's level was already almost two feet lower than the path inside. But those two feet or even three were consumed by the curbstones, so that a careful eye and a good jump were surely enough to mount astride.

Lost in thought, the son hesitated for a little while. He said, "To be sure." Then he said, "Basically it's only a symbol. Like the big gate down there; it's half-rotten: a good kick would knock it down. And after all what's the use of all these walls, bars, barriers, gates? They're even less effective than the 'no spitting' signs in the trams. At Pastrufazio. Oh! the twenty-seven million bipeds . . . my equals before the laws of Maradagàl . . . aren't restrained by that . . . I mean, from hawking up their souls, on the sidewalk, at every turn. By the way, Doctor, isn't saliva an internal secretion? What's the need of spitting it out all at once? I really thought it was an internal secretion—but surely I'm mistaken. I thought it a juice, a viscous substance, rather swinish, oh yes, but which the Good Lord had endowed us with to salivate properly that swinishness called croconsuelo—moldy, yellow, verminous . . . to chomp it properly, the stinking, the nauseating . . ."

"Why, it's the king of cheeses! They've even baptized it Rex . . . with the trademark patented." (The doctor was mistaken: Rex was quite a different cheese, imported from Europe.) "In any case, to return to the wall."

"Of course . . . to return to the wall. But what can I do, Doctor? I'm tired . . . I'm ill." The doctor didn't believe it. "The meager, hard-won savings of a lieutenant in the field . . . under cold stars . . . the loved one is underground . . . in that face there was a light . . . a smile . . . under cold stars . . . in the drought of the rivers and among the shards of the infernal mountains

. . . the wretched little salary of the weary, bedeviled
engineer. And here are these walls: I've had to pour my
life's blood into these ruins, here . . . in the plastering of
the walls . . . the taxes . . . plugging up the hole, the
mortgage. Now I'm tired, I'm ill."

Grief had dissolved the unrepeatable years. The
guardians' madness had lacerated the child. Death was
left.

"And, after all, what walls? What enclosure?
Didn't she tell me herself, one day, that in these villages
the people are as good and simple as country bread?
You know them better than I. They're good people,
aren't they? A bit rough, perhaps, a bit guttural in expressing themselves, that's sure—halfway between the
cave stage and the pile dwellings . . . but good people.
In the war they made a fine showing. They died as if
they were drinking a glass of water. Nailed to the spot.
And in peacetime they've never caused any trouble, poor
devils."

After the variations of a more or less inspired tan-
trum, he suddenly looked like a child, pleading to be reassured, appealing to the grown-ups' authority against
the horror of the dark, to be calmed.

"Good people . . . good people," the doctor snickered, thinking of the invective of a moment before and
the peon's glowering.

"When they don't wield their knives, of course,
they're good people."

"But I never heard of anything . . ." the son repeated. "For that matter, my mother is stubborn, that's
sure . . . a thousand times! I must have told her: keep
someone in the house, at least at night. Keep a maid, a
peasant, a dog, whatever you like . . . but have somebody
there. You might need help . . . feel ill. She's no child,
not by a long shot.

"Keep only one maid, I say, instead of having fifty

women clumping about the house in their clogs. But have that one stay the night. Peppa, the laundress who does the sheets, if you like, since you get on with her. Oh! the recruits of Pomerania, at their medical examination, would cut a sorry figure, compared to Peppa."

"Her! The very sight of her would be enough. . . ."

"That Peppa! To deal with a criminal she doesn't need a musket or a knife, not her! She'd take off a clog and wham—end of thief." He seemed to be completely consoled at the idea of Peppa. The Pirobutirric feudal domain guarded, guaranteed, confirmed by Peppa: seeing the lack of wall, of bottle fragments, and with all the felonious nature of the curbstones revealed, and the infamous José. A few moments before she too had figured in the roster of base and wicked, Peppa; now she was a Michelangelo-esque spirit and bicep, with victorious clog brandished and hurled in the night, with shoulder, from the opening of the nightshirt, white, fulminating. "The other day—her father is over seventy . . . and he fell to arguing . . . down below . . . in their field . . . with the water men . . . you know, the ones for the artesian well, those two lice from the city administration . . . who go hunting for water where there isn't any . . . with the excuse that they were in the war.

"Well: she heard them arguing . . . and saw them, too—from the window . . . while she was tidying up Mama's bedroom. If you had seen her! She flew. A hen hurling herself on a snake, with all her feathers sticking out.

"Of course, of course . . . that would be the practical solution. But it's not even to be mentioned! A waste of breath. I get on very well by myself, she says, and I don't need anyone. At night I like to sleep. And what if they strangle her in her bed? I don't want maids in the house, at night.

"And during the day?" He numbered them with his fingers: "Peppa, Battistina, Pina the dwarf from the cemetery, José, Giovanna, Beppina the *sans-culotte,* Luigina, Marietta on temporary leave—I almost forgot Giovanna—ah! Gaetanina." He unfolded two more fingers. "One who does the sheets, another the stockings, and this one for the linen . . . and that one for the colored 'garments' . . . or for the fish . . . and Luigina to iron . . . and Marietta to prepare the tomato conserve . . . or with the excuse that she brings figs . . . when she won't even eat." His face became wretched in the vacuity of the report, like a maniac, at Cogoleto. "But she gives them to the coffee-colored grandson . . . so that he will condescend to glance over that bit of owls and cabbages with a final x . . . to learn a few words, wrong . . . with that wonderful accent he has, the grandson—it makes me sick just to hear him.

"*Maître corbeau sur un arbre perché*—Oh! *nolite margaritas.* La Fontaine for such an idiot. And my mother, my mother! And she gives him figs, peaches, sweets . . . the idiot. And she pets him. The more idiotic he is, the more she pets him. And chocolates. And she smiles at him, as if she were his Mama . . . and biscuits, words of praise, and even the final kiss, at last . . . because he's been so idiotic, superbly idiotic. And, he hasn't understood a thing. And all of a sudden he's asked to go and weewee . . . and she's waited for him, to come down from his weeweeing, patiently . . . and they've started again to try to read—that is, to make him read—and *crêpes* promptly became crap, and Mama burst out laughing. And she was happy; happy! With that idiotic little puppet, who's popped up from God knows what hole, after what grim mechanics.

"He didn't understand a thing, he scratched his knees, dug into his nose, stuck his pen behind his ear.

And instead of the whip, which he deserves: sweets, figs, biscuits, words of praise . . . until he'll fall ill with a bellyache, the beloved grandson; and we'll have to pay also for the bellyache of the grandson of the medical colonel, poor darling! Also the funeral of the grandson, the tomb, with an angel dropping a rose over it, the solemn Funeral Mass . . . with eight priests, with the orphanage in procession after them, the full complement.

"If he only would die, really! Since I'll have to pay . . . pay . . . after the bells, after the mortgage, after the subscription for the public commemoration of Ca-çoncellos . . . for the jubilee severance pay of Caçon-cellos' maidservant. She must have contributed too, I imagine, to assuring a peaceful old age to the faithful Giuseppina—since this Lukones means summer people. And summer people mean paying: and Pirobutirro means paying, donating, giving, giving away . . . away, away, away! Everything that can be given away, given to others . . . to the beloved others. And if the grandson dies, of indigestion after the figs and the chocolates, I'm the one to be blamed. And I'll have to pay, as always. Pay for his place in purgatory, the idiot's. Because the guilt will be ours, the Pirobutirros'. And so we'll have to pay. Since we're guilty of everything. The guilt is ours for it all . . . whatever happens . . . even in Tokyo . . . in Singapore . . . the guilt is ours. It belongs to the Piro-butirros, marquesses of Lukones. And we'll have to pay. Pay everything to everybody." He abandoned himself again to his delirium. Coercive ideas girded that skull with their iron crown. Only a psychiatrist, and one who knew in detail the torment of that miserable biography, could have attached a tag to the illness. But the good doctor smiled: "Come, come . . . thank the Lord."

"If a man is stuck on the spikes of the gate, because he's a thief, and was climbing over the gate to break in and steal, well . . . we're responsible! And we have to beg his pardon, cap in hand, and assign him a pension for the rest of his natural life; because he spiked his scrotum coming to steal. Ah! Christ, Christ . . . what a thing it is, the right, a man's packet of rights."

It really had happened, years before, behind the garden of one of the more rusty villas, full of nettles and lizards, toward Iglesia; some young people out to steal figs had roped themselves together like climbers, one Sunday, over the spikes of the garden gate: and one, run through, a few days later was cut off in the bloom of his manhood by the consequent tetanus infection. The distraught parents, a few years later, were awarded three thousand by the heirs of the owner (who in the law's delays had also become defunct, in their turn), though they had attempted to make a killing, and their representative, lawyer Buscaglione, repeated eight thousand: and then, enraged, nine thousand five hundred at the second appeal.

"Come, come, Señor Gonzalo!" the doctor said. "Everything looks black to you, even the sun!"

"They're good people, they're good people. But are you guilty of having a house? I said, a house?" He raised his index finger under the doctor's chin. "That they would like to have themselves? That all of them would like? Then pay. Pay the taxes, the upkeep, the guard, the bells, the hearth tax, the special supplement A, the special levy B, the firemen's benefits, the municipal pharmacists' fund, the parish tax, refuse removal, when there's no refuse, no sweepings to sweep . . . since even the sewage is used by José, even that, from 'his' sewage tank . . . immediately, for 'his' tomatoes, on 'his' cabbages." The doctor stood and listened to him, head bowed, lashing himself.

"And what the devil? Would you like even to be

exempted from taxes, now? Why, if you really read the Gospels, as you insisted a while ago, you can see clearly for yourself in the Gospels what is written. It's written . . . that taxes must be paid."

"Absolutely. I admit that. Tithes are sacrosanct. Caesar is sacrosanct . . . that is to say our beloved Congreso. But why the peon, why pay the guard? Since he doesn't guard a damn thing . . . not the Gaul borders, since he had gone into hiding at Imatapulqui, nor the garden of the house, where nothing but hay ripens . . . or the onions? The peon isn't Caesar. He's a pig. He steals my trousers, and my sewage. He's the murderer who will climb the wall, or the gate. He isn't Caesar, he's a thief. Why pay him as well, the thief, who comes to steal? When to come and steal he sticks his testimony on the spikes?

"Pay the thief, pay the guard! If the thief steals, pay him all the same, because the guard isn't guilty! If the guard steals, thank the thief for being less of a thief than the guard. The important thing is that, in any case, you must pay."

"Have you subscribed to the Nistitúo?" the doctor interrupted him curtly. He threw out this question in the shortest possible way, to break off once and for all these ravings which had bored him far too much. All for three pesos![14] Really! It was too much. He seemed to be asleep on his feet, with his eyelids like brackets. Legs apart, his hands resting on his stick, a sleepy Roland on the hilt of a rachitic Durendal. This time his speech was brief and sharp, like a sleeper's, one who sleeps but too loud nevertheless not to be master of the human condition and of the notorious chatter of mankind. And he blurts out at the opportune moment the few words, cutting off sharply, but charged with value. That is, with sound judgment. The eyelids, upper and lower, covered almost entirely the reddened bulbs, which were supporting brackets to the falling line of his gaze.

"The Nistitúo?" the son asked, with new apprehension in his countenance.

"Yes . . . the Nistitúo. That seems to me the only thing to be done. What could be more sure than that . . . for one who sleeps . . . at night . . . in an isolated villa?"

"And where is this Nistitúo? Whom should I approach, just in case, if I chose to subscribe?" And the doctor remained silent. "Yes, I mean . . . where do you pay . . . the office where you make your declaration: I want the little slip of paper tucked into the lock of the gate, every night? In actual fact, I mean, where must I go? To Prado? To Iglesia?"

He asked all these questions at random, for the pleasure of asking them (or at least, so it seemed to the doctor): to appear a bit more decent in that umpteenth ferry ride from delirium to rationality, or also to cause obstruction, since in reality he knew very well where it was that one had to go to pay. You paid at home, you paid Palumbo, who took care of everything himself, even the signature, in his role as agent and propagandist for the Institute, proxy, night guard, and collector. Still, in the grip of a certain inner irritation, the good doctor wanted to inflict a final torment on his Pepa's suitor manqué.

"Where do you have to go? Why, to the Vigilancia para la noche . . . its headquarters are in Prado. You . . . forgive me for saying so . . . but you really are creating a storm in a teacup. In Prado, in Prado. At the top of the village, up above, in Calle de los pájaros . . . haven't you ever been there? You know . . . at the end of Corso Pastrufazio, but quite a bit before the monument . . . on your right . . . those thirty steps or so . . . where you start panting to reach Nuestra Señora de los Milag-

101

ros. Well: on the first landing, to the left, where there's that little doorway . . ." The son didn't recall, or had never climbed up that far. "Why, of course you recall! Of course! Next to the barber. Just opposite there's that other doorway, the green one, with a little peephole, and as soon as it's opened, inside the walls are all tiled . . . you know very well."

Tiled meant porcelain. The son received this porcelain with an automatic interrogative, carried out by his eyebrows, which on their own initiative moved up toward the middle of his forehead. The rest of his countenance remained inert. "It's more hygienic," grumbled the doctor, his mouth shut. "Well, just opposite is the Nistitúo . . . Señorita Gamberoni." He shrugged. "Dolores! Who doesn't know Dolores? They call her the recruits' godmother." His tone became harsh, discourteous. "You go to Dolores: and on the spot, once you're there, tell her you want the night service, you too, that you want to do what all the others do. Put your pájaro there in her hand . . . and it's all done. Go, go, and you'll see: afterwards you'll feel much calmer."

"Pájaro" in the Maradagalese lexicon signifies the twenty-peso banknote: and is derived, they say, from the springlike hue of the bill, between sparrow and canary; others say instead it stems from the fact that the republican eagle, crouched on the sword of republican Justice, looks more like a fledgling sparrow, so fat and sly and greedy.

They approached the gate; Señor Don Gonzalo was silent, aware of the quack's insolence. The gravel, beneath their shoes, did its duty, both for its lord and master and for the guest. From the invitations to live, with Pepa at the wheel, there, they had descended to mockery, to the ill temper of the disappointed father; of

102

course! Dolores! The recruits! And yet, the idea that the doctor was going away increased his suffering. The white walls would go on stewing in their hot inanity; caravans of ants ran over them: black, minuscule crumbs of motion and of being.

Mama hadn't come back!

He suffered also, en masse, all the other insolences of others, of the distant, the rich. He suspected that even Mama, his mother, must hold him in contempt: he remembered certain attentions she had lavished on people truly worthy of esteem, such as the violinist for example—though he was dwarfed, big-nosed, and terribly coarse. That year she took him under her wing, and invited him to Lukones. Raised into the glory of the villa, the dwarf! Surrounded by chicken livers. He had introduced himself to Gonzalo, a boy, with a circular hole in the upper part of his right shoe, corresponding to a callus: peremptory, whining, he had expatiated on the calliopean syndrome.

And, generously, glug glug went the flask, from the neck, turned at once into a horizontal, amid the splendors of the tablecloth.

At the fish he began to hiss through his teeth, because he removed the bones from the junctions with his fingers, spitting them out again on the floor; which, all around, was covered with spittle and fish bones. When the moment of the croconsuelo came, he used his knife to place croconsuelo on his tongue (and he slobbered over both together, in a sole lick, the goo and the blade). Boy as he was, he then uttered some rather hard words. "Use your fork!" He challenged the notion that for croconsuelo the knife was better. He enjoined him to go and eat in the kitchen, with Carolina, and the violinist had turned pale, but Mama, with great tact, had pro-

103

tected his sacrosanct condition, which was that of guest. More than as guest, he was sacrosanct in that maternal preference.

That sudden memory made his heart pound with anger; he clenched his jaws; desperately he imagined how he might order from the hemp mill a special order of rope, with a 250-pound breaking point.

But Mama, where was she? The brief road, perhaps, was, in her weariness, an endless journey. Mama had gone away, from the house, from the sun.

From his pain he seemed to return to fear—like a stray mongrel roaming about without plan, following the first smell the street offers him, and suddenly on his back falls a searing firebrand. The doctor realized he had gone to excessive lengths. He regretted that stupidity about Dolores. Having walked forward, he turned, for he was at the gate. The peon came and went without looking at them, dragging his clogs, a little kettle in his hand for the chickens, busy with his chores.

"For that matter, you don't have to go all the way up there . . . I mean . . . to la Gamberoni. All you have to do is tell Pedro, I mean Gaetano, the first morning you hear him go by here. Have him give you the receipt at once. When you've paid the first month, it's as if you had signed the subscription contract. They obligate themselves for twenty-five years."

These twenty-five years were soon an obsession for such a fanatical lover of freedom, who would have liked to choose, to construct his destiny from minute to minute.

"Because they have only one contract . . . a contract form . . . which comes no doubt from the regulations. Because they stick to the regulations. In fact, when I think about it, there must be a law—"

"I don't think . . . a law," the son blurted, flushing,

with harsh severity. He had, of the law, a *sui generis* concept; not learned from reading the edict, but consubstantiated in his being, biologically hereditary. And it cost him an effort to recognize the species of the law in an abuse or an arbitrary act, even more, also, in an imposition. But, in considering an abuse this provision of the guard, he was surely mistaken. Perhaps he suffered from what Sérieux, Capgras, and other contemporary psychiatrists have effectively called "interpretative delirium," distinguishing it from classical or hallucinatory delirium, as well as from delirium of imagination.

"Law or no law," the doctor rebutted, "what does it matter to you?"

"But isn't that pest there enough?" the son said, "when I pay lodging, taxes, wood, electricity, service? So that he might condescend to wake up . . . if somebody came to steal . . . whereas, instead, if they really did come, they would catch him . . . knocking down those few almonds . . . then blaming it on the frosts, on the fog, the hail."

"But they all do this."

"And after he's poled them down, do I also have to pay the Nistitúo?" Again he had changed ideas, manner, words: his anguish was again harshness. "There's nothing to steal! What do you expect them to steal, in this house of poverty? A few odd forks? My Cervantes? What would thieves make of a Cervantes, in the Serruchón?"

The doctor could find nothing better than a shrug.

"In order to sip my Ariosto in peace, in bed, my Boccaccio, when even the clapper of the bells has grown drowsy, after its propaganda; in order to enjoy my classics sprawled in my bed, stretched out full-length like a Caliph, why should I have to pay a pájaro per month to Gaetano?" (In the past several years he had

105

acquired some sort of knowledge of the Italian language.) "Pay the invisible patrol of the Nistitúo? When there are only the crickets, in the countryside, all darkness, to punctuate the world's time?"

"Who can tell?" the doctor said. "If they take it into their heads that there's a job to be pulled off . . . you can be sure, a gate doesn't bother them. A bit of money is always kept in the house. There's the silver. Your mother, too, with those diamonds . . . everyone talks about . . . since they all see them . . . even from a distance."

The normal man, doctor though he may be, easily forgets he is talking to an ill one. The son, in his grief, saw a bride of the years of President Uguirre, when there were still horse-drawn trams, and her husband, with the glitter of the presents, leading her to blush with joy, and to smile. Alive in her hopes, she addressed the years of life, she questioned with the trembling flower of her person the warm breath of the future. But old women, on the dark roads in winter, have their diamonds torn from their lobes. (The dead sons do not defend her, assumed, memoryless, under the crosses of the Cordillera.) Their poor person, from whom the torment of childbirth has been erased, and the torment of death, bent, weakened, does not deserve pearls. In the darkness a dungheap gapes.

The doctor repeated: "Who can tell? In any case it's a greater security."

"Are you afraid there's no security?" the son implored. "These are calm villages."

"Oh!" the other man sneered. "As if they were Christians, here in Lukones . . . those who will flash the light in your eyes! There are also a few stolen automobiles in this world. No? And they know how to drive, never fear, they can handle a car, don't worry about that! And also with the lights off.

"Last year at Carpioni's, up in the farmland, then at Brocchi's. At Brocchi's it was small pickings, I grant you that . . . half a dozen rabbits . . . a few hens . . . and it's hard to understand how they managed to keep them quiet. They must have strangled them on the spot. This year at Brugnoni's, at Carpioni's, and another attempt at Teresotti's, two months ago. Now, the Carpioni and Brugnoni thefts, it seems to me, were two master strokes. Don't you agree? And the family, imagine, the Carpionis, were downstairs eating salad! On the ground floor. You know? The lettuce from their garden, which had just been awarded an honorable mention at the horticultural show at Terepàttola . . . a first honorable mention." The son's face became serene again; a ray of good humor sustained him. The doctor went on, unperturbed: "At Brugnoni's, then, they found the police dog had died . . . a real piece of luck. And so they were able to pick the place clean . . . silver, tablecloths, napkins. It isn't like living in the city, mind you, where a thief, the minute he starts robbing, has people coming up the steps . . . and in the street, afterwards, immediately he has a crowd after him . . . so, if they're delayed . . . the police . . . But here! Before anybody jumps out of bed! Fat chance! Here you're alone, in the dark, off in the country . . . precisely . . . as you said just now. Except that the crickets are no use."

The peon clomped again into the brief scene of the garden triangle, before the whiteness of the house, busy, with his trousers clumsily tied over his hips, sweating, depositing cakes of compressed dung after him on the gravel's chirping, as if to mark his itinerary, as they flattened beneath his quadruped walk in the clogs, which had turned into slippers they were so worn. A cat followed him and then preceded him, at a trot. The man entered his master's house through the official entrance, without closing the glass door, which a draft, suddenly, slammed. The cat had slipped into the house, alert, a velvety little shadow between the man's feet.

The doctor, with this talk, behaved as if he wanted to amuse himself by frightening a child. In reality he wanted to seem informed, to amaze Señor Gonzalo with the certainty of his news: to assert, then, in spite of everything, that the police of the arrondimiento were peering into the darkness, in full efficiency. He was a public official, a functionary of the Ministry of Health; he felt a solidarity, to some extent, with all the other functionaries and officials of the province, and perhaps of the Republic; he enjoyed special benefits in official circles of the Serruchón, excepting the benefit of earning a salary sufficient to meet the needs of living. His dentist's office, in Prado, was guarded free of charge by the Vigilancia; the decayed teeth he extracted from the jaws of the Pradese, every Tuesday and Friday, had not aroused greed; no automobile-borne band had yet moved in the night, to make its prey.

Gonzalo, in that being of his, in that undulating graph of his with exaggerated extremes, composed of an alternation of contrary moods, a succession of opposed humors, now saturnine, now Dionysian, now Eleusinian, now Corybantian, was perhaps far from thinking of thieves qua thieves—*ut jugulent homines surgunt de nocte latrones*—but he was grieved at the thought of Mama. Thieves, in his anguish, were the symbol of an offense which could be committed against his mother, or, more precisely, of a failure of succor in her indigent solitude. But everything had failed her, his mother.

"To be sure . . . frogs are no use," the doctor meditated. "There's that one!" the son replied, "to satisfy the law's desires . . . he has to suffice": he nodded toward the door where the peon had vanished. "He has the revolver Mama gave him; he has a shotgun, which he borrowed from the Besteiros; if you ask me, he's a pig. So it seems to me he will suffice."

"Very well . . . but it's a question of doing one's best to cooperate . . . each according to his power. To join, all of us, in an idea of civil solidarity . . . yes, after all . . . civic duty."

"I won't pay anything more, neither to the Celts nor to the Indios." The doctor was about to be convinced perforce that Señor Don Gonzalo was mad. "No. I don't believe in the guard, just as I don't believe in the omniscience of the volcano Akatapulqui,[15] as you know well, the volcano god worshiped by the Incas, the god of sulphur and of flames . . . who looms up and shoots off, there, in the darkness . . . after the squalor of the Cordillera."

"What do you believe in, then?"

"In the Institute for the Progress of Letters . . . surely not." (It was an inter-American institute, fallen on hard times today: which was under the jurisdiction of the League of Nations and, in those years, provided the daily bread of at least a hundred employees.)

"I don't believe in the guard . . . who flies past . . . like a shadow . . . sticking his little paper in the lock . . . of the gate; who has two hundred and fifty villas, and their respective woods, to cycle past in the darkness . . . scattered over three or four communities."

"Well . . . but still you know there is somebody watching . . . and he's a public official."

"What can he watch, with two hundred and fifty villas to watch? I mean villas, huts, rectories, and convents, of both sexes? Would you please tell me what he can watch?

"When he slips along the Besteiros' wall, at Lukones they can dance the tango as much as they please, no? The villa robbers. . . . When he reaches San Juan, on his outward journey, I imagine, or Lukones, at the dirty stable of Manoel Torre, let's say, who can tell what the devil is going on at Villa Brocchi, at Villa Teresotti? And when he finally slips his ticket into the lock at Villa Brocchi, what are the toothbrushes up to at Villa Giuseppina? The ghost, on this occasion, can satisfy every whim that takes him, flouting all the assize courts of Maradagàl: mind what I say—it's the moment, the very one, if he chose, to follow the caprice. They say he's a kleptomaniac . . . that he has a weakness for toothbrushes."

The doctor smiled at this allusion to the theft, considered supernatural: not so much because of the remarks themselves, as because of the tone of severe violence and indignation with which Don Gonzalo had uttered the invective, mistaking the ghost for a political enemy. Among the versions that received greatest popular credence about the methods and imaginable author of the theft of the relics (toothbrush, slippers, and rubber douche), there was also the belief that it had been the ghost himself that stole them, with his own hand, on the night of a Friday the thirteenth. The supposition, for that matter, had had a beneficial influence on the takings of the "lotería nacional."

"I don't believe in the little slip of paper . . . I don't believe in it! And besides, this damned Nistitúo is for the night—only for the night. And then they could come by day . . . or the moment the cock has noticed the egg white . . . there . . . from the gaps of the east . . ."[16]

"Egg white?"

"No: I won't pay. I won't pay! Enough of this paying." He had gone mad.

When he went to the cemetery, he had to walk past the gate of the Villa Agostoni, which was thoroughly subscribed to the Nistitúo and deeply observant not only of the laws or legal decrees and the respective regulations, but also of the simple suggestions and recommendations that the alcade from time to time wafted into those zephyrous villas, on whatever day, in spring or in autumn, when the most propitious opportunity arose. And the pebbled open space before the Agostoni gate, in which you could read "salve hospes" in white pebbles among the gray ones, was all sprinkled with little pink slips, like tram tickets. They were the slips that the Nistitúo, through the guard's personal care, thrust every night, one per night, into a low point of the gate: which was a series of long poles, with gilded spikes. And a breath, toward dawn, from the pines, from the lindens, scattered them in a brief and silent diaspora. "I don't believe in the little slip of paper."

"But you surely believe in a good Browning."

"Not even that. In any case day before yesterday I heard Peppa telling Mama a long story. One of those stories only she can tell, in a low voice . . . a kind of miracle . . . at the Pastrufazio hospital. But I didn't understand the end. I confess that to you. And besides, since he's disabled, how can he be a guard?"

"Disabled?" He opened his eyes abruptly, the good doctor. "But he's cured! For some time! More cured than you! And than me." He had picked up his ears, if one may say that, in a bound toward joy, like a little horse at the crack of the whip. Like a water tank under pressure, which the moment you turn on a faucet under its belly, whoosh, pees forth such a whistle that you can't cut it off again, not even with a monkey wrench.

A joy, a pride: for they helped him to live, to be the most informed "personality" of Lukones or perhaps even, let's see, of the whole area. From Prado to Iglesia, to Ranchito, to Vaqueiras. To have drawn from the sources, from the first spouts, from the repositories of

111

the record, from the heads of the office. To drop, plonk, as if it were nothing, all of a sudden, on the thirsting curiosity of the interlocutor, the huge drop of the palabra oficial. He had led the conversation around to that theme, and right up to that point, who knows? to reach a moment of importance and pride, for those ten minutes of condescension, which would enlighten Marquess Gonzalo Pirobutirro de Eltino . . . in a low voice . . . concerning the question of the day . . . oh! not with the "I hear tells" of the populace . . . but with data in the possession of the authorities, communicated to him by those same authorities . . . to him . . . to him alone . . . under the seal of discretion.

If it hadn't been for this character's spleen, the conversation could already have taken place, in the most decorous fashion, from Professor to Marquess. Some people, in fact, instead of doctor, called him professor.

At that moment, however, they heard pebbles spatter away beneath a rubber wheel, as if in a clotted sparkling—a bicycle—from the road along the hill. Someone got off it, an official; and, from its hinges, the gate gave forth its rapid creak, all rust. The man in uniform entered, his legs slightly bent in his boots; one would have said a rider; his belt, the bandoleer stripe, and the revolver's holster, of shining leather, had brass buckles that seemed polished with Sidol.

The two tiny eyes flashed, like a blade. He said, "I was looking for the Señora," with two fingers, calmly, at the visor of his cap. Then, however, he took off the cap, and the cranium was round and bald to perfection, but with unexpected modulations of hue: from the lower forehead, bronzed, to the crown, very white.

"What do you want?" the son said.

"It was for the Nistitúo. She told me that, this year, she would want it, too, the lady . . . like Señor Agostoni, like the Villa Brugnola, back there." And he motioned with his thumb. "I came by Wednesday before last . . . but she said, come back later."

"It's our guardian angel," the doctor said good-humoredly, as if to introduce him.

"Besides . . . the alcade also . . . urged her to take steps in time . . . not to overlook—"

"It's not obligatory," the son said.

"To tell the truth . . . the law of February twelfth . . ."

"I don't intend to concern myself with this business."

"For the province, in any case, there's the decree No. 5888, of his Excellency the Governor, dated July 22, 1932."

"What about the nonsubscribers then? . . . I want to remain free."

"But the villa is in the Señora's name . . . Pirobutirro de Eltino. At least that's the way it's down in the lists." (A hint of irony, in his voice.)

"What lists?"

"The tax lists. And the Señora spoke to me this past spring, too. She said this year she really wanted to subscribe." In his eyes he had a steady, arrogant glare, behind a first veil of deference, almost of affability.

"My mother is not in," Don Gonzalo said, irked, looking at his main buckle.

The man in the leather rigging turned his gaze up to the windows and then, below, to the door and the curve of the terrace, as if to make sure.

He was really a dog.

At this new insolence, Don Gonzalo's mind was suddenly rekindled entirely, in his favorite and secret idea of the noose. His mouth said nothing. Ingredients of the wrath, in that spirit, were severity and helplessness. The

113

bearer of the gubernatorial decree No. 5888 climbed up two steps (he had remained standing on the third), put his cap back on, settled it on his head with both hands, and said: "Very well . . . I come back when your Mama's in," with a tone, however, that to Señor Gonzalo seemed one of challenge, or of downright mockery. So he let his fantasy rage, for another minute or two, his jaws clenched, on the noose's breaking point and on the various methods of hanging, lingering over the most consolatory details. He even allowed the rope to break eight or nine times, before it worked as it should; then finally he bade it hold fast.

But the auspicated pendant from the Great Gallows galloped instead on his bicycle and descended at once toward Lukones, tires pinched by the stones, which shot away from beneath his wheels as if from so many slingshots awakened in the earth.

The doctor coughed a bit; he had, in his throat, and then also in his nose, a fairly well-selected cough. Then a few monosyllables, a more happily respiratory guttural or two: so that he was able to bring his patient back to the idea of the miracle, or rather to the scientific interpretation of the so-called miracle. They went out of the gate. Don Gonzalo now looked at the turn in the road, toward El Pinto, in the distance, from whence he expected to see returning Mama's black parasol, accompanied—who could say?—by Pina, or by Peppa. Despite this he seemed ready to lend himself with sufficient seriousness and decorum to the desires of his informant; he seemed indeed to regain his composure, and the doctor was overjoyed by it: it was that which concerned him most of all. He said: "But your Mama is late coming home! She can't mean to spend the day at the cemetery!" The doctor had at his disposal certain facts that were

114

absolutely not on the market—he was proud of them—given him by Colonel Di Pascuale: to him alone, two days earlier, on the occasion of the most recent supplying of peas, under the bond of the most absolute secrecy.

These were precisely the facts that he began, little by little, to allow to drip forth, like drops of a pharmaceutical henbane into the ear of the patient, with that characteristic grumble of his and with eyelids toward the ground, combined with a certain detachment from the event, with a certain subterranean magnificence, as a secretary to the Secret Protocol, with an intention of adjustment, of authoritative straightening out of the epos.

In the son's spirit, all invectives were calmed, all sketches for invectives, spurts, and rekindlings of flame in general: against public tax collectors or beneficiaries of private salaries, against the various bipeds, male or female, who had been guilty of being baptized in the name of Mary Virgin and Mother. They were granted peace from the scourging imagination of the persecutor, as they were granted peace, perhaps, after their puchero, in the high hour of the day.

A tardy hen, one of those who lays her egg at one in the afternoon, broke the silence, from the vastness of which gurgled forth once again (like a need hastening toward fulfillment) the hot, baroque moan, uttered in intoxication and in impudence: cockadoodle, cockadoo—dull—do dull do. On the "salve hospes" of the Agostoni, surely, the lizard lay dully in the sun: more Augustony it could hardly be! The hospes, for those powerful savers of the cent, was yet to be born, however. Nor, once brought into the world, would it then have been easy for him to cross that threshold—doodle hospes, doddle hospes, do!—to cross that gate eternally shut in the sheaf of its spears, of that pebbled and deserted entrance, scattered with little pink slips: the petals of decree No. 5888.

At the doctor's report, Gonzalo gave way. "In order not to sleep . . ." Any excuse is good, in the villa! the villa! for the poppied victims of boredom. Special information! The story of the cure had gone like this.

At the Central Military Hospital of Pastrufazio, before the Second Reexamination Commission, Palumbo had recalled the facts, already repeatedly put on record thanks to the local commissions: expounding, with the dramatic accent of truth, in absolute narrative coherence, the terrible stages of the "bombardment," culminating (for him) in the atrocious explosion that had reduced him to a state of complete deafness. This Commission of supreme appeal, composed of twenty-two superior medical officers, assisted by a solicitor, by a secretary, and by a lieutenant-colonel of artillery (of the Third Siege Train) as consultant, and presided over by Major General Huberto Ramirez y Fonseca, had found impeccable everything that Palumbo had adduced, deciding in consequence that his position as a disabled veteran was safe from any attack of the Fiscal Council. But the medical colonel Di Pascuale (descendant of a family of Italian origin, immigrated into Maradagàl toward the end of the last century) had had, however, some doubts. "That character wants to make a fool out of me," the brave[17] and zealous officer had said, in the dialect of his forefathers.

Still, how do you prove that a war-deaf veteran is not deaf? That he can hear perfectly with both ears? If you reflect only a moment, you can see at once—just a minute's reasoning is enough—that the problem is anything but simple. This character can't hear. Why not?

116

Because a lacerating grenade went off near him, on Hill 131. So he can't hear. And, if he can't hear, there's not much use in your saying, "Yes, he can hear." How can you prove it? He flings Hill 131 in your face. It's that Hill 131 that screws you. Were you there, on Hill 131? Well then?

He gazed at him for a long time, Colonel Di Pascuale, from his heavy chair down at the end of the table; then, asking the floor, he stood up, and he spoke briefly, proposing a suspension, which after a short exchange was granted by Fiscal Council. The exchange's only effect was to place, as they say, pepper up the ass of Di Pascuale, exasperating his triple punctilio as officer, as physician, and as an Italian by origin. Also because his most petulant contradictor was a little doctor, beardless, though a major, who gave himself airs as if he knew more about the situation than Di Pascuale. More than him? Ha! As soon as he was in his office, in his chair, and he felt beneath the pepper the pillow of Señora Rosa, "Just hold your horses!" he said, with a look in his eyes! holding out his hand in the direction of Palumbo, who wasn't there, naturally. A scribe raised his head from his scribbling. "Yes, Colonel, at your orders, sir!"

"Who's ordered anything? Just keep cool." He had the strong, solid mind of the Samnites, and the lower lip advanced a fraction of an inch beyond the upper one; as if the man were meditating upon a certain stubborn resistance of his, an "¡Aqui estamos!" in the supreme guardianship of the Maradagalese internal revenue.

Palumbo had "forwarded an application" to be released from the hospital, at least temporarily; he asked for thirty or forty days, as a minimum, since he was to marry, and he had to settle a number of matters that the war had left up in the air—so he stated. And he had

117

renewed the application just a few days before, alleging that the person whom he was to marry couldn't wait indefinitely. The doctors, indeed, believed that he had to repair urgently a specific situation, as was frequent in that year, especially among the rural classes, after the victory over Parapagàl. In reality, it was a question of a widow, with fairly solid roots, table linen, sheets, a farm very, indeed very much in order, who, therefore, didn't lack for suitors. And the widow, in a few words, had sent a message to him that he wasn't to keep her in suspense like this; he was to make up his mind—take her, or leave her. The war by now was over. If he had become deaf, she would take him even deaf, provided he made up his mind. Otherwise she would consider someone else. He, naturally, was rather on pins and needles, in view of the turn events were taking, because this was really an opportunity and it would have been a shame to let it slip through his fingers, like this, just because of the caviling of Colonel Di Pascuale. But Di Pascuale would hear none of this, and two days after the meeting of the Commission he signed the order for him to be put under "special medical observation." "God curse him!" muttered Palumbo through clenched teeth. Two months of observation!

They seemed eternal to him. But he became hardened to the situation. No trick had been clever enough to catch him out, not him! in any possible lack of sincerity. Not the sudden announcement, made to him by the colonel in person, of the death of his uncle Mahagonès, who had named him his heir. So said the telegram. (Heir to a silver chain, some chairs, and a stuffed owl, as it later appeared.) Nor the sudden firing of a blank pistol, which they carried out in the office, behind his back, treacherously, one Sunday, during a terrifying thunderstorm. Nor their showing him a fifty-peso

118

note, or a newly minted pájaro, on the table, saying to him sadly: "The Ladies' Visiting Society has given it to you: take it, ¡anda!"

Nor their charging some poor woman, less filthy than the usual, to call him, in a low voice, in the street below the horse chestnuts of the Fortaleza, one evening or another when he didn't have a cent in his pocket and had instead plenty of quicksilver in his veins: "Hello, sweetie, hello, handsome," etc., etc. "But I wouldn't take any money from you, I like you: all I want is a little loving," etc., etc. How that girl's South American eyes opened, in the stupendous evening! They looked like the night's sapphires. And they dropped in his lap gratis. But, being deaf, he hadn't fallen.

The weeks were consumed slowly, evilly; Palumbo by now believed he had been forgotten in the Central Hospital of Pastrufazio by the delays of procedure, and of the military bureaucracy. Tattered and greasy novels went the rounds of the wards, losing from time to time a few more pages, exploited by some patients without other resources to deal with the sudden effects of their bodily ills. Becoming enriched, from one reader to the next, with ever-new layers of filth, as well as with hairs, wax, and dandruff.

The comrades, sometimes, summarized for him the curious plot.

Also in the ward, in the yard, he had narrated more or less to all, willing and unwilling, shouting, as the deaf do, to all "who came within range," about his uncle and about Hill 131. So that by now they all knew him. "Hey, 131!" they shouted at him, without, however, his hearing them, poor devil. "So long, 131! Say hello to your uncle! See you in civvies! See you when you're on your pension! Hurrah for the Army!" No trick had worked. In the end he became torpid, as if resigned, in a kind of moral doze: even the widow, after all, since she was in such a hurry . . . it must be said that she was also a tramp. Better off without her, that one! "After all," he made an effort to convince himself, "things aren't so bad here, at Central!" But then anger over the wedding, the linen, the farm, seized him again: the convalescent leave, the thirty days plus travel time, at least! Then he had them write to the widow that she was to be patient, that the final examination, the last suffering was near; that the pension was sure, not even General Ramirez by now could screw him out of it. Sixth degree, fifth category. And the widow, on reading those letters with the four-leaf clover in them—phew phew!—wasn't entirely insensitive to that cry of grief[18]—a "government pension" was always a government pension, even if it was of the fifth category, or perhaps of the ninth.

And so the days ripened, one after the other, like tasteless pears: a few cigarettes, a few tasks assigned by the quartermaster on duty, to shift forty pounds of rubbishy papers from one floor to another, to shine some brass handles, the iron door handles of the verandas, with pumice, leaving them, after rubbing and rubbing, all shiny and scratched. Every second Friday the peacock-colored entrance of the Hospital Visitors of San Giovanni (Nepomuceno) bringing two Tuscan cigars, and two Umbrian chocolates.[19]

This saint, who is venerated in Pavia in the middle of the bridge, is also in Maradagàl the patron of river boatmen and of bridge builders. Bridges, however, are not to be seen, in Pastrufazio, in view of the Biblical proportions of the flood that sweeps through there, by the name of Guarany: and its span must be about seven miles. But the Saint is venerated there and is the local patron, as Ambrose is with us. Because of the river.

And, even more, for having the same name as General Nepomuceno Pastrufazio, the second "founder" of the city, the libertador of the windy pampas—where he rode about like a monsoon, with his kerchief around his neck—and of all the pre-Andean plain: terror of the gringo and of the Indio, that is, a bit of the one and a bit of the other, though constant, unfailing friend of the aboriginal Incas—the generous Incassi[20] as our good poet Parini calls them.

Colonel Di Pascuale, one morning, sent for Palumbo, "that character." "Which, Colonel?" "Which?! That one! I told you." "Ah! I know. Freguglia!" "What Freguglia?! That other character . . . 131 . . . the one that can't hear!": and when he had him before his desk, at attention, he wrote in blue pencil on the first sheet of his pad: "Tomorrow we will be send-/ing you home and you will have-/a month's leave. Does that make you-/happy?" And he turned the pad around, so that he could read. As I have noted, because of the application the colonel was aware of Palumbo's ardent wish. And Palumbo, now reassured about the sixth-degree pension, longed for nothing more than to be able to cash it and enjoy it thoroughly, supported by the widow, monthly, in the peace of regular installments—after so many odd hills and so many storms on the mountains.

He raised his eyes to look the soldier in the face. The poor deaf man flashed joy and gratitude from his eyes, moved around the table: and, grasping the colonel's hand, his left, he fell to his knees, all of a sudden, like a beggar in a plaque by Tintoretto; and he took to covering it with kiss after kiss, to the amazement of the clerks speedily reawakened from their forms, at those kisses, alas! of a man to a colonel. Kisses upon kisses, in that ardent, irrepressible effusion, which is of the humble and the pure in heart, as well as of the young,

121

whose impulses burst forth so spontaneous, so "moving," that there exists no protocol or regulation, no captain or colonel, however stern, however caviling, that can restrain them. That transport typical of native, and I would say virgin, souls which, by virtue of contrast, so strikes us *littérateurs*, dry, passive (save for the brief parenthesis 1915–1918), all concerned in our meanness and trivia and hair-splitting, far from the sufferings of the people, and lacking, not only pensions, but all vital spirit.

Colonel Di Pascuale was moved, in his turn, in perfect fashion. The hard, squared chin, and the lower lip which protruded a fraction of an inch beyond the upper, seemed almost to tremble with repressed emotion, in an access of virile compassion, descended, surely, from the hard mountains of Samnium. He even managed to express, from the two apposite saccules, two half-portions of tears absolutely paternal: which dried, slowly, below, on the ancient parchment of his cheeks, like the minimal water of the wadi which is lost in the glistening of the Syrtes; and after a few very chaste attempts to withdraw his hand, he didn't really withdraw it until many kisses and much saliva had sealed it with plebeian gratitude, inside and outside.

Then, on the second sheet of the pad, having torn off the first, he wrote further: "Come to collect to-/morrow your pass and tick-/et: your leave begins-/12 noon." And this time in red, because he had picked the pencil up by the wrong end.

And he smiled at him again, briefly, paternally.

The deaf man was profuse with renewed benedictions, now incorporating several saints, among them San Rocco, San Basilio bishop, and San Giovanni Nepomuceno, and his dead forebears, predominant among them the neodefunct uncle Mahagones, as well as the Madonna, and specifically the Madonna of Pompeii, much venerated in Maradagàl where there is a lack of local Madonnas of any efficacy: for there isn't one, in those hangar-churches with tin roofs, who seems to glow with the slightest light of miraculous comforts. Palumbo couldn't stop invoking prosperity and good luck, and grandchildren of both sexes, upon the somewhat bent shoulders of the elderly doctor, and colonel *malgré lui*, dear and good figure among the clutter of old papers, to make you sneeze with their dust, or within the smell of clothes and stale sweat of the examination rooms. The colonel pushed him gently toward the door and nodded his head, yes, yes, yes, still without uttering a word, since it's useless to talk to a deaf man; he had actually, by the Blessed Mother! two daughters-in-law pregnant, at that moment, one more swollen than the other: and his third daughter, the last, had given birth the month before, which had caused an incredible round of toasts.

The dawn of the next day broke, and all the bugles of the hospital sounded what there was to sound. Reveille, assembly, change of orderlies, inspection sergeant, corporal of the day, coffee, doctor's rounds, convalescents before the Commission, rejected to the quartermaster, arrivals in the reception hall, suspected malingerers under observation; and then brooms, registry, X rays, electrothermy, heliotherapy, kinesitherapy, bath; and then further, urine, blood, sputum, feces to be analyzed; then launderer, wardrobe, dispensary, Holy Mass for Catholic patients, those in condition to attend; and at eleven, double blast for General Ramirez, etc., etc.

Every celebration or operation, act or fact, entrance or exit, rise or descent, ingestion or emission—liquid, solid, or in-between—everything had its special gurgle in the pipe of the bugle, at the top or bottom of the scale.

Among the offices the sentries had been making their

rounds for two hours already, their trousers loose, scratching the pavement with the nails of their shoes, in their bored delivery of an envelope, or of a paper; all the seats were already occupied, by what normally occupies them; and, at certain moments, when the words and the doors and the footsteps fell silent, in conjunction with fits of coughing, catarrhs, and blowings of noses, then, those young men heard the shy tips of their own pens, pre–high school, creaking along, squeak-squeak, against the hard surface of the paper, from which there rose to the nostrils a smell of paste and of old romantic ink, notary's ink, from the inkwell, in the celebration of the various syndromes and clinical decursus of Freguglia's dysentery and of other infinite dysenteries of infinite Lopezes and Gomezes and Gutierrezes, distinct from one another only because of their serial number, in three digits, because mere baptism couldn't distinguish them by itself. The clinical files, the reports of the observation and the commissions, the forms of the regiments and the detachments, poured into those "writing rooms" with ever-new additions, with more and more energetic orthography and orthopedics, in the registry offices "which were the ganglia of the whole kit and caboodle," according to the (shouted) definition of Warrent Officer Pastorino.

At ten Colonel Di Pascuale heard a knock; he said, "Come in," his tone one of irritation. But no one came in. Then a clerk got up: and he brought in Palumbo.

In the center of the office, standing, his collar undone as usual, the colonel was speaking and almost arguing with another, rather young, colonel, who began to raise his voice and to contradict him, more and more harshly. He, now and then, drew his head down between his shoulders, as the turtle does, and raising his wrinkles halfway up his forehead, with his hands open, he said: "Now what am I supposed to do?" and similar expres-

124

sions, more or less Maradagalese, to indicate inability to do anything and a desire to wash one's hands, or rather one's hams.

There was also the quartermaster of the ledger, erect, his face all spotted by a case of acne, waiting for orders: a bundle of papers under his arm and a sheet of paper in his hand, doubled by a second sheet. Colonel Di Pascuale, after a while, when he had glimpsed Palumbo, said: "Excuse me, excuse me just a minute" to his fellow colonel, and turned. "What do you want?" he asked the deaf man harshly, as if he were seeing him for the first time.

Palumbo didn't answer, because he hadn't heard, being deaf. And he questioned, in his turn, amazed, grieved, his superior officer, with those poor disabled-veteran's eyes, disabled in both tympana! now abstracted from the muddle of acoustical significances, of a speechless world. "Ah! You want your pass?" the colonel said then, all of a sudden, when he remembered the matter. "Hey, Quartermaster, where did you put this boy's leave papers?"

"Here they are, Colonel!" the slender quartermaster said, with his facial springtime of pods; and he held out the papers that he had in his hand all ready: "Ah! All right!" The colonel took them, went to the desk, dipped his pen, bent over, and signed absently: with his spirit still engaged in the argument, obviously, with his fellow officer, who went on talking to him all the same, tormenting him with constant objections (to what had already been asserted by Di Pascuale): a dog who won't ease his bite. "Now what are you trying to tell me? That they haven't barred the promotion of Fagioletti Onofrio?" etc., etc. There was a hail of "plan of advancement" and "promotion for merit," ("special" being understood), with constant returns to Fagioletti Onofrio.

That argument had sincerely embittered him, poor

Di Pascuale. He handed the paper back to the sergeant, ignoring the soldier, and turned again to his colleague.

The quartermaster handed the two papers to Palumbo, pass and train ticket, saying to him (in a low voice, however, out of deference to that quarrel of his superiors): "Here's your pass: fifteen days plus two days' travel time."

"But he promised me a month!" Palumbo blurted out hastily, in anguish.

Colonel Di Pascuale turned as if an asp had bitten him: he looked at him; he went over to him.

"Ah! a month?" And he paused for a long while, staring at him. "A month, I promised you?" The face of Palumbo Mahagones was scarlet. The other colonel, now, also smiled at him, diabolically. The quartermaster's face, a bit less yellow than usual under the maroon scum of the pimples, looked at him from the second line, as if apologizing: "Your sins, you know, will find you out—but—it's not my fault." The Central Military 051 hadn't, surely, been his invention.

"Well, boy, let's get it over with once and for all—with this play-acting about being deaf. If at first you don't succeed, try, try again! Here there's testimony—two good eyewitnesses, as the law requires" (the clerks were silent)—"Colonel Zeppola"—and he gestured as if to introduce him to Gaetano, as one would do in civilian life—"and this little quartermaster of mine . . . a fine boy . . . fine. Hey, Quartermaster, did you take your yogurt? I told you . . . with all those buds blooming in your face?"; then again to Gaetano: "The witnesses that you're all well . . . the Madonna of Pompeii this morning has worked a miracle for you. You ought to thank her with your face on the ground! All right, all right. Congratulations. So you can go on leave . . . unlimited leave . . . and the pension remains with the government."

126

He turned to Zeppola, shaking his head, up and down: "Our poor government . . . which pays so many pensions . . ." and he waved his hand in midair, as if to say, "Plenty, and that's the truth!"

All of this, naturally, took place in the Maradagalese language, except perhaps for some spirited Neapolitan remark, uttered casually. But Doctor Higueróa had still fresh in his ear his conversation with the colonel, all full of humor and unprejudiced dialect. It seemed then that Palumbo, the quartermaster, and Zeppola himself understood Di Pascuale's speech perfectly, either because of their long familiarity with it in the office, or because, and this is more probable, they were also of Italian origin, as would, in fact, appear from their names.

In the son's spirit, in any case, there was stamped again the vivid image of the old medical colonel, whom he too had had occasion to know, if not exactly at the Central Military Hospital of Pastrufazio—the image of the old doctor, and colonel in spite of all, with the squared chin, the collar insufficient to the perimeter, with the little hook every so often unhooked, around his neck, so that he seemed almost bandaged by a white military bandage. Bandages that he had seen, he Gonzalo, on those lying outstretched; but never white, on the mountains.

Poorly dressed (if one may say so), after the children and the grandchildren. Firm in his resistance behind mountains of papers, after those others, those mountains—loyal to his duty, which is everything, everything.

Through this duty, it was asserted by many rumors, and all of them well founded, he had by now recovered for the revenue of Maradagàl several millions of pesos, after having patiently, laboriously extracted them, as

127

you extract the marrow from the ossobuco, with that special little harpoon spoon that looks like a dentist's implement, he instead from the chain of little bones, or from other bones or sinews or kidneys or bladders of certain robust young men, with too great a tendency however (according to him) to award themselves a premature pension of the fourth degree. Or sixth, as the case might be. At their age!

It must be observed, furthermore, that the just severity of the law, excluding from benefit the nonpossessor of qualifications, and the firmness assumed by the decisive commission in applying this highly sound order to the case in point, had and have an ethical significance, and achieve a social result, which altogether transcend the value of the thing disputed. Those thirty or forty young men, in fact, instead of receiving from the Maradagalese government an advance subsidy for sloth and idleness, with the false motivation of having suffered the war in their own flesh—which turned out instead to be as perfumed and intact as that of the most flourishing idler, or, if afflicted, still injured and poxed by a war quite different from that with the hated Parapagàl— those young men, I was saying, were stimulated by their nonpension to reflect seriously on their own situation and to seek, I would say, a different and more worthy means of subsistence. The position of night guard in itself is, to begin with, an honorable and socially positive employment. Some others, then, among those vigorous aspiring pensioners, but in fact pension rejects, and Mahagones especially, tried something even better: cooperating with all the energy of their spirit toward the progress, indeed the growing development, of the firm organism of the lucky firms, which were instinctively prompt in taking advantage of their cooperation. Making himself, I am referring to Mahagones, not only guard, but also hawker, procurer of lightning contracts, and lightning collector, or one might say *à la fourchette*, for the same firm. And learning above all, in cases of emergency, even to write his own name. Cooperating in the best fashion in the success of the most disparate enterprises—whether in the inserting of little pink-colored slips, every night, in the holes of locks, Agostonian or Giuseppinian or Teresottian, or in detaching more substantial and detailed slips, violet, baby blue, or pink, from a pad with stubs, or in detaching them, month after month, identical—though they were apt to represent, month after month, a modulated, rising income, that is with positive differential, if one may take the word from the mathematicians—that is, affected—this income, by propitious (however modulated) increment and leeward tide.

This increment and modulation of increment, unnoticed by the subscribers' pockets as they represented a *quantité différencielle très-petite,* lead the firm in one of the most secure progresses that can be expected in the affairs of man. Melchoirre Gioia[21] could not have excogitated a better.

And finally, in affixing to these receipts his own signature, through the agency of a gnawed, breech-loading stub of a pencil, they bear witness to the fact that when there's a will there's a way. Will, will! It digs cash from the walls, in the villa. In all villas! From the salve hospes: from the tail of the lizards.

PART   II

I

She roamed, alone, in the house. And were those
walls, that copper, everything that was left her from
a lifetime? They had told her precisely, black and cruel,
the name of the mountain—where he had fallen—and
the other, desolately serene, of the earth where they had
borne and placed him, his countenance restored to peace
and oblivion, deprived of all response, forever. The son
who had smiled at her, brief springtimes! Who so
sweetly, passionately, had caressed her, kissed her. A
year afterwards, in Pastrufazio, an army subaltern had
presented her with a diploma, had delivered a little
book, asking her kindly to affix her signature in another
ledger: and in so saying he had handed her a copying
pencil. First he had asked her, "You are Señora Elisa-
betta François?" Blanching at hearing her name spoken,
which was the name of her torment, she had answered:
"Yes, I am." Trembling, as if at the fierce exacerbation
of a punishment. To which, after the first horrible outcry, the dark voice of eternity continued to summon her.

Before he went away, when with a clinking of the
chain he gathered to himself, after the book, also the
gleaming sword, she had said, as if to detain him, "May

133

I offer you a glass of Nevado?" clasping her fleshless hands one to the other. But he would not accept. It had seemed to her that he strangely resembled the one who had occupied the brief splendor of time: of time consumed. The beats of her heart told her this, and she felt she had to love again, with a tremble of her lips, the reappearing presence, but she knew full well that no one, no one ever, returns.

She roamed in the house; and sometimes she opened the shutters of a window so that the sun would enter, into the great room. The light then encountered her humble, almost poor clothing: the little expedients with which she had been able to medicate, resisting tears, the humiliated dress of old age. But what was the sun? What day did it bring above the howling of the darkness? She knew its dimensions and its pattern, the distance from the earth, from all the remaining planets, and their progress and their revolutions; many things she had learned and taught: and she knew Kepler's matheses and quadratures that pursue in the senseless vacuity of space the ellipse of our desperate grief.

She roamed, in the house, as if seeking the mysterious path that would have led her to encounter someone: or perhaps only a solitude, shorn of every compassion and of every image. She went from the kitchen, now without fire, to the rooms, now without voices, occupied by a few flies. And around the house she saw still the countryside, the sun.

The sky, so vast above the dissolved time, was shadowed now and then by its grim clouds, which misted rotund and white from the mountains and gathered and then darkened suddenly; they seemed to threaten anyone who is alone in the house, her sons afar, terribly. That happened also in the end of that summer, on an afternoon in early September, after the long drought that everyone said would last without end: when about ten days had gone by since she had sent for the woman with the keys and, accompanied by her, had wanted to go down to the cemetery. That threat wounded her deeply. It was the impact, it was the mockery of unknown powers, or beings, unknown yet inexorable in their persecution: the evil that rises again, again and always, after the limpid mornings of hope. What dismayed her most, as a rule, was always the unpredicted ill humor of those who had no cause at all to hate her, or to offend her: those in whom her trust was so pure and so enthusiastically placed, as if to equals and to brothers in a higher society of souls. Then every succoring experience and memory, value and labor, and support of the city and of people, was suddenly erased by the desolation of the mortified impulse; the inner strength of her awareness became lost: like a little girl struck by the crowd, overwhelmed. The barbarian crowd of lost ages, the darkness of things and of souls were a murky enigma, before which she asked herself in anguish (unknowing, like a lost child): Why, why?

The storm, and that day too, was used to traveling with long howls through the frightful gorges of the mountains, and it debouched then in the open against the houses and the works of man. After every gloomy hoarding of his rancor, through all the sky, he gave free rein to thunderbolts, like a rowdy captain of mercenaries in wrecking and looting, to swill amid sinister flashes and reports. The wind, which had carried off her son toward oblivion-making cypresses, at every window seemed to be seeking her, too, her, in the house. From the little window over the stairs, a gust, bursting in, had gripped her by the hair; the floors and their beams of wood creaked as if they were exploding; it was like hull plating, like a ship in a gale; and the closed, barred

135

windows were swollen by that furor out of doors. And she, like an animal already wounded, if it hears above its head again and again the ferocious horns of the hunt, huddled as best she could within her exhausted condition to seek a refuge, below, in the cellar: going down, down: in a corner. Overcoming frighteningly that void of every step, trying them one after the other with her foot, clinging to the banister with hands that were no longer able to grasp, going down, down, below, toward the darkness and dampness of the bottom. There, a little shelf.

And the darkness yet allowed her to discover, groping, a candle, softened, a little dish with some sulphur matches, set out there for the hours of the night, for those coming home in the late hours. No one came home. She urged a match several times, another, on the sandpaper: and then, in the yellowness at last of that tremulous perception of the pavement, there, a further fugitive, a shard of shadow, horrible: but it immediately recovered itself in the immobility of a snare: the black of the scorpion. She huddled then, her eyes shut, in her final solitude: raising her head, as one who knows any imploration of kindness is vain. And she shrank into herself, close to annihilation, a grieving spark of time: and in her time she had been woman, wife, and mother. She hesitated now, terrified, before the weapon without valor that she too used to reject it, the shadow. And they followed her even there, where she had gone down, down, in the dark depth of every memory, they hounded her, the explosions, ferociously, and the vandal glory of the storm. The revolting snare of the darkness: born, blacker stain, from the damp and from evil.

Her thought knew no further whys. Why! Forgetting, in the extreme offense, that an imploration is possible, or love, from the charity of people: she no longer remembered anything; every ancient succor of her people was lost, distant. In vain she had given birth to children, had given them her milk; no one would acknowledge it within the sulphurous glory of the storms, and of the chaos, no one thought of it anymore; over the distant years of her womb, over her torment and the erased sweetness, other events had descended; and then the clang of victory, and the orations and the pomps of victory; and, for her, old age: this last solitude, to close the final skies of the spirit.

The drip of wax fell, scalding her, on her trembling hand. The icy breath of the tempest, from the little window over the stairs, inflected and laminated the tiny flame, making it stray over the humidity and the greasiness of the wax, attenuated, that blink of the wick, like the farewell of death.

She could see nothing anymore. All was horror, hated. The thunder weighed upon all things and the flashes of the electric storm hastened in their wrath, roasted in renewed moments by the slats of the closed shutters, above. And there was the scorpion, reawakened, who had proceeded, as if sideways, as if to skirt her, and she, trembling, had withdrawn into her sole being, extending a damp and weary hand, as if wanting to stop him. Her hair fell over her forehead; she dared say nothing, with dry, bloodless lips: no one, no one would have heard her, under the din. And whom could she address, in this changed time, when so much hatred, after the years, was addressed to her today? If her very creatures, in the years, had been a vain grief, flower of cemeteries: lost! In the vanity of the earth.

Why? Why?

From the dark depth of the stairs she sometimes raised her face, even in those hours, to recognize over her head silenced interludes of the storm, the stupid nullity of space: and of the falling evening, from the eaves, outside, drops, like weeping, or the compassionate silence. She imagined that the sudden shafts of every gust, having run through each room, had come out like a belated band to take refuge toward the plains and the night, where they joined their migrant swarm. A shutter banged against the wall of the house, slapping it. The trees outside, she could hear, gave off rare drops toward night, washed as if by weeping.

No one saw her, descended into fear, below, alone, where the yellow of the wick quavered, faded within the shadows, from the shelf, drying slowly in its liquefied wax. But if someone had ever chanced to see her, oh! even a rogue! would have felt in his spirit that this upraised face, petrified, did not even ask to be allowed to implore anything, from vanished remoteness. Scattered hair misted from her forehead, like a breath of horror. Her countenance, barely, emerged from the shadowy binding; the cheeks were conduit to the impossibility of tears. The bending fingers of old age seemed to dig down, down, in the mold of darkness, the features of one who disembarks in solitude. That face, like a specter, turned from the subterranean darkness to the supernal society of the living; perhaps it imagined help without hoping for it, the word of a man, of a son.

This name rested lightly on her spirit: and it was a dear apparition, a suggestion almost of morning and of dream, a lofty wing that flew over, a light. Yes: there was her son, in time, in certainty, in the knowledge of the living: and even after the changing, after the rush of the years. He walked among the living. He trod the paths of men. Her first son. The one in whose little body she had wanted to see, oh! days! the defective proof of nature, a failed experiment of her womb after the received fraud of the seed, reluctant at having suffered, at having generated what was not hers: in a long and unhealing darkening of all her being, in the toil of the mind, and of the viscera opened then to the slow shame of births, in the mockery of the wise traffickers and the merchants, under the structure of imposed duties, so nobly anxious for the success of society, to the suffering and the wretchedness of the honest. And he was now her son: the only one. He proceeded through the arid roads below the flight of elms, after the dust toward the evenings and the trains. Her first son. Oh! only the squall— lash of whistling skies over bent crops of the countryside —only terror had been able to separate her in such a way from the truth, from the well-founded security of memory. Her son: Gonzalo. Gonzalo had not, no, no! been awarded the funereal honors of darkness; his mother was horrified at the memory: away, away! from the inane obsequy the dirges, the vile weeping, the lamentations: tapers, for her, had not lessened their height among the pylons of the cold nave and the tombs of the shadow-centuries. When the song of the abyss, among the tapers, summoned the sacrificed, calling them down, down, within the wormy pomp of eternity.

An automobile's horn, from the highway, and the vacuum of all things. All was silent, finally. The cats, at the usual hour, certainly, had penetrated the house by the entrance only they used: velvet presences, they stared at her from the halfway point of the steps, with eyes in the darkness like topazes but slashed by slits, aligned pupils of their hunger; and they addressed to her, meowing, a timid greeting, an appeal: "The hour has come." Domestic order and charity called her back upstairs. And she, forgetting her own, became immediately concerned at the suffering of others, as always: she climbed up the steps. The clogging feet of the peasant resounded on the pavement above: returned from his purchase of tobacco and perhaps, she hoped, of salt. He called her in the darkness, spoke to her of provisions and of the fire, informed her of the time, the devastated harvests; he proceeded, with renewed clashes of his voice, to unlock the door, the windows. Reassured, she saw again, sweet and distant, clear expanses of the village and in her sweet memories flowered again those words from always: "They open the balconies—the family opens terraces and loggias"[22]: as if the restored society of man were reappearing to her after a long night. And the manservant, there, before the cats, was going about her house: from his own hearth to this other, so spacious and cold, carrying sparks, thyrses; and then on the stairs; behind the quadruped progress of the clogs, doors and shutters banged. And stalks and branches were more or less everywhere along the virile dropping of his itinerary. And the wind had become lost toward the plains, in the direction of the Pequeño.

From the terrace, on summer evenings, she could see on the distant horizon the smoke from the farm houses, which she imagined populated, each one, by the woman of the house, her husband in the barn, and the children. The girls, in clusters, came back from the factories, the looms, or spools, or tubs of the silk mill; bicycles had brought the apprentices back from the anvils, or they had returned behind their father with the swaying oxen from the field, and he had guided and braked with his rudder the low wagon, its short sides bent and opened over little wheels with greased and silent axles, laden with possession and with labor, logs, and grasses—on whose peak, as if forgotten, rested the weary scythes, in the shadows of the evening.

They were rustic offspring, come, numberless, from work to the fire, to a spoon: to the poor chipped bowls which rewarded their day.

Very distant flashes, songs, came to her from outside the house. It was as if some housewife had set her copper pot to dry in the farmyard, to reflect, shining, the sunset—perhaps as a greeting to her, the Señora! who one time, like them, had been woman, wife, and mother. She envied no one. She hoped for all those women, all, happiness and the calm strength of sons, that they would work, health, peace; good marches in the morning where the captain commands them; that they would soon find a bride, returning from the regiment, in the aromatic thicket of the girls.

So, every day, she found a reason or a pretext to call to her the laundress, the daughter of the baker, the woman who sold lemons or at times some rare oranges from Tierra Caliente, the eighty-six-year-old mother of the manservant, the wife of the fish peddler. (There was reason to suppose that the required series of garments was not completely present on the latter's person.) They were poor pikes, dark, with pointed snouts like the desire of the poor, and grim, which had swum and swum through green poverty toward the silvery glint of the Durendal; or tench, great yellow fish from the lakes, of a greasy and stupid viscidity, which even among carrots and celery still tasted of mud: after the hour of sunset harpooned with the line in the Seegrün or in that other valley, very sweet in autumn, of the abbot-poet, or in that other, still farther on, of the painter-disciple,[23] when it reflects, under liquefied clouds, the serration of the mountain, upturned.

With carrots and celery, over a slow fire, was the long casserole of the pike; she stirred, in that mush, with a long wooden spoon: a thing came out full of bones, of celery, but rather good to the taste. When the task was done she merely tasted it; she was happy: she gave it all to the women. The women praised her for her talent in cooking; they rewarded her for her goodness.

She envied no one. Perhaps, after so much valor

and study, after having toiled and suffered, and having fulfilled without tears her geniture, so that they might dispose, the strategists of the Republic, of her finest blood! as their reason prompted them; perhaps after the burning rush of every day, and of the years, weary ellipses, perhaps time prevailed—the gentle assuager of every renunciation—oh! it would lead her where one forgets and is forgotten, beyond the houses and the walls, along the path guarded by the cypresses.

Rustic offspring, levy of perennial daily bread: let them grow up, let them love. She considered herself at the end of her vicissitude. The sacrifice had been consummated. In purity; of which God alone is knowledge. She was pleased that other men and women would be able to pick up the vital meaning of the fable, still deluded, with their hot blood, into believing it necessary truth. From the distant horizon the smoke of the houses rose. None of them would bear her spirit anymore, or her blood, in the empty days.

But Gonzalo? Oh, the lovely name of life! A continuity which was achieved. Again it seemed to her, from the terrace, that she could discern the curve of the world: the sphere of lights, revolving; among periwinkle-colored mists they vanished on encountering the drowsiness of the night. On the world, bearer of harvests, and of a song, the quiet illuminations of midsummer. It seemed to her that she could watch it still, from the terrace of her life, oh! still, for a moment, being a part of the calm evening. A sweet lightness. And, in the lofty sky, the sapphire of the ocean: which Alvise had gazed at, trembling, and Antoniotto of Noli,[24] rounding capes of nameless reality toward the appeared dream of archipelagoes. She felt caught up in the event, in the ancient flux of possibility, of continuation: like all, near to all. With

her thought, with her sons, giving herself she had overcome the darkness: gifts of works and hopes toward the
holiness of the future. Her consummated task brought
her back into the path of souls. She had learned, taught.
Belated bell strokes: and the slow wick of vigils had
been consumed by the silence. Along the interlines dawn
insinuated itself: noble paragraphs! And she, in sleep,
repeated its sentence. Generations, cries of spring, play
of perennial life under the gazing towers. Thoughts had
aroused thoughts, souls had aroused souls. Grieving
fatherlands ferried her toward the harbors of awareness,
ships for the Tenebrous Sea. Perhaps, thus, the atrocity
of her grief would not be vain in God's sight.

She clasped her hands.

Gonzalo, from his work, earned enough to live on.
Recently she had gone by Modetia;[25] the shirt maker in
Modetia was supposed to make him some cotton shirts—
the seamstress had written, in fact—she would cut them
out with the greatest care, she felt under such an obligation, dear Señora, after all her goodness and kindness.

Gonzalo! Her older son was not a pensioner of the
government, except laughably, for a little medal: the
lowest and most laughable of medals. (But this is what
the experts might believe, not his mother's certainty.)
No reason existed, for that matter, why he should be a
pensioner of the government. His tympana were afflicted
by another ill, now, not a traumatic laceration, but
spoiled by another tedium, one would have said, different from the inscrutable fog of deafness. She couldn't
understand the way he had reappeared to her, oh, in a
dawn of ashes: amid the merchandise and the mud of
Pastrufazio, and the invincible machines. He was unharmed, with poor years inside the gray chevrons of
return. Perhaps his war, for him, had not been dangerous. He told nothing, ever: he spoke of it with no one—

143

certainly not with children, if they surrounded him in a moment of their pause, belligerents or scratched, overheated admirals, with bayonets of tin, and not even with the ladies in the villas, who were, it was said, among the most distinguished gentlewomen of Pastrufazio and the most epos-thirsty, and in consequence the most enthusiastic drinkers of nonsense.

Children, moreover, he seemed to regard with outright hatred. A grim sternness came over his face if he found in the house even one, like that poor silly child—the mother smiled—with his *caillou, bijou.* Oh! "her" Gonzalo! It was too obvious that the arsenal of glory had refused to place him on its roster. Plautus, in him, would not find his protagonist; perhaps Molière. The poor mother, not wanting to, saw again the distant figures of the Misanthrope and the Avare, all laces and frills below the knees, in the old book, in double columns, of her adolescent mornings, of her so fervid vigils: when the circle of the little lamp, on the table, was the orb of thought and of clarity in the intactness of the silence. In the old book, with its odor of the old ink of France, with bonnets, laces, and Maître Corbeau. It was obvious. After regained victories, the printers of funereal glories hadn't had enough of their mortuary woodcuts to sing of a veteran without hendecasyllables—funeral lights and inscriptions and little flames and *perennis ardeo*— all engravings had been used up, on the covers of the cadaverous poems. His dead companions, Gonzalo never, never would have used them to poetize so gloriously, his brother, distant smile! His name locked in him, the desperate memory.

The vendors of frills had no fripperies at any price that they could sell him, nor caballero's braidings, nor ribbons, nor buckles, for his silent way. The hidalgo

144

avoided the salons, the opinions of the patriotic ladies. To the long tea, as if that were not enough, he preferred the lonely road of the Recoleta. After these unfortunate facts had been verified, the esteem of right-minded people began really to give him a wide berth. And one fine day, indeed, when his notebooks in the Faculty of Letters had been put in final order, and his Engineering, his native Pastrufazio could not help defecating him.

But these notes were external to his mother's love, as also to her language: in the anguish of her spent days she had never acceded to the conversations, to the jangling conglomerations of society.

She thought with sweetness of this, her first son, seeing him again as a child, studious and thoughtful, and now already bent, bored above the wandering of the paths. She came back inside, from the terrace, into the large room. The flies had resumed, now that the storm had moved away, their flying over the table: where there were the newspapers, with the new events, which had followed others. So from year to year, from day to day: for the whole series of years, of days. And the pages, quite soon, turned yellow. When the flies, for a moment, paused in their roundabout, and also the great green fly, for a moment, then in the labile cosmos of that unexpected suspension she heard more distinctly the woodworm creaking, creaking toilsomely, with little nips, in the old walnut secrétaire which she couldn't unlock anymore. The path of the key had become lost in the succession of her attempts, or, perhaps in the grieving shadows of memory. In it there must be the picture . . . the pictures . . . the mother-of-pearl cufflinks . . . perhaps also the two letters—the last!—the sewing scissors, the black fan, of lace . . . the one they had given her in the swamp, when she had taken leave of her colleagues, of the few girls, her pupils . . . more than one ran a fever, all wanted her kiss. But she was not lacking, por suerte, an extra pair of scissors: three pair, in fact.

And then the wedding.

If her thoughts descended, from the memory of those two children, to the closer years, to today . . . it seemed to her that the cruelty was too great: similar, fiercely, to derision.

Why? Why? Her countenance, in those pauses, turned to stone in anguish; no heartbeat of the soul was possible then; perhaps she was no longer a mother, as in the outcry of birth, torn, distant; she was no longer a person, but a shade. She remained there like that, in the room, with pupils blind to every compassionate return, the fleshless immobility of old age, for long strides of time. And the dress of poverty and age was like an extreme sign of being led before the faces of the portraits, where fatuous winged creatures, on the void, will circle within the surviving tomorrow. Then, like a ritual of the season, suddenly, the hour arrived from the spire, freeing in the vacuum its lost, equal strokes. And it seemed to her an unnecessary, cruel reminder. In the ended time of every summer, across the world that had left her like this. The flies traced a few circles in the great room, before the portraits, under the horizontal shafts of the evening. With one hand, then, wearily, she rearranged her hair, whitened by the years, spread from her forehead without caresses like the hair of King Lear. Survivor of every fate. And now in the silence, as the sunset descended, the tempests of possibility had vanished. She had learned so much, read so many books! By the little lamp, Shakespeare: and she still spoke some verses, as from a broken tombstone forgotten syllables are scattered, and in the past they were the light of knowledge, and now the horror of the night.

146

In the sky the mists had been scattered, and the smoke, up from the neck of the chimneys, with the pot below, of the poor suppers of the people. They had scattered like a goodness from the earth: toward the evening star, through the bluish air of September, up, up where the blond light is, from the black chimneys that rise with the strength of towers beyond the shadows and the blued hills, behind trees, over the distant chimney pots of the farms.

She had heard the rumbling of the train, the whistle of arrival. She would have liked to have had someone near her, at the approach of the darkness.

But her son appeared only rarely at the threshold of the house.

II

*H*is tall form was outlined, black, in the frame of the French window, from the terrace, like the shadow of a stranger: and, behind him, in the sky, two stars seemed to have helped him on his way there. Splendid Dioscuri over a stripe of amaranth, distant, in the quadrant of beauty and of knowledge: saved fraternity! His mother noticed him, but couldn't see his face against the rectangle of light. He came in then, and was carrying a small valise, the usual, the one of yellow cardboard costing forty centavos, like a traveling peddler of handkerchiefs. In the same hand, rolled, the old umbrella. His mother said, "Oh! Gonzalo, how are you? Oh! look!" and uttered, with a sob of joy, the names of the two stars, her hands clasped, as a greeting. But she thought that only the first applied, in the correlation of fortune and stars as symbol of an earthly presence; because the other, so bright, so pure, was nothing but a distant thought of the night.

The son barely greeted her, as he did every time, tired. Nor did he smile at her. She did not insist in seeking his gaze; she didn't ask him about his journey, or about the storm. Her heart hammered in uncertainty;

148

she busied herself preparing, on the table, the kerosene lamp. But she didn't succeed at once, in fact she botched it, with damp matches; she coughed, at lighting some; which immediately went out against the blackened chimney of the wick. Her rigid, almost inert hands were unable to grasp precisely; it was difficult for her to insert the glass cylinder in its exact metal ring of shining brass, like a lace of forgotten customs: and this instead was meant to hold it to the base. She would have sat down, she was trembling . . . but she had to think of her son. When the lamp was able to light the room, at last, she thought she would have to fall . . . the last glance of twilight, already very far away, was abandoning the furniture, with low, cold glints on the credenza, on some metal trays. That pallor of the lamp, truly, had not added much. She closed the glass panes as best she could—the window was very tall, on the terrace—shuddering.

Her son, upstairs, was washing; replacing a brush in a drawer. She heard his footsteps, muffled, above the ceiling.

She went into the kitchen to prepare something for his supper. It was absolutely necessary; also she had to demonstrate the functional efficacy of the villa, especially since, after all, the villa was without a cook or any sort of maid. Otherwise he would have seized upon that pretext to grow heated about the inanity of the country: and he would have become involved in the worst caprices and tantrums (the thing, by now, a sad rite: the poor mother knew that well). He would have repeatedly held up to shame the villa, cursing it along with the furniture and the chandeliers, with the memory of his father who had built it; crowning with obscene vituperations all the fathers and all the mothers who had preceded him in the series, back, back to the procreator of Adam. He would have descended to blasphemies, which she couldn't

149

hear, to accusations too true, perhaps, to hear, involving in the mad turpitude that bestialized him in those moments even the sacred name of Pastrufazio (the Garibaldi of Maradagàl) and Prado, Lukones, and Iglesia, and the respective spires, with their bells, the mayors, the pastors, the coachmen, and gradually all the accursed Serruchón and sons of guns (so, approximately, he expressed himself), all the infinite villas of the Serruchón, the gutturaloid Calibans of Néa Keltiké, filthy, whom he would have hanged gladly, had he been able, from the first to the last.

His mother, on the contrary, from the moment when the masons started work in '99, had incorporated into herself, immediately—enflamed splendor of youth —the serpentesque triumph of "her" villa over her Keltikese rivals, girls who didn't believe in the possibility of a villa (for the very mangy Pirobutirros).

And that pride, that thyrsus of glowing coals that she had been able, on a faroff day, to insert into her soul, to spite the psuedo-sisters-in-law and the psuedo-nieces that later had grown to intoxication and to radiant omnipotence, within a resplendent, haunted age, without measure or boundary—the idea of possession and of the supposed victory drained like a cognac of fire and of life with every new morning, with every splendid day.

That had been enough for her, during forty years, to allay desperation, to keep at a crouching distance, beyond every torment and every wretchedness, beyond every tattered jersey of her babies, every bell toll, every glory, every tench, the dirty grin of death. The Matrix Idea of the villa she had appropriated for herself as a rubescent organ or prime entelechy consubstantial with the womb, and therefore inalienable from the sacred wholeness of her person: like a wardrobe or hatrack of

De Chirico, carnal and external within the dreaming heart of the lares. To that pituitary[26] sum, recondite, noumenical, there corresponded externally—jewel or prime cock crest beyond the confines of the psyche—the objective villa, the datum. Operating in her, during forty years, were the tireless hormones of anagenesis—what woman takes, in life she gives back—that unperturbed constancy, that happy ignorance of the abyss, of the curbstone, so that, never say die, from pumpkinhead, they manage to produce an engineer; the formidable capacity for absorption, for introduction of absurdity into reality, which is characteristic of some of the best of women—the most resolute, the most vigorous of intellect. Such women, even if they aren't hysterical, impound their milk, and the stubbornness of a whole life, to constitute in a thesaurus certain, historically real, a commonplace product of the encounter with human stupidity: the first that they find at their feet, not to say between their legs, the vainest: ephemeral symbol of an emulation or a reverence or an acquisition which will count for nothing: large diploma, villa, yes Madame, plume. It must be added also that the majority of men behave exactly like them. And it is really one of the wonders of nature, if you choose to consider it in its methods and results, this process of accumulation of volition. It is the automatic progress of the somnambulist toward her triumph-catastrophe: from a certain moment on, the hysteria of pique succeeds in forming their sole reason for existence; in such women, it leads them to falsehood, to crime, and then the banner of the useless, with the fraudulent mug of falsity, is borne forward, forward, more and more obstinately, more and more uselessly, against the desperate anger of the other side. The liberating darkness arrives, which remedies all sides.

Impotent anger was in him, in the son; a pretext having been offered, it immediately was freed in words, tumultuous, vain, and wicked: in fierce threats—like a madman's scream from the depths of a prison.

Something for supper! The mother, trying to recover herself, looked about the kitchen, empty and cold; she opened a door of the cupboard where the shadows had fallen asleep on that faint whiff of lard and leftovers: in the kitchen there was almost nothing, not even an egg to prepare for him. The stentorian behind of José's hens arrived rather rarely at such a glorious expulsion. He kept more than one, but they each laid their egg in turn: and often, at that, they dodged their turn. The son would have flown into a rage over this, too: so then she would have to skip the matter, the eggs. In the past, on other occasions, he had become infuriated at these defaulting hens of the lousy Serruchón: and he had accused the rooster of genetic nonfulfillment and of perversion, the hens of being Lesbians and whores; then his fury had calmed down with a recollection of Livy, *"gallinam in marem, gallum in foeminam se se vertisse."* And, atrociously, snickering, he had drunk the rooster's health! But he hadn't actually said to his health, he had mentioned a part of the body: he had sung the praises (mocking her, his Mama) of the scoundrelly cock, better than all the fathers of lousy Keltiké, he had yelled, "that way they wouldn't generate any Keltikese." She trembled again, humiliated; the mockery still resounded in her ears. Then he had cursed and recursed all his relatives, including those who had never existed in the eyes of the law, in the fear of overlooking one, male or female. No, no; her son's desperation, at times, knew no bounds.

There was, in the drawer of the table, in the other room, the place-setting, of silver, that she had destined for him as a boy, buying it second-hand from the old and kindly Señora Teotòpuli, overpainted. She smiled slightly, at the memory. A bit dented even then, yes, "that's so": and the fork with its tines a bit crooked, "that may be." But her son would have mocked with new obscenities, and fierce gibes, clenching his teeth, both the fork and the Señora Teotòpuli,[27] whose rouge—weaknesses! Who amongst us doesn't have some—constantly became muddled with tears and nose blowings, at the least weeping, drooling down over her withered face, like macaroni sauce. But was it worth becoming upset, over this? Gonzalo, perhaps, would become upset at the fork, at seeing those tines, so crooked and so soft. He would have risen from the table, would have . . . Perhaps he would have hurled away the knife . . . against a portrait, maybe the most visible . . . his uncles—against the portrait of his father! Perhaps . . . No, no! He had never done this! She had always used that place-setting, without paying any special attention: for years. Having returned into the dining room, the mother looked for the silver now, in that half-light, in the table drawer: but, her eyes and hands weakened with age, she couldn't distinguish the pieces, among so many, and grasp them at once. That clanking irritated Gonzalo: who from his own room, on the floor above, shouted at her: "Stop that!" She stopped short, holding her breath. In her uneasiness, she thought of turning to someone, to José, to ask them to help her stand on her feet; she was ill; she had swallowed something half an hour before, a cup of broth with some country bread sliced into it, half an egg she had had bought in the village. Now that little bit came back, enough to soil the shoe cleaner, which was a worn doormat at the edge of the dining room; but, for that matter, it couldn't even be seen. The pavement, a bit farther on, was also soiled with a few

153

spots. The son must have heard her heaving, confusedly, and must have believed it an attack of coughing, because he cursed again from upstairs: "Are you consumptive, after all?" His mother took care to clean the floor before he came down, with a bit of ash, with the broom. There was some sawdust in the kitchen, but she hadn't the strength to draw out the bucket, where it was kept, under the table against the wall, to pull it over the crossbar: which bound, at a low height, the two front legs. She erased, as best she could, in haste, the signs of disorder: with the broom, with a bit of ash.

For years she had sensed, about her son. In the city, too: where she lived, except during the summer. The rare times that he appeared—the lost son—there was always the same grim idea.

The poor mother had slowly understood. Now she saw the darkness of that soul. Slowly, for having wrestled at length in her vivid hope, in her joy: before giving way to understanding. An impious sentiment, one would have said a deep, and very remote rancor, had been swelling in the spirit of her son: the only one, who still appeared to her, at times, when they met, smiling at her and calling her "Mama, Mama," if still it wasn't a dream, in the streets of the city and of the earth. This sorrowful perturbation, stronger than any moderating entreaty of the will, seemed to come out on occasions and on pretexts from a deep, inexpiable zone of shrouded verities: from a torment without confession.

It was the obscure sickness of which histories and laws and the universal disciplines of the great chairs persist in having to ignore the causes, the stages: and one bears it within himself along all the resplendent descent of a lifetime, heavier every day, without medication. Perhaps it is the "invisible sickness" of which Saverio Lopez narrates: told to him by moribund words of the Incas: and he speaks of it, with the *nihil obstat* of his superiors, in the final chapter of his *Mirabilia Maragdagali.*

He knew no peace, Gonzalo, nor would he know it—his mother, seeing to those pans, felt forced to despair—his face, distraught, revealed that, at certain moments, he could not get the better of his delirium.

He never drank liquors. He didn't smoke. It wasn't even thinkable that after the toilsome hardship of his days, so grudgingly rewarded by the Compañia de Distribución, there would be money for the costly alkaloids of which there had been reports, until then, in the newspapers, more or less all, both of Maradagàl the victor and of the defeated Parapagàl; they were also mentioned, whenever possible, by certain avant-garde literature, between rebellious and satanical, which had occupied the newsstands in the stations. Moreover he worked, however reluctantly, just as mothers dream their son should work—that is, giving orders to those under him: in his hours of leisure, after having distributed millions of kilowatt-hours to all the spinning mills of the Nevado Bajo, to the victorious factories, then, finding a moment for himself, he opened his books, weary, without having the time to read them to the end.

At certain hours his will seemed sick. "With a bit of good will," his Mama would say to him, smiling at him, planning to bolster his spirit, and to bring a little serenity into that countenance. "The will . . ." he answered, "which is indispensable to murderers. . . ." That frightened her; she tried to change the subject. Perhaps he was tired. It was very probable that the war had changed him, and, more, the news that his brother would not return. And yet he didn't complain about the war; he never spoke of it with anyone; he hadn't been wounded.

155

No one, certainly, asked him about the "glorious exploits," dark mountains, no one among the[28] swaggering kids whom Mars had saved for later, in view of their tender age. They gained nothing, these youths, by granting their gray-haired rivals this preferential status in competition, this too-valid attenuation in the Scales. Attenuation, that is, of errors, defaults: of a bewildered course. The little Scales of the highly measured Scruple were occupied only, in those years, with balancing, amid bagatelles, the disputed identity of the Martin redivivus, known as Martin Guerre or the widow's Martin,[29] passing from season to season through all the most subtle needle eyes of the law: as the stubborn *gendarmerie* fought for him with the marriage bed no less stubborn, and no less greedy to be able to creak for him.

But it is best for everything, everything to be weighed in the balance.

The son seemed to have forgotten, beyond all imagining, the torment of those years, youth reduced to ash. His rancor came from a grimmer remoteness, as if between him and his mother there were something irreparable, more atrocious than any war: and than any frightful death.

When he came down, with a book, the soup seemed to be waiting for him on the table, at his place, in the circle of the kerosene lamp: from whose tenuous dominion the steam of the bowl evaporated and was lost in the darkness, among the great ribs of the ceiling, and the dark flooring. The Spanish-style beams were festooned with cobwebs, like stored sails, kept in reserve, hung up, proceeding over the Sea of Shadows.

That wick, so tired and humble, immobility shut in its glass cylinder, under the glass shade (which was a cone of an opaque whiteness around the mechanism of

156

the lacy metal ring) seemed to him to be all that his mother granted him: in the house inhabited by the woodworm, in the depths of the solitary countryside. It was, in any case, everything that father and mother had considered sufficient, as well as useful, for the life, the progress, the happiness of their sons. And yet they too had known well, dammit all! what certificates, or invitations, what sort of pentacles or greasy talismans were of value at doors, in opening to mortals, and even to the maize-fed pithecanthropoid, the doors arabesqued in gold and heavy ivory,[30] the revolving doors of the Odéons. Tides of men and of women! With distinct swim of deluxe hairdressers, madames of public houses, manufacturers of motorcycle accessories, and cockades. Toward the tins of Liebig[31] peptone trains of cows, from the northwest; open cars with central catwalk that the melancholy-eyed gaucho, superintending, walks long. Such did fortune appear to them, in South America. Tempestuous sea against the battered rafts of lost, laved people, with sargassos of Chinese or of Negroes' arms above the ferment of the waves: Armenians, Russians white and red, Arabs who had gained a sloop with knife in hand, true Levantines with a cargo, on their shoulders, of fake rugs, from Monza: and on the poured-out bellowing of that tobogganing horde with no Christ now or devil, the multitude flagellated against the shore by the onrush of the wave, there, there, at last! The wan triumph of some undertakers, very few, one in each city of Maradagàl, who benefited from the most prosperous among the Maradagàl licenses and concessions: the corpse monopoly. Such as, for example, the Flejos firm. The zinc coffins sold at thirty times their cost to the affliction of the grieving, during a thirty-year period, had enriched them with the most legitimate among all the sources of income. And then too females, females, after the zinc

157

and the Recoleta; females! Like coasting vessels restored, overpainted, with the bassarids' laughter open
over the thirty-two teeth to their ears; a creased little
skirt, of half-wool, to tegument with a diez-peso mystery
(fifty-five of ours) the wretched mechanism of their tail-
wagging: the shitty rags of a Negress would have had
more tone. Or else, at the opposite extreme, the fat
butchers, like moustached rats, making rat-salami; tow-
ering over the high marble, with chopper, the butcher-
scimitars; or flushed middlemen, in the market, howling
"sobre el ganado"; or silk dealers in dinner jackets
swollen by the prosopopoeia of the full complement of
Keltikese virtues, with eleven wattles, though unable to
produce a single z from between their teeth; electricians
nearsighted as artichokes; priests (Presbyterians) in
ball dress, brachyskelic[32] with their trousers filled with
contraband saccharine, cuckolded engineers, physicians
of the tripes, and of the kidneys, and specialists in the
buttywuttocks; guards, thieves, gas-fitters, asthmatic
madams, plasterers and plasteresses of every stripe! And
the specter of the Bard terrorizing the chickens, after
midnight, in Giuseppina's chicken run! Lousy Jonah!
This sea without rest, outside, washed against the harbor
of madness, broke over the mad shores offering its perennial foam, drinking again its wicked backwash. Mer-
curial pomade or apocryphal gospels, there, there,
toward the haunted splendor of the Odéons: with behind
them the warehouses of Flejos y compañeros.

The famished saraband whirled under the electric
globes swaying in the Pampero, amid myriads of soda-
water siphons. The light of the upturned[33] world drank
in its uricaemic crowds, perfume-salesmen at the mercy
of Progreso, urethrae leveled by soda-water. "¡Mozo,
tráigeme otro sifón!" A jolly foolishness animated the
faces of all; the women, as if they were scratching acne,

or with gestures of apes who have passed a cacaruette[34] or two from hand to hand, powdered themselves at every dish: they ate minestrone and lipstick. And all hoped, hoped, in their jollity. And they were full of confidence. Or else, authoritative, they were silent. At the table; chests out, shoulders straight, packaged in the starched apparatus of the dinner jacket as if bandaged and in the supreme swelling of certainty and of biological reality. From time to time they made the siphons piss: and the virilely micturating siphon bestowed on the idler's hand a kind of gravity. And they gargled, baritone in timbre, glabrous, with the mouthwash of memories: boasting of imaginary nights and the lucre of diamonds sold (but never existent): silent was the face-falsehood of the female, on the subject of the true income.

The son, standing, near the table, looked, without seeing, at the modest display, the scant steam it was exhaling: as his old mother still hunted for some fork, a plate, a pretext, in the sideboard and the kitchen cupboard. She was again uneasy.

Boys: with legs like two asparaguses. Idiots in their heads worse than if they were made of tubers, speechless of any sort of language: after twelve generations of Indian corn and of Indian poverty with dirt-green feet emerging also from the bastard Ark of the generations, to try to stammer out some mean boast in the marketplace: the crooked forum of Pastrufazio! Come down, down, from the stinking cheeses of Monte Viejo to the more resounding failures of the Uguirre,[35] silent and acephalous in Castilian, deaf to Latin, reprobates in Greek, inept in history, their brains below zero in geometry and in arithmetic, unsatisfactory in drawing, even in geography they were unsatisfactory! One had to waste one's breath for weeks, for years, to make them understand what a map of victorious Maradagàl is! And how maps are made: and they still couldn't make it, poor darlings!

And yet they came down like a kind of oil to their bannered launching, launched finally into nonsensedom with full honors and every sanction: keels tallowed with stupidity. The more witless they were, the happier and smoother the ways beneath their bottoms, down, down from the green croconsuelo of Monte Viejo to the swelling tide of the avenida, with their full complement of cock-crest. Some wrinkled old woman could always be found, in the old-women's shop, with six or even seven teeth left in her mouth, to break the propitiatory bottle over the prow of the illiterate: in order to create those rebounding shards that the rite requires, God willing, with that tuft of spume. (The calf's cheeks, in any case, had to be daubed with a suitable amount of adulating saliva, whimpering over him and drooling on him, at every new trumpeting, the admiring mucus of a pyriform nose, highly affectionate and highly soupy.)

And as, ass-backwards, the ship descends, so they, the majority, like ship or lobster, and precisely because they are lobsters, ass-backwards, thanks to their nonqualifications, descended, slipped happily into the world, painted up with a new splendor all their own. And others, in whose florid cheeks under the nardous shininess of their hair, you could lightly perceive an adolescence of cotton flannel, and of rosbiffe. Flowerbeds of rosbiffe! All of them, all entered the light: the light of life was folded around them, poured over their greased heads by the patient generators of the Cordillera, which pour their light over the plaster paradises. All, all! Turks, pancake vendors, Circassians, guitar-playing beggars of Andalusia, Poles, Armenians, Mongols, Arab medicine men in bowler hats, Senegalese big-lips with club feet, and also the Langobardòi of Cormanno, im-

160

migrating from Cormanno (Curtis Manni), to achieve, even in the new world, the record for foolishness and lack of imagination. And the agent of the perfume firm, of Greek lineage; and the other, the Jew, from the house of carpets. Who sold also, on his own, in his leisure hours, pictures, although second-hand, lots of rags for paper, and heretic furniture of the sixteenth century. All, all.

All had their life, their woman; and they had allowed themselves to be launched; and they were in a position to be taken seriously—each in his field, and even the man who operated the clay pigeons. Many in evening dress. Everybody believed, really, that he was something serious. Members of the Maradagalo-Parapagalese Grand Orient, many adorned themselves as a further help, with frills, little beads of carnelian or of polished bone, assorted trimmings. The Free Masons of the Scottish Rite, on the occasion of their annual meeting, there, at the end of Saenz Peña, Number 3225, could be seen with something coming out of their jackets, swaying between their legs, a kind of tassel of sheep's wool; or else, across their checked vest, more tassels, but a bit smaller, and ribbons, and green braid, and a two-colored or orange frill. Some of them, also, on holidays or patriotic anniversaries of old England, appeared bedecked with buttons of exceptional shininess, or in eighteenth-century dress, with wig: two days later *Fray Mocho* published the glory and the magnesiac splendor of the horseshoe banquet, amid a downpour of cockades, ribbons, goblets, flowers, braid, Masonic turbans (these, however, only he saw, Gonzalo, in his delirium) with feathers of Amazonic parrots: and their women in bird of paradise. And flabellate fans of ostrich feathers, tinted pink, over the buttery bosoms: and little plumes, and pinfeathers. And in the harsh season, that is roughly from Santa Brigida to San Balafrone, silk dealers and portly engineers could hardly wait to put on their great furs from beyond the Circle, of the strangest bears, sables, seals from Pitt's land, kangaroos from Australasia, and opossum. Some times they had diadems of jewels over their hair, the women: and their husbands with collars and a medal of tin, in zincotype, which was then nothing but the image of Mazzini, his neck all bandaged in his collar-cravat, in white, cylinder block: his beard carefully bipartite and scissor-cut, two swollen bags below the eyes: some instead preferred to decorate themselves with a face of Disraeli, with sideburns, or of old Sarmiento. And from that rigging hung bangles in the form of triangles, or 33, or a little hammer, little silver trowels, or even gold ones. Others added to a flannel, Prince of Wales-like elegance, little gold chains, on their wrists, very fine, and a gold watch, on their wrists: and, attached to the chains, various baubles: little medals with a sacred scene, enameled, or a four-leaf clover in high relief, in a nice enameled green; or even both together, namely Madonna and lucky charm, since you never know, on the spot, who might best come to your aid, to get you out of a mess. Or, instead, a little horseshoe, but of gold, however: with dots of white pearls for the nails.

Wristwatches! Some had real chronometers—that is (they explained), measurers of time: with a third, fourth, and fifth hand, very fine: the last was actually filiform, which started off at top speed only by your pressing, tick! a secret little pin, with the pad of the thumb: and it was for races, at the take-off, that is at the start, which from time to time they pronounced in English: or at the end, by a head, by a nose.

The quadrant, black, with the months and the quarters of the moon in a scarlet-red line, or in twilight gold, with the seconds, the minutes, the years, the hours, the hegiras, in green and lemon-color; and in sapphire-blue the revolutions of Uranus. So that such a chronometer on the wrist of the tobacconist, if anyone barely notices it, and one can't help glancing at it, places its wearer in a supposed mathematic-geomantic elite, or geophysical, as if one were to say a priestly astrological caste of Egypt or of Chaldaea, a closed orphic-pithagoric community, possessor of Copernican contraband two thousand years before Copernicus—whereas most of the time it was a question of a completely normal and highly solvent citizen of Brusuglio,[36] who had moved across the ocean "with his talent and his will power." In the ascending phase, therefore.

The mother, now, having gone out and come back several times, was also standing, almost trembling, her hands clasped over her lap, waiting for her son to sit down at the table. Racking her wits in the darkness of the kitchen, from the bottom of a forgotten pot, her tenacious hope had managed to root out some pickles: and with those three little greenish peppers, withered, arranged in a chipped plate, a coffee saucer, she had come back into the dining room and had set the plate on the table, in the devout attitude of Melchior who sets, as an offering, before the Babe, the precious pot of myrrh. A sorrowing agitation again hammered out its fleshless minutes: the old and worn minutes! Filled only with heartbeats. Gonzalo continued to stare, like a sleepwalker, without seeing them, at the food, the tablecloth, the circle of the lamp on the table. Very little steam, now, came from the bowl, toward the pinnacles of shadow.

Where was her humiliated knowledge going, with the torn edges of memory in the wind, without cause now or end? Where were busy minds active about truth, with their rightful certainty, illuminated by God?

Black waiters, in the "restaurants," wore tailcoats,

though full of stains: and the slab of starch, with false tie. Only the slab, of course: that is, without that, the most imposing of all pectoral dignities, ever becoming rooted in a totalitarian harmony, in the necessitant physiology of a shirt. Which was lacking entirely.

Affected by a tiny shudder, the ladies: the moment they heard themselves honored by the appellation of Madame by such obsequious tailcoats. "A mixed chocolate-vanilla for Madame, very well, Madame!" It was, from nape to heel, like a thrashing of sweetness, "the pure and hidden joy" of the hymn.[37] And also in the men, for that matter, the secret itch of complacency: up, up, from the groin toward the meninges and the eyeballs: the illusion, almost, of a moment of marquisial power. All the strikes were forgotten, abruptly; the shouts of death, the barricades, the Communes, the threats of hanging from the lamp posts, the purple at Père Lachaise; and the black and clotting rennet on the Goyesque abandon of the outstretched, the spent; and the uproar and the blockades and the wars and the massacres, of every quality and of every land; for one moment! For that moment of delight. Oh! sweet pang! Furnished us by the reverent tailcoat: "A lemon and soda for the gentleman, yes sir! Lemon and soda for the gentleman!" The marvelous, sumptuous cry, full of obsequiousness and a touching concern, more intoxicating than an Elysian melody of Bellini, reechoed from commis to commis, from slab to slab, enriching with new dextrogyrate spells the marquisian[38] hormones of the orderer; until, having reached the pantry, it was: "a lemon and soda for that prickhead at Number 128!"

Yes, yes, they were very highly considered, those tailcoats. Serious gentlemen, in the "restaurants" of the station, and to be taken seriously, ordered of them in perfect seriousness an "ossobuco with rice." And they, with eager motions, agreed. And this, in the full possession of their respective mental faculties. All were taken seriously: and each held the other in great esteem. Those at table felt themselves companions in the elect situation of their poops, in the usucaption of an elasticity fit for the importance of their behind, in the dignity of command. Each was pleased with the presence of the other, a desired audience. And neither chanced to think, looking at his neighbor, "What a fool!" Beyond the Himalaya of cheeses, of fennels, the maître announced the departures: "¡Para Corrientes y Reconquista! ¡Sale a las diez el rápido de Paraná! ¡Tercero andén!"

What's more, the fruit knife was dull. They couldn't manage to peel the apple. Or else the apple skidded off the plate like a stone from a slingshot, to roll among distant feet. Then, with resentful voice and offended dignity, was when they said: "Waiter! This knife is dull!" Between the brows, suddenly, an imperatorial cloud. And the waiter ran up, breathless, with more ossobuchi: and revealing all his consternation, his complete involvement, he humbly laid his appeal at the foot of Their Lordship's wrath (in a more than sedative tone): "Try this one, Señor Caballero!" And the cloud had already passed. And "this one" was even duller than the one before. Oh, rage! while all the others, instead, went on chewing, snorting upon the excoriated bones, wetting their tongues, their moustaches. With a slight smile, oh! a shade only, a tickling of irony, the last and very elegant couple, he she, very faraway, seemed to continue to perceive that apple, finally immobile in the center of the aisle: shiny, and green, as if De Chirico had painted it. Over which, cursing in whispers, à la Bolognaise, the successive waves of ossobuchi-tailcoats stumbled, though with sharp downward kicks, and almost rebuttals, from one to the other: like Meazza, like Boffi.[39] There were some goddammits blurted out like viper's spits, not so whispered however that one couldn't understand what they were: from behind piles of ferried plates, or bowls of mayonnaise, or heaps of asparagus from which melted butter dripped down on the shiny pavement; followed then, all, suddenly, by unexpected windspouts of risotto, toward the rescuing shore.

All, all: and more than ever those gentlemen at table. All were highly esteemed! And none, ever, had ever thought of suspecting that they might also be fools or, let's say, three-year-old children.

Not even they themselves, who still were deeply aware of everything that concerned them, their ingrowing nails, and their warts, their moles, calluses, one by one, their varicose veins, their pimples, their solitary hairs: not even they, no, no, would have formed of themselves such an opinion.

And that was life.

They smoked. Immediately after the apple. Preparing to release the fascination which for a long while now, that is from the period of the ossobuco, they had gradually been accumulating in their person (like static electricity in frictional machines)—there, they, all were certain that an unforeseen decree of theirs would surely have struck the important spark, released the lightning bolt and explosion of Lordship on the suitable atmospheric distributor, of shifted forks. Cascades of clanking cutlery! Of teaspoons!

And they were in fact about to arrive at that unforeseen, and therefore very curious act, which was so insistently evoked by the tension of the circumstances.

They extracted, with absent nonchalance, from their pocket, the silver cigarette case: then, from the cigarette case, a cigarette, rather full and massive, with a mouth-

166

piece of gold paper; they tapped it lightly on the case, shut in the meanwhile by the other hand, with a tatatap; they raised it to their lips; and then, as if annoyed, while a faint horizontal wrinkle was outlined on their forehead, beclouded with lofty concerns, they replaced the negligible cigarette case. Having moved on to the ceremony of the matches, they discovered some finally, after having searched in two or three pockets, a little folder of them: but, opening it, they ascertained that all had been torn out, whereby, with pique, the folder was immediately expelled from the boundaries of the Ego. And derelict, there it lay, in the plate, with the peelings. Another, in the end, came to the rescue, dislodged finally from the 123rd pocket. They unsealed the stamp-seal, ubiquitous image of the Internal Revenue Who Is One and Three, until they had bared in that miraculous little comb the Urmutter of all little sulphur-headed spirits. They detached a unit, struck, lighted; smoothing in new serenity the forehead, already so overburdened with thought (but very foolish thought, concerning, for the most part, articles of costume jewelry in celluloid). They replaced the no longer necessary folder in some other pocket: which? oh! they forget it at the very moment of the act; to have an excuse to renew (on the occasion of a contiguous cigarette) the highly important and fruitful search.

After which, the object of dumbfounded admiration on the part of the "other tables," they drew the first puff of that exceptional smoke, of Xanthia, or of Turmac; in a voluptuousness of sybarites in 32°, which would have evoked the pity of a constipated Turk.

And so they remained: elbow resting on the table, cigarette between index and middle fingers, emanating voluptuous arabesques; mingled with miasmas, this we know, from the happy bronchial tubes and lungs, while

167

the stomach was thrown into a state of joyful murmuring, and went ahead like a desperate amoeboid in mauling and peptonizing the ossobuco. The peristalsis came off with a triumphal progress, appearing a kind of song and triumph, and distant prescience of the drum, the triumphal march of Aida or of Carmen's toreador.

So they remained. Looking. At whom? What? Women? Not even. Perhaps gazing at themselves in the mirror of the others' pupils. In full exploitation of their cuffs, and of their cufflinks. And of their faces like ossibuchivore dummies.

Much advertising of tobacco, or of liquors, of the oiliest and yellowy-greenest had been inspired, in all South America, by the elegance of the cuffs of their shirts. On the back cover of *Fray Mocho,* for example, you could frequently see a cigarette's smoke being exhaled from some character's mouth toward the ceiling, that is toward the physical limit of the page: in faint whorls, very elegant, and the elbow was on the table, and the oily little glass. And the cuff, and the "aristocratic" fingers, and the cigarette, were high and enviable before the virile mien of digestion (of osso and buco), with moustaches, though appropriately trimmed. Ardent, dreaming, souls of the young, mostly runners in offices, of the young and hairdresser-working classes, dreamed of arriving at this: some day! "From the Apennines to the Andes."[40] With that cigarette between index and middle fingers, that little yellow glass on the table, that cuff, those cufflinks. Oh! yes, yes! That man, really, you could see had reached the point where he could say of himself: "Yo soy un hombre." That was no fool's face: no, no.

The son, standing, his eyes wide over the lampshade, remembered precisely that his hairdresser's apprentice, some weeks before, in Saenz Peña, had mur-

168

mured into his ear: "Como me gustaría, sabe Usted
señor don Gonzalo . . . asentarmi a tomar una copita de
licor . . . por la tarde, en una mesa . . . ese . . . del Donisetti (he pronounced it like that, Spanish fashion) viendo
pasear a las guapas en toda la calle . . . a los caballeros
. . . a los coches . . . sabe Usted, ese benedictín . . .
supongo que Usted (he had to smile) todas las dias . . .
podrá permitirse este lujo . . . Permítame, señor ingeniero (and he cut off, snick, a hair from below his
nose)—¿sabe Usted? Come en aquella réclame que
vemos en todas partes . . . Un gran artista la hizo, ¿no
le parece? . . . con esa mano levantada . . . y la copita
por adelante . . . y el cigarillo. ¿Quiere Mag-nesia? . . .
encendido. . . ."[41]

The r's, like guitar strings, vibrated in all their
harsh violence: the stupendous idiom, parecido a una
luz, a una llama, exhaled from the yearning, from the
warmth of the lips. The teeth made one think of a ferocious purity, distant, toward the snows of the Sierra.
The melancholy eyes (on the jars of all the pomades lay
the sunset) glistened with an extraordinary hope.

III

No one knew the slow pallor of denial. Wet nurses torquated with filigree or amber, scarlet broodhens among the children: eyes and curls of children in the peaceful gardens. And clamorous chanters in their choir stalls, where, designed by Scamozzi or by Panigarola, the intarsia had become worn, the single image was articulated into the narrative, became an epic. And Saints of silver, mitred bishops on the pulvinar, drink the rich cloud, the drunken denseness of glory. But time leads also the moments of negation toward shut souls, shadowy prompter of a law of shadow.

The hidalgo was in the room, facing lamp and bowl. He had washed his hands, had put away some clothing, or a brush, in a drawer, upstairs.

His secret perplexity and secret pride rose to the surface within the woof of his actions in a negation of nonvalid appearances. Nonvalid depictions were to be negated and to be rejected, like false specie, counterfeit money. Thus the farmer, the wise gardener strips the fine plant of its drooping leaves, or plucks, unripe, the fruit which has grown flabby or withered despite surrounding nature.

To seize the lying kiss of Appearances, to lie with her on the straw, to breathe her breath, to drink in, down into the soul, her belch and strumpet's stench. Or instead to plunge them into rancor and into contempt as into a well of excrement, to deny, deny: to be Lord and Prince in the garden of one's own soul. Closed towers rise up against the wind. But the progress of rancor is a sterile footstep; to deny vain images, most of the time, means denying oneself. To assert the holy faculty of judgment, at certain moments, is to tear possibility: as one tears an indecent paper, reading lies written in it.

The hidalgo, perhaps, meant to negate himself: claiming for himself the motives of grief, the acquaintance with grief and the truth of it, nothing was left to possibility. Everything was exhausted by the theft of grief. Only the contempt for designs and appearances was safe, that tragic mask on the metope of the theater.

The mother came over to him with an ineffable tenderness, put one hand on his arm, her fleshless hand. (He was taller than his mother, already bent.) "Won't you eat something, dear?" she said to him, almost imploring, in a murmur of love.

Then he stirred; as if to break, brusquely, the weary, the useless pattern of actions: as if a secret rancor forbade him to know the truest tenderness of all things, maternal succor. He broke away from the mother. The passionate gratitude which blossoms in every conscience seemed to become extinguished in him. Was this too, perhaps, to be negated? To go alone toward the night? He went out into the vestibule: his mother heard him opening one of the cupboard doors, rummaging in the large bookcase.

Then he went up to the bedrooms, perhaps to fetch or to take some books there. Coming down again, he handed the mother some newspapers he had bought for her, saying to her in a respectful but opaque voice: "I've brought you the *Gaceta*, the *Fray Mocho* . . . *El Mundo* . . . if you like, there are also the evening papers, the *Razón*. . . ." She accepted and looked at the pack of papers; her eyes became clouded in moved gratitude, happiness, and weeping: she raised her emaciated face as if to await a greeting, a kiss, as if until that moment she had been prevented from being Mama! The son then clasped her to him, desperately; he kissed her at length. An old silver brooch, with a garnet, flower of the maternal years, adorned (and slipped from) the poor trappings of old age.

Meanwhile there came in, clogging, the poverty and fetor of a peon. He was bearing two little logs for the fireplace, and a bundle of dried banzavóis stalks. The storm had chilled the fields, held now by the night. They lay silent, stretched along the measures of the darkness, under gloomy sapphires. The peon groped with his head inside the mouth of the fireplace; then he stood up: it seemed as if, any moment, his trousers were to fall, they were so low over his hips with respect to his belt. From his person and his pants there was released a good-natured odor (so tradition would have it), but certainly odor it was, thoroughly Serruchonese, as "Oh la, José, how goes it?" not laved for years. Rightly, for that matter. No Diocletian had constructed baths in the solitary countryside.

The hidalgo, even in the spreading shadows of neurosis, did not demand special ablutions of the villeins of the Serruchón: for them, after the decease of Caracalla, Holy Baptism seemed to him sufficient cleansing. Only he perceived the odoriferous fact with a certain consternation and at times with wrath. In the case in point, then, he knew that the peasant could have kept himself a bit more in order. The rising delirium of rage

172

allowed him to identify in that indecency a premeditated ostentation of poverty, a demonstration of a trade-unionist nature: demanding some further *largesse* from the masters in aid of that same poverty. For some time now the peon had said and repeated to the Mama, and had given him to understand, that the (scarce) income from the scant land, lashed almost every year by the hail, should rightly be complemented by a salary, perhaps even according to the law: considering that the peon was not in any sense a sharecropper, since he didn't limit himself to working the land, beating down nuts, reaping, harvesting, sawing, and gathering the grapes; but his very presence on the property, in the situation of a master's villa, which was convenient to his masters, and not to him, caused him to assume the economic and legal position of "watchman of the villa." Even in bed, during the night, with the wife, he snored and wived in a watchman's nightshirt. Thus he asserted: and he went on snickering, caviling (with the mother), thanks to many a "so I believe" or "if I may say so."

Now, a watchman is entitled to wages. The regulations, too, demand it: there were explicit orders.

This suspicion had the effect of infuriating the hidalgo: a black rage boiled in his soul, in the pot of miserliness. To be obliged by law to pass on a share of one's own emoluments to the honor of the almond beater! The idea put him into a fury without precedent in the long history of his tantrums. He was embarrassed moreover by his natural shyness, and, more, he was perhaps restrained by his fear of bureaucratic complications, a flurry of yellow franked envelopes and of summonses to the beadle's office, tobaccoish, which were the foreseeable aftereffects of a possible refusal.

Six million Maradagalese bureaucrats terrorized his spirit, alien to official windows as an ocean of embers might terrorize the cautious prudence of the serpent. He did not like the triple ledger of the Paleologues. His mind, which arranged in order necessary facts (which were not, that is to say, appearances, or in other words false substitutes for the Pragma), had a horror of the cavil and all the procedures of inanity. But is contributing to the daily bread of the poor, perhaps, a form of inanity? His Germanic, or Hunnish, blood served him as a quite convenient excuse for harsh refusals.

Certainly, those trousers and those clogs led him to despair of his own clemency. His mother, needless to say, was indulgent toward the rustic claim, as usual: everything that was born of the Villa, or of the Villa-Idea, was a manifestation and mode of the Being, sacred pimple on the neck of the Being-Beast. Even the smell.

If he, the son, ventured some word of reproach at that olfactory exhibition of the valerianates, formates, and caprylates of the Serruchón, God forbid! The peon's reflexes could easily be predicted: first of all a gesticular and facial mimicry of a distinctly hebephrenic character, accompanied by intestinal borborygms of a paleo-Celtic ventriloquy, with sequences of guttural explosions of a savage sort: then, on the pilot-surge of the Celtic cataract, suitably stirred by the agitating blades of a kind of Parkinson syndrome, there into the darkness of the room would pour the no less horrifying request for the payment of a salary. Now, of ancient date was the pact that the rustic was entitled to gather "*pro domo sua*" all the fruits of the earth (almonds and butter pears excluded, of which the latter ripened on their own, without anyone's having to tend them, with the sole assistance of San Carlo di Arona): and that he, master and marquess, was left to deal with the Collector of Internal Revenue, and with the individual Taxes: that is with all

Taxes: municipal, provincial, and federal, and others still which in turn would present themselves at the door, in the progress of time and of provisions—a not at all unlikely situation—from the first centavo to the last. Excluded then from the harvest were the fruits of some trees, nearest the house: cherries, some loquats, a few agriots: and the above-mentioned almonds, which however the peon, an all-too-early riser, was accustomed to beat with stick and pole during the night, complaining and inculpating the hail, not much, no, and passing quickly, but sufficient every time; to cause the ruin of every drupe. The rustic had the usufruct also of lodging with luminous windows over the countryside: a good lodging; which the late marquess had incorporated into the Villa, and protected by a single and egalitarian Roof, thus equalizing in principle and in fact the habitation of the peasants with the habitation of the gentlefolk, not to say marquesses and masters. He, then, the son, but even more the Mama, requited the peon with special tips for special services: and always rather generously compared to the recalcitrant parsimony of the Lukonese landowners, some screwed by the rust of the years, others quite alert in matters and provided with half a palm of sharp nose, but all equally miserly about prices to be paid and dogged in the guardianship of what was theirs: they never ceased fluting and 'cellofying, full of idiot enthusiasm, the healthfulness, the peacefulness, the oxygen, and the low prices of that blissful vacation spot, of those hills sloping so gently up to their respective Enrichetta, or Maria Giuseppa, from the azure basins of the lakes.

The peon went out, came back, clogged like a madman between corridor and kitchen. He, the son, gave him some castoff suits, one or two a year—worn linen, shoes

175

—which were things or stuff still decent and in any case capable of annulling the Franciscan purity of the image (if *robba* or stuff meant suit, as is not the case):

lo villanello, a cui la robba manca.[42]

Such in fact, he thought, is the social function of the hidalgo, and even more of the marquess, in whose name is enscribed, in the ledgers of the Maradagalese registry, the ownership of a Serruchonese villa: to stuff the rustic's pudenda into his own ex-trousers, paying the taxes on his account, after having intensely loved him, deeply bowed to him, sweetly caressed, celebrated, sniffed him, extolling his odorous virtue in the Pastrufazian haunts, and having expelled an appropriate portion of erotic drool in perceiving the harsh stench, the pungency of his feet and armpits, and of something else.

Clogging, as if with a grace note of pedestrian castanets, leaving everywhere pancakes of dry manure that kept scaling off from beneath his clogs, the good man had gone and come back several times for some matches; which then he couldn't succeed in lighting, however much he rubbed them more or less everywhere, cursing, on his thighs, on his behind, and also on the floor, on the wall. And meanwhile he imprecated against the Compañía de Fósforos. (It holds the Maradagalese monopoly for all kinds of matches: kitchen, safety, sulphur.) The flame, ignited by the blasphemy, finally started crackling in the brushwood, in the miserly bundle of thorns and in those few dried stalks of banzavóis from the year before. The victor burst forth then with some amplificatory propositions violently accentuated in syncope. At every eruption of the sound one could see his Adam's apple go down and up along his neck, with the promptness of an elevator in a Manhattan hotel. Letting himself go in a jerking agitation of the shoulders and of the head, he celebrated his bravura as a fireman, lamented the damage of the merciless storm, and the damp, and September, and how costly wood is nowadays, and a lovely fire (sic) is good for the bones, etc., etc.—statements the mother received benignly as if pleased by such a worthy ratiocination. Nothing in fact so softens our pituitary, and sweetens us to clemency, like the good sense of the humble and the healthy discernment that at times transpires from their logos and proceeds in the labyrinth of their vocal impulses.

Poor Mama! She would also have contributed to the development of the theme, on a level of naval parity and great cordiality (which was a characteristic of the Pirobutirros), if she had not perceived in time that her son's humor was again about to change. That oaf in clogs gave himself airs as if he were the patron and the provider in the situation. The son looked at him, gripped by a blind rage.

The dried stalks, the thorns bitten by a rabid, tiny, glory, had gradually kindled and were consumed in two minutes, between the two iron firelogs, crackling and spurting shots of sparks on the floor, as if the fatuous soul of a pumpkin were celebrating his passage in that slight and credulous flame. It gave off low, yellow lights, at the legs of the chairs and of the table, of a soft transcience, as if stirred by a flabellum of mystery: dusty penumbras occupied the inhuman happiness of the ceiling.

No increase of temperature took place in the room, before that apparatus operating by heresay, of no thermal yield, the foolish and absolutely senile fireplace. An ancient epoch was required, and rich tresses of beechwoods from the mountain, instead of the clumps and bumps of the bald sierras or the splintered mountain of Terepàttola, to have recourse to such a poor contrivance.

177

The man in clogs began again. Gonzalo arrested his gaze on the endangered trousers:

"I've told you before I don't want any speeches. Spare us your concerns, and your talk. You make too much fuss, over a few dry logs!" The mother began to fear: on her face anguish was again visible.

The peasant blanched, but recovered himself: and noted that the masters, to give themselves importance, want people to speak in a low voice in the drawing room, as in the confessional.

"You must get out of this house, once and for all: go away!" The man looked at him. "Go away: do you understand? . . . go away . . . and make sure not to come back. . . ."

"What does that mean?" the man asked, dumbfounded: but he immediately frowned. "Gonzalo!" the mother's face implored, pale in her wrinkles, as if behind the bars of finished time. She clasped one hand in the other.

"There's nothing to be said," the son added. "Leave us in peace. . . ."

"Ah!" snickered the fireman. "It can't be a thing that's decided like this . . . all of a sudden. . . ."

"Get out of here!" Gonzalo said with an unexpected violence: and he opened a door, as if to make the command more firm.

The peasant went out after some gulping of words: which burst out in jerks of the apple (Adam's) and in a brief agitation of hoarse, indistinct sounds, as of a mute who had tried to protest.

Gonzalo, then, sat down at the table: and he began to raise the spoon to his mouth, without the entrance of the liquid's marring the genteel form of the silence.

The peon was almost never drunk: and that fact endowed him with a certain superiority over his predecessor, who also employing the same name of José, and the nickname of Estrella, every day fell deeper into the clutches of the demon: the one that makes his home, it seems, one two or three fingers' length, below the neck of every flask.

Normally incapable of a gaze that wasn't the oblique glance of mistrustful avidity, from time to time, but as infrequently as possible, he brought an egg to the mistress: and he celebrated with few blasphemous and bestial accents both its rarity and its extreme worth, in very difficult times for hens. On occasion he added a few rough leaves of a kind of chicory, hairy as nettles, or a half-head of emaciated lettuce.

Gonzalo continued to swallow his soup. A posthumous attempt of his mother's to introduce the beloved José into the antechamber of clemency had had no effect of any kind. Then Gonzalo offered himself a glass of water; then he stood up, opened the French window, and went out on the terrace.

With his hands in the pockets of his jacket, he raised his face, as if to look at some stars. But he didn't even see them (as one doesn't hear words repeated too often) in the superfluous banality of the sky.

After some clear, completely limpid days, the mother seemed calm. Glimpsing him, her weary face contracted into a smile, but the light of that smile was extinguished in an instant, as if at the sudden collapse of an effort. The week's passing brought the lights of autumn nearer, shrouding the hills in it, the villas. In that region of Maradagàl, so similar, in many of its aspects, to our lost Brianza, they seemed the lights of the Brianza lakes. A faint, gilded veil of sadness along the line of the hill, from the plane tree to the elm: when from it, darting, a sparrow flies away: and the tops of the ancient trees, pensive consolers, before the gates of the deserted villas dismiss their weary leaf.

Gonzalo had gone away and come back several times. With his little valise of imitation-leather-colored cardboard, enamel cufflinks, costing cuarenta centavos. For the last year or two he had sworn to himself that he would buy a watch: but he had never found in himself the moral energy necessary for the purchase. He would have liked so much for someone to give it to him. Who? He hadn't the least idea; really, who?

Many years before, when he took his degree, his Mama had wanted to give him one, of gold, that a Russian refugee, or Armenian perhaps, had offered her at a rather favorable price. He became terribly upset: because there were more necessary expenditures (so he justified his rage) and he wouldn't hear of second-hand objects that had belonged to others. His mother, frightened, didn't carry out the transaction.

On that occasion he burst out in horrible vituperations against the Russians and people of the Levant and singularly against "that" Russian. He mistook his geography, in his rage, and his mother then, timidly, corrected him, as one holds out a hand to a child having a fit of temper: hoping that the correction, as on other occasions, would distract him. He greatly admired his mother's memory and knowledge, was moved by them; he was proud, enthusiastic, that she should know so many things and could call them up with such promptness, exactness! But that time they were of no avail. He went mad at the idea. If the Russian were to turn up, he shouted, he would welcome him with revolver shots. There was no likelihood of his turning up, since the Russian was in a little city of the provinces (toward the great bend of the Río Tinto), where the mother was head of a Normal School. He took from the wall a painting, a portrait (as he did also in another access, years later), and flattened it against the ground. The sheet of glass broke. After which he stepped on it: trampling as if he were pressing grapes in a vat, he reduced the glass to tiny pieces. His heels drew a kind of moustache on the portrait, two frightful bruises on the portrait. He accused his mother of exploiting him, her son, as a means or "pretext" for giving some money to the Russian.

His mother, disfigured by pallor, her bloodless lips trembling convulsively, drinking desperate drops, remained with her hands clasped over her lap, not daring to lower her eyes to the tormented memory of her husband. She looked before her, into the incredible, refusing the images as if all living were an outrage: to one who cannot be rescued from her silence!

Many sacrifices she had endured for her sons; so that they could finish their studies, study still further, take doctorates. Now she wanted to show him, with that gift, her tenderness and her pride at the good outcome of a whole career of studies, at his degree: the only one achieved, poor Mama! The other had in fact been granted in memoriam, the shade had taken it for himself. But nothing happens without a reason. A mere whim of iniquity is barely thinkable in a spirit that is not cruel. Though we take it upon ourselves to give the most severe assessment of the aberrant violence de aquel perdido, tenemos todavía que abrir el ánimo al residuo de una duda; y este sobrante caritativo es en el concepto y quizás en la inquietud que un mal tan profundo tuviese en alguna parte su origen, aún recóndita y obscura:[43] that there was a reason or a cause, or several reasons or several causes, perhaps, unknown to humans, irreparable, why the spirit of the hidalgo should be so devoid of all joy.

His degree misted away without celebrations and

181

no one had even bought him a Cinzano. Immediately upon being plucked, the flower of the fake vellum scroll began to wither, with its dry seal, in the great herbarium of the attestations received.

Now the new torment of the wall had come to join that of the terrace (it was losing its stucco, from below the vaulted ceiling, winters and rains harassing), of the damp stairs, of the ferns, of the scorpions, of the unsafe doors and windows, of the shaky gates. He found people in the dining room, like grass snakes, admitted there by a plebeianizing affability or villa-esque permissiveness, both of which led him to anger. Attached to the evidence already is the chart of sadness; in all its details the scene of violence has been drawn. The terrace to one side, that is toward the mountains and the antarctic configurations, was at the level of the garden, whereby the house seemed to rise, corresponding to an embankment (the declivity, in terrain that is farmed, is expressed in embankments) —about twelve feet, the height of a storey. So, before one side of the house and in the slope of the hill that los Toscanos call *a bacio*, or shaded, es decir en el declive de la colina hacia el Norte (en España), o hacia el Sur antartico (en Maradagàl), a little triangular open space, con guijarrillos, allowed every intruder the opportunity of coming directly on to the terrace, through the little iron gate, after a brief chirp. The outside wall, symbol more than munition of private possession, could be straddled and easily scaled by an agile boy, with scant scraping of the knees, it was so dwarfed and asinine, and lacking also, along its withers, the ritual fragments of bottle. Snarling georgophiles are wont to bejewel their own encloistering: "wholly devoted to his work and to his family," as one learns later, some fine day, from the unexpected announcement of their funeral. But the older marquess, with a guirlache parecido, would have felt he

182

was insulting the right of intraspection and the good faith of the populace, which looks, enjoys, and doesn't touch. And the little wall, this too there was occasion to note, did not run parallel to the house (whence the triangle), but instead graced it obliquely, running down like a diagonal. So that one corner of the building, that toward north and toward evening, jutted to within six feet of the enclosure.

Beyond the wall, a rough road: rocky, steeply descending, with crescents of broken dishes, or of a bowl, among the pebbles, or oblivion of a rusty tin, emptied, of course, of its ancient tomato sauce or mustard; at times also, under the livid metal of a pair of drunken horseflies, the extruded shame of Adam, the coiled turpitude; this time, really, the result of some guirlache de almendras, a huge one! ... to be placed on the scales, by God, to see what they weigh; appearances, for that matter, about which the magnanimity of our sensory system, helped by honorable decoration of circumstances, can do nothing, in truth, but pretend not to have perceived.

Traveled by rare pedestrians, the road: and sometimes, in descent, by some country cyclist on his mulecycle; or ascended by the fearless rural postman, scrambling under rain and superwind; or limped over who knows in which direction by certain hebdomadal beggars, male and female, ragged apparitions in the great light of nothingness. As autumn misted away, there chattered bands of roguish boys, barefooted, en busca de higos y de ciruelas, who manage to divine through telepathy beyond every enclosure: of garden (excepting the priest's garden) or of lordly park. There ventured also, with September, a few whorish old automobiles, exhausted by their excesses, by their years, having taken aboard perhaps a whole excursive family, with two quarts of peepee apiece in their tank against the first

183

stop, kiddies boys and girls, and the old rooster behind, sprawled in the poop, who stifled with the paternal authority of his behind the two blades of grass, the two older daughters. It seemed as if a Mechanics, bearer of hams, were hurling itself against the absurd, exploding, shooting stones from beneath its tires, lacerating, with the roars of its motors and the cries of its battered Argonaut-women, the delicate web of all philosophy.

Curbstones of gneiss, outside, protected the wall from the jerks and the long scratches of the axles, of the wagons of gravel, and at the same time debased its stature, already wretched; the carts have protruding hubs, blackened with grease, and they descend to the valley, jolting over the pebbles.

Farther down, within the valley, lay the charity of the village, whence, after the seasons and the sorrows, the trembling smoke of the poor is exhaled: on the anvil you could hear through all sunlight the blacksmith's hammer beating, beating: bending, bending, it marked the hour of siesta, in the silence of everyone's labor taking upon itself alone the travail. From the cave of the forge the strokes were repeated to the mountain: the mountain's reply plunged over all things; from the void time it deduced the name of grief.

And from the tower, after desolate intervals, the bronze number took flight, the dark or resplendent hour.

PART III

The Third Part, unpublished in Italian, was written immediately after the preceding sections, in 1941. The translation has therefore been made from the manuscript, which the author was unwilling or unable to reread. (Translator's note)

I

*T*he son, on the terrace, setting down the little tray on the low column of the railing, his eyes toward the hills' sadness, began to sip the coffee: which was very strong and maternal, unlike what was usually produced by the most distinguished ladies of Pastrufazio. He seemed calm. He looked into the kitchen, to carry back the crockery: and also to ascertain, cruelly, that the ceremony of cordiality and goodness was being celebrated according to the customary program. But he was calm. And the discourse of the two beclogged creatures, so curious, interested him. There darted from his head another irritation, which had stopped as if in the storeroom, the backroom of his brain. But what? Ah! what? Hm! when he was reading the *Parmenides?* Ah! yes, that Peppa was sowing fleas in the house, having collected them, the best of their kind, at the "Municipal" wash tubs. They were really unrivaled fleas, of an incredible vitality, with rainbow leaps over the Eiffel Tower. Into his spirit, excited by the coffee's alkaloids, the gospels crept: "Love thy neighbor as thyself." But the evil one prompted immediately: "Including fleas?" In any case, he stood there and listened.

The report was a bituminous epos, all roars and

breaks. Gutturaloid at the source, the poverty of expression from time to time became canalized in a labored, monosyllabic, oxytone rhythm. Constant interjections and constant shrugs, underlining the drama, with howls, a gloomy array of Celtic *ü*'s, and gargled cachinnations: and, then, denials and smiles with happy remarks. The mien of the narrator and of his *commère* were a part of the drama, like the chorus in Euripides, but here strutting bedecked in critical peacock feathers and according to a rustic arrogance, probably conspired, forgetful sometimes, yes, of the barber, and oblivious of all talcum, but properly exhaling urea, lipoids, valerianates, borneols, and derivates of caprylic acid and of isobutirric acid.

Those vocal emissions and those gestures, according to the basic theorem of modern physics, were the equivalent of considerable electric energy released in (useless) labor: with what showy play of all the muscles, the Maradagalese facies and shoulder blades believe they can compensate for the nonexistence of a linguistic substance.

The peon, in the most dramatic moments, would also have spat gladly: but with the pseudo-mistress present, he didn't dare: since the ejection of yellowish liquid from the mouth (extroflected in a momentaneous phallic proboscis or simply contracted) constitutes an act of such open and disgusting analogy that even a peon of the Maradagalese Cordillera would perceive its unsuitability.

The kitchen was dominated by the gleaming uselessness of the pensioned-off copper, hanging on one wall: there was also the casserole for fish, a yard or more long; opposite, the hearth, without fire. Benumbed by the list of ancient winters the andirons guarded a little pile of ashes, waiting for eternity.

The andirons, the heavy chains, the basin, the rush-bottomed chairs, in the marquess' house, were given the most respectful treatment: only the sons, in a little while, would vanish without a trace.

They had grown up under the hood of the Maradagalese virtues.

And the tale managed to unfold: in short, a theft in the castle of Trabatta. The Nistitúo de vigilancia para la noche had examined it repeatedly, during the fine weather, in the zephyrish species of the most loquacious and brilliantined propagandists: oh! these weren't Celts, no, no. Old Trabatta, naturally, had told them to go to the devil every time with his wiped lips, aspirators of lucid syllogisms. Their dove-colored flannel trousers and their chalk-colored canvas shoes costing eight lire had made no impression on him.

With his white beard, thick and parted in the middle, with his pince-nez on his slightly turned-up nose which seemed to smell the stock-market listings among the rhododendrons, he had about him a somehow wiped and financially elegant air. He was one of the most moneyed creatures in the whole province: shut up at times in the Castle, to enjoy his pears, ripening and therefore hard as rocks: he gave them copper sulphate, then sulphur and calcium, and there were some little pots with water and honey tied to the branches, where the worst wasps remained stuck, so that the pears, when the ripening was complete, which occurs after San Carlo and after Sant'Ambrogio, cost between eighty and a hundred and twenty lire apiece, like those of the lamented marquess: only he could allow himself certain luxuries, whereas the poor marquess had a hard time keeping his head above water.

Putting aside the Celtic dialect in favor of correct Maradagalese, he spoke and expressed his ideas clearly;

he aspired concatenating sorites: resuming at the beginning every time, to be even more wiped and precise.

And he had sent them to the devil. A hundred lire per month? Why, who did they take him for? And yet the price would have been two hundred. For the nightly guarding of the castle, in fact, yes, Señor Trabatta, believe it or not, this was already a minimum offer, a friendly price: a sacrifice that the Nistitúo was making, joyously, simply to have the honor of assuring his sleep and at the same time of complying with . . . of standardizing the requirements. Yes . . . obeying higher instructions.

"But the law doesn't state any obligation," Trabatta said at once.

"That is, well, you must consider the gubernatorial decree 5888."

They should have asked two hundred, according to the price list, reduced, however, to one hundred: and that out of sheer kindness. A hundred: considering the dimensions of the tower: and considering the fact that the lightning rod also served as antenna for the national flag on solemn occasions. According to the laws of Maradagàl the two functions should be divided, that is assigned to distinct organs: since by all logic the antenna of the national flag (and even less the flag itself) must never serve as lightning rod. It would be, speaking Horatially, really a *miscere sacra profanis*. However, the Nistitúo could turn a blind eye, since the Governor had authorized them to turn it. Moreover the flag's dimensions were five by eight, that is to say, adequate for the resources of Señor Captain Trabatta. So with such a flag, it would be a good idea. "To pay more than the others?" the old man said. "Then come out and say it: this is another tax. You make me hang out the flag in order to slap a tax on the flag: and one on the lightning rod. . . ."

"A tax? Why, not at all. The owner has a right to accept or . . . rescind."

"Then what is it to you? I mean what significance has the flag for you?" the financier had asked, removing his pince-nez and carefully drying the lens, his eyes narrowed to zero, replacing the careless sentence with the more polished one, and aspiring.

So, after the wrangling they had gone off, disappointed yet another time.

Now, God is great.

Like the Thina of the ancient Tuscii, the God we have is one of those who knows his business well: with certain pigs, he isn't in any hurry; he lets them have their way, and even pretends he hasn't noticed a thing; he looks in the other direction, because in the meanwhile he is taking care of others, for as far as troubles are concerned, if you start looking for them, you find more than the fleas in a dog's coat. And the other goes on, goes on believing that all is going his way: then He, all of a sudden, wham, flings at his balls the prima manubia, which is a warning thunderbolt: a zigzag whore of a yellow flash, terrifying, with a blinding burst of flame and then a sharp report, that makes your flesh crawl.

The other, ha ha, acts nonchalant . . . yes, he assumes an I-don't-care attitude . . . but meanwhile, at heart, he's already begun to realize that his legs are wobbly. And sometimes he also feels a certain damp warmth in his drawers, and, when he has changed his clothes, the laundress later enjoys that jam. After a while, however, since he sees everything is proceeding as before, he starts up again, the louse. And this is the very time, then, when Thina flings the second trump at him, the peremptorium, and keeps the third in readiness for immediately afterwards, namely the annihilating thunderbolt, headlong. This is the definitive thunderbolt that leaves, where the crook was, a blackish spot on the ground, singed, which sometimes gives off a brief smell of sulphites and ammonia: and nothing else. Nothing else, you understand? Nothing else, nothing else except a brief smell of sulphites and ammonia, which a gust of wind annihilates in the air. Nothing else.

And thus, more or less, it had befallen Trabatta, guilty of wickedness toward the Nistitúo para la noche.

Peppa the laundress succeeded then in being able to egurgitate, with some Manzonian glug glugs like a female turkey, that the preceding night Señor Caballero Trabatta was in his bed sleeping, as he is accustomed to do every night. And while he on the second floor was sleeping, or rather when he had reached the stage when "he snores like a whore"—those were her very words— "they had entered his study," on the ground floor, and had rummaged in everything, at their leisure, and then they had gone off through the park, scratching and pricking themselves surely in the thorn hedge, and according to all the evidence they had reached the Iglesia Road. This runs all along the valley, flanking the Seegrün, which is a long and solitary little lake where the tender canebrake croaks at one end, in the evening, with frogs, under the icy constellations of the Pole. And certainly on the Iglesia Road, motor running, an automobile must have waited for them: which in the Celtic-Turkassian dialect of Keltiké is said "col motor pizz." This is quite different from the Maradagalese language.

Caballero Trabatta, then, had wakened, since in his sleep he thought he had heard footsteps on the ground floor: although they were muffled, steps of Alpine climbing shoes. And perhaps it was a dream. In any case he had turned on the light, had slipped into drawers, slippers, and robe, with a capuchin's cord at the waist, and within, a certain virile palpitation, a financier's. He took his revolver from the bureau, and a flashlight, and releasing the safety, had first gone to waken José and then both had descended the steps together, one beside the other, turning on as they went, one after another, all the lights of the house.

Reaching the study, in that festive ballroom glow into which they had exalted, one light after another, gradually, the whole Castle, a splendor that surely caused a nocturnal peak on the indicators at the power station, and though Captain Trabatta persisted in hoping it was all a "sensory illusion," there were instead really ahi! drawers and papers and books and bills helter-skelter with the letters of his poor Teresa: the drawer of the desk had been forced, the letter opener and the blotting pad on the floor along with the picture of his children at their First Communion, and everything in disorder. A tossed salad to make you disgusted with this world. While, notwithstanding robe and underwear, an ironic little breeze blew from the window—the western window, which was in fact flung wide on the darkness, its aperture punctuated by the cold stars aloft, like candles, over the black spot of the mountain. He, before going to bed, he remembered clearly, had locked and barred it. The devil!

And the safe—*Adieu!* And the eleven thousand lire! For just at that very time he had to pay the last installment of his taxes. And the diamonds of his lamented Teresa . . . His eyes grew damp. Then saying "poor Teresa, my poor Teresa!" he had telephoned to the sheriff, but before he could be summoned to the other end of the wire, it was dawn, and toward nine the police had set off along the road, on foot . . . the police!

"It'll take more than that," José said; "by now they're safe and sound in Parapagàl." And he pointed to the mountains, traversed by the busloads of tourist-brotherhood.

God is great! And the Nistitúo de vigilancia seems to worship historical nemesis, like Giosuè Carducci. Despite that, Caballero Trabatta, going down to the village in the course of the morning, around eleven, had already declared to the pharmacist, to the tobacconist, to the butcher, to the baker, and to the town clerk, that he would not submit to any imposition, to any blackmail (he didn't use this word, but he allowed it to be understood), never. He hadn't chosen to make himself any clearer, since he was a man who knew his way around in this world. And he hadn't even been able to say, "But what does this idiot Mahagones do?" because, rightly, Mahagones would have been able to answer him: "You aren't a subscriber, so you can't expect anything."

Mahagones, in fact, since he had assumed the guardianship of the zone and therefore of the villas adjoining Trabatta, who were subscribers, had also achieved a special ability in excluding from his guard the nonsubscribing villas: they, quite correctly, were abandoned to their fate. How he managed to exclude them, no one knows exactly: perhaps in passing them, he shut his eyes and turned his face in the opposite direction. But it is certain that he observed so scrupulously and so effectively his obligations that there had never been an instance of a subscriber-villa suffering the slightest outrage. The subscribing villas moreover were so pitifully lacking in china and in bed linen, that the thieves could scent from a distance the useless effort and they allowed them to enjoy their subscription in peace, under the starred frying-pan of the night.

At a quarter to twelve Caballero Trabatta had al-

ready engaged two young men of the village, cousins—
and Peppa named and described them: trousers, stature,
appearance, finances, jacket, kin, address, trade which
at present turned out to be nonexistent—who were not
war veterans, given their youthful and vigorous age, nor
ex-deaf veterans miraculously healed by the Madonna
of Pompeii, but they looked as if they could face the
devil, even if he came along the road from the rectory.
Captain Trabatta surely wasn't short of mattresses, nor
of sheets, nor urinals, nor double gun permit. And years
would surely have gone by before the Nistitúo de Vigilancia could have trapped the new subscriber with its
special offer including lightning rod, to slip at every
dawn in one of the many spindles of the gate the reas-
suring paper:

*Nistitúo de Vigilancia para la noche
de la Provincia del Serruchón
Autorizado por decreto del Gobernador
General No. 224488-14-5-1933*

Against the fire and the sureness of the dawn the
"serrated" (sic) peaks of the Serruchón rose, high;
spurts of shadow were dying instead in the great channels on this flank, toward the little hermitage of King
Agilulf, which appeared, gray as stone, and the cliffs of
the mountain, in the somewhat clouded field of the old
binoculars . . . They suggested edelweiss, flowers enu-
merated by the dawn's pallor, Carmelite flowers, and on
the dampness and the clefts of the rock, matutine lichens
which would have made Sbarbaro[44] pensive. . . .
Everything, from the terrace of the villa, seemed to
flee toward its destiny like the rolling trains which, already with the first trampling of the day, were lost,
piping through the moor—and from the faintly saddened

spirit those words could have risen to the lips, the immortal prelude of *The Betrothed:*

> *so that there is no one who, on seeing it (the Serruchón), providing he faces it, for example from the walls of Pastrufazio that look to the north, does not promptly recognize it by its name alone (that is, its serrated line) from the other Sierras of obscurer name and more ordinary form. . . .*

A few days later the mother had occasion to receive another visit from Peppa. The good woman, as Giulio Carcano would say, was shown in by the peon who acted as psychagogue in clogs and marshal and master of ceremonies; although, through the little gate and the plum-tree path, along the wall that ran behind the house, and then on the ground-level terrace, passage was perfectly easy for any simple and limpid soul as well as, for that matter, any more tenebrous one, who had had the notion that it was a good moment to pay a visit to the few members of the family when they were in night dress, or busy in cutting the nails of their lower extremities.

Anyone, any outsider could have appeared, black and sudden, in the frame of the window of the dining room, without asking leave and without encountering obstacles in the path of familiarity and of "we have nothing to hide." The older marquess, builder of the villa and of the ground-level terrace, was and felt himself so pure, and, under the protection of feeling himself pure, he so loved the people and placed such faith in the people of the Serruchón that when it came to locks or bars or bolts or bits of bottle on the walls, with which certain rich old men arm themselves against the temptations of their fellowman, he would not even hear them mentioned. Besides, he was by no means a rich old man, since, after the construction of the villa, he never knew what it was to have a red cent in his pocket.

The peon then showed in Peppa, as he was accustomed to showing in all visitors after having looked them up and down suspiciously and, if necessary, having rudely questioned them. But it is well known that a certain guardianship is universally exercised over old ladies in villas, by their old and faithful servants, of whatever sex. Immediately afterwards the mother also received Poronga the carpenter, who wanted to make a rustic offering of a basket of mushrooms (very mossy, in September, in the Maradagalese Cordillera) which he knew how to gather, nonpoisonous, beneath the chestnuts, after every shower, and guarding himself in advance, with a little ficulne staff,[45] from the coffee-colored softness of the asp; which, coiled upon itself, might seem to the unwary a simple and innocuous turd: woe to him, however, who might step upon it. Excluding infallibly from his harvest the Boletus Atrox Linnaei, which resembles the Boletus Edulis the way a crook resembles his own identity card, Poronga, then, in working hours, built also stools and tripods for the ladies in the villas, who, after having inhaled with full lungs the countryside effluvia, made more piquant by the activity of Poronga's most industrious sebaceous glands, and after the exchange of well-founded and deductive assertions of loyalty toward villa holidays and the Serruchonese earth, they paid him, moved, a few lire the pair. With Poronga there entered the dining room, besides his trousers and his feet, also a mushroom-worker's soaked shirt as well as the patches that carpeted the seat of those tottering trousers, which one would have said were on the verge of capitulation at every word, but which, instead, who knows how? managed to function for yet another minute

197

. . . and another, yes, yes . . . and so from one minute to the next.

Miles of walking and other testimony exhaled in the room. Then the fish-selling Beppina had arrived, with a *B* instead of a *P*,[46] known in the whole area for her custom of peeing in a standing position, in the fields, on the most populated and proliferating anthills, since the garment which should have prevented such an operation or at least have made its sequel irksome was in no way to be listed among the trappings of her person. She entered the room barefoot, mumbling of devotion and rustic spontaneity, offering a yellow tench, enormous, from the Seegrün, which she held, hanging from a little iron hook. The iron, at its other extreme, was bent into a ring wherein the woman had inserted her middle finger. To the glory and wonder of those present, she raised the dead animal, its eyes clouded by an Acherontic lassitude and its mouth open and rotund, as if it were prepared to allow a cream puff to be inserted into it, and instead it was hanged by its palate from that hook.

"Oh! fifteen pesos, more or less," Beppina whined. "What's that, nowadays, fifteen pesos, Señora, what with the war and all . . . after the victory over those dogs of Parapagàl? Oh! if he were only here, my poor Angelino, to see it, a fish like this . . . my grandson, you know . . . the son of my poor Gina . . . he loved fishing for tench in the lake . . . Angelino . . . yes . . . yes, that's the one, right, heee . . . yes, that one, to be sure! . . . hee hee, the one who played with your poor boy, hee, when they were babies no bigger than that, hee, that's the one . . . yes . . . no . . . of course . . . I mean, yes . . . or rather . . . to tell the truth . . . no . . . : he died of typhoid when he was on leave . . . but it was because of all the hardships of the war . . . the bad food . . . Ah! That war!"

198

The mother wanted to say yes; the desperate automatism of her impulses brought tears to her old eyes: to which only some yellow photographs had remained, beyond the coming and going of the flies. In a little while, perhaps, the vain tumult of time would have made her eyes like those . . . If it had not been for the dignity of the eyelids, which fall, fall, like Caesar's toga, over the stupor of death . . . Mushrooms, the tench . . . yes . . . poor creatures . . . it seemed to her, at the close of her years, that the victory . . . charity . . . yes, memory required this too . . . this too was proper . . . In the trembling of her tears she began to admire with delicate expressions that yellow belly of that repugnant and marshy fish. (She wanted to blow her nose, but looked in vain for a handkerchief.) With pitying sweetness, she obliterated the turpitude of the appearances. In memoriam.

Some of the peon's hens then, or chickens, or whatever, keenly perceptive of the idea of Friday, which for them was what for us would be a kind of festive interlude between a sermon and a moral lesson, had progressed, scratching, along the plum trees, pecking at God knows what, and having arrived at the back of the house and at the terrace, as if they, too, were a part of the beloved population, some had even the air of contemplating a downright passage of the Pillars of Hercules, entering there, as if it were nothing, into the dining room . . . But, before the chickens, which flapped away in terror, suddenly in the frame of the French window there was outlined the little woman of the cemetery, and she was, or seemed, a black cockroach on the blazing cement of the terrace: wife to the dwarf sacristan, a seventh month's child, of Santa Maria (the parish), to whom the Town Hall, jealous custodian of the public finances, had entrusted, for economy, the management of

199

the cemetery and the keeping of the dead at half-price and had named him indeed the chief municipal grave-digger on half-time and half-salary, after his Church duties, naturally, and with the allotment of a fixed emol-ument of approximately eight lire per month, in Mara-dagalese valuta. Although, when it came down to the practical matters, he couldn't manage it, tiny as he was; and having dug half a grave, exhausted, he ceded pick and shovel, each time, to the pubescent young manhood of the village who, for half a flask of wine, concluded the job for him, who was eternally glabrous like a baby. To be sure, the bottom of the grave had to be reached some-how because the dead aren't joking, and they want their fine hole ready when the deadline falls.

The little woman, whom everyone called the hunch-back's Pina, but who in reality was Giuseppina or in-deed Giuseppa, along the little plum-tree path and the terrace, after a light creak of the gravel always found a way to slip into the house, kitchen or dining room, avoid-ing the formalities of protocol, such as ringing a bell (which didn't exist) or asking, "anybody home," or else, "may I come in"—all nonsense, these things, from a past time and custom.

She succeeded even in eluding the suspicious peon, she had so thoroughly mastered the cockroaches' tech-nique. Moreover, since it was Friday, the peon's eighty-three-year-old mother, afflicted with hemiplaegia of the left side, came to observe the fast in the Señora's house and there was surrounded by the most cordial care and revivified with the fattest croconsuelo that had ever stunk upon Mother Earth. Lacking teeth, she was in a position to gum it with the highest productive result, treating it with saliva and wine on her lisping tongue.

The peon had not taken part in the war, if not in spirit, having been declared, thanks to his activity as a "farmer," exempt from the obligation incumbent upon the Maradagalese soldier to receive volleys of Parapagalese machine guns in his belly. Many other farmers, his peers, had had to go and even to fall, in the war, but not he, luckily. Still, in the mother's spirit and one might say even in her viscera, the mother-son relationship had become so identified with the war-death-of-son relationship, that she could no longer conceive of a mother except as a lump of inhuman grief surviving the victims. And moreover the peon's mother, hemiplaegic, had in her day wept for a son, who wasn't the peon, but another son. He was indeed the first on the list among the war-dead, on the plaque in the cemetery, because his dead last name began with A.

The French windows of the terrace were opened wide and fixed to the walls with brass chains. The meeting of the fleas and the conspiracy of the more volatile valerianates had enlivened, in the dining room, the bland equinoctial serenity: April entered the room, like our September, from the windows, and some flies, gnats, and crepuscular horseflies, rather decadent in tone the last-named and to tell the truth a bit suspect,[47] buzzed and circled, with a bored and remote manner, over the aromatic basket of those young mushrooms: to whose vital freshness they attributed also (in their imaginative ignorance), the smell of feet and perhaps of other pieces of skin, which were fairly putrid and sweaty, truly, Poronga's.

The hens, the chickens, strutting, pecking, and God knows at what, seeing the nakedness of the terrace, approached the doorway. The sun stewed their brains. Perhaps, although in vain, they were looking for someone to lash them suddenly, as the wrath of God is wont to do, ready to flutter off in an eddy of mad cackles, losing a few feathers, their commanding brains lost, in the schizophrenic syndrome of terror; which is simultaneously torment and inebriation of their privileged natures. They had eyelids at two-hundredths of a second, with brief, very rapid horizontal shifts of the head, where, in fact, the brain was supposed to nest. The olea fragrans had short and glossy leaves under the September sun; sky occupied beyond the fields by a distant bell; leaves, the olea's, of an enameled green; bent, the delight of free-hand drawing classes: from its flower-crumbs, very white and succulent, it gave off a heady reminder, though unique, of the climes of lordship.

The sun and the light were declining toward their sweetness, when the son descended from the *Symposium* or perhaps from the *Laws*, and, unforeseeing, opened the door of the room. He saw his mother, her eyes reddened by tears, holding a circle; standing; and all around, like a conspiracy that finally has caught its victim, Peppa, Beppina, Poronga, chickens, peon, the old hemiplaegic of Fridays, the gravedigger's dwarfed and humpbacked wife black as a roach, and the tomcat, and the tabby drawn by the whiff of fish; but they were staring at Poronga's little dog, filthy, which was now trembling and showing signs, the coward, of being afraid of the two cats, after having sniffed at length and libidinously the shoes of all and having peed under the table as well. But the thread of piss had then progressed on its own toward the fireplace. And on the plate, the dead fish, stinking. It was enormous, yellow, with flabby and cyanotic eyes after its shamelessness and nudity; with the rotund-open mouth as if they had given it to suck, to finish it off, the rubber gas pipe. And in the basket the feet-smelling mushrooms; in the air flies, including some horseflies, two bumblebees, one or perhaps two wasps, a crazed moth against the mirror; and he estimated immediately, clenching his teeth, a suitable contingent of fleas. His anger, an infernal anger, still did not change his face. He had a special capacity for hatred without physiognomical alterations. He was, perhaps, timid. But more frequently he was considered an imbecile. He felt mortified, weary. The old obsession of the crowd: the horror of his schoolmates, of their feet, of their croconsuelo lunch; the stink of "recess," the foolish deviltry; the long processions toward the clogged urinals, in order, two by two; the imperative schoolmistress who said that will do to anyone who took too long: some then postponed the remainder until a better occasion. The disgust that had gripped him as a boy, through all his years of school, the scorn that in the months after the war he had directed against the voices of so-called mankind; through the streets of Pastrufazio he had seen himself hounded, as if he were an animal, by their infuriated charity, of men: of association, of a thousand. He was one.

The years! and the property persisted on the hill; and in the eastern sky the Serruchón persisted, orographic totem of his people, splendor, red dolomite waiting for the Copernicus of Pian Castagnaio[48] to lend it a sun with contrary sunset, a Phoebus-chariot with feedback of flame. The butter-pears grew heavy within the gilded hull of autumn, hard as rocks: until San Carlo, suddenly, employing well his big nose wins them to the drooling of Donna Paola Travasa.[49] One night, all of a sudden. Of what was San Carlo not capable? Teeth, for that matter, aren't needed for the butter-pears, after San Carlo, or two or three at most.

The whole chalice, go ahead, allez-hop! he wasn't the "transeat a me" sort. The whole chalice of idiocy: drain it, allez! to the dregs. Without even stammering back up phew phaugh, clenching his nose between his fingers as when you quaff the purge, the oil. All the foolishness, all the clogging residue of the years had to be the sole thing, to count, to avail, in the world. And it was in his house now, the whole congregation, as the marquess, prescient, had dreamed: "For my sons, the villa, the pears, for my sons." A pity that one of them had gone up in the air, the fine air, in that way: but gravity had worked, the 9.81, with two red lines on the lips of the nostrils, and the eyes, opened, in which the sunset was dying . . . With his lips he seemed to want to drink back his own blood . . . because it doesn't look nice . . . from the nose . . . blood . . . two red lines . . . from the nose. The congregation: as Papà and Mama loved it, in the house, clogs of the dear peons, male and female; they gutturalized their variations, a hundred percent Indo-European belches after jubilation of upturned, mad Faith-propagating church bells: from the tower. Five hundred, prewar five hundred. The clitoris-clapper was the glory, enormous, of the rejoicing village. Five hundred pesos; five hundred. Only five hundred. His jersey, the son's, when he was fourteen, against the breath of the north wind, which in school they called the Borea, had four open windows: this big. And it was necessary to eat little, to grow up healthy, slender. But for the future; the villa, the villa.

Inside the house, now. Populace and fleas, which moved Mama, after her younger son, in the distant years, had looked at those running up to him. With eyes shining, open. Open, still. In the stupor of the dream with no more answers. The fairytale. It was clear, now, splendid, endless, as in the child's book. Two threads of blood descended from the nostrils to the lips, half-parted: opened to the unspeakable truth.

And the piss in which Peppa clogged, from Poronga's dog, filthy, flea-ridden; in which the old woman without drawers slopped, as if it were hers, that piss.

And the pancakes of compressed dung which had scaled from beneath the quadruped clogs, now set to marinate in the piss. In the room where only he and his mother should enter and hold fast; and wait. Their souls should, alone, wait, as if for the return of someone, in the years . . . of someone who hadn't been able to finish . . . to finish his studies . . . Or perhaps they were waiting only for the flight of the kindly angel shaped by the night, by the silent eyelids, by the wings of shadow. . . .

The studies, perhaps, had been finished . . . He had come across with a degree all the same, Colombo[50] . . . with seals, with Victor Emmanuel . . . Laurea ad honorem, the doctorate of the dead. . . .

In the house, the son, would have liked to cherish the jealous reserve of their two hearts alone. Wrath gripped him. But the observation of that obscene plurality overcame him: he felt mortified, weary.

In those days the letters of some acquaintances had arrived. They urged him to complete a work of his, which they, in perfect good faith, supposed a novel, and, what was even more moving on their part, a good novel. If one were to believe their cordial words, it would seem that Maradagàl could hardly contain its longing for his novel, whereas in reality the great landowners of the Serruchón, who had immigrated into the country from old Europe during the second half of the seventeenth century, were concerned only with breeding and shearing the merinos of the Cordillera.

But he was a man, despite appearances and the cardboard valise, of rather strong judgment and, I might say, sharpened. No illusions.

He knew very well what would happen after all the effort and the futility, after the war and the peace and the frightful grief; at the bottom, at the bottom of everything there was, waiting for him, the broad path with the

poplars, smooth as oil. With the poplars of the tergiver-
sating leaves, in the blond light, the asphalted *allée* of
the Recoleta, where the huge electrified beetles slipped
in silence, seeming themselves black shadows, with silvered, trapezoidal trunks. The zinc casket, inside, which
was obligatory according to the Maradagàl law, represented a monopoly of the City Administration, which
charged the grieving families eight hundred pesos. Eight
hundred ... No griever, to be sure, after him, and he
snickered to himself with joy just to think of it: *absint
inani funere neniae luctusque turpes et querimoniae;*[51]
the City Administration would be screwed, this time.
They would have to throw in the zinc for nothing and
carry him to the Recoleta gratis, and hurry it up too:
because his supposed nobility of spirit after a few hours,
and amid general scandal, would begin to emanate an
unbearable stench. The City would have to carry him to
the Recoleta at its own expense, ha! ha! A fierce laugh
gurgled up from his stomach, he was laughing with his
tripes. Eight hundred lire, the zinc casket. The City of
Pastrufazio this time would have to lump it.

He knew, he knew.

Despite this he enjoyed daydreaming at times: and
he allowed himself to receive a kind of caress, from
whom? from whom? if not from the vain light of a
thought, ephemeral as the ray of autumn's sun.

He imagined that some society would present him
with a little watch, a wristwatch, since no woman had ever
thought of it, ever: no woman? Mama, poor Mama.
He daydreamed that the Maradagalese fatherland would
encourage him to perfect his scrawl of a novel:

> *e te molesta incita*
> *di poner fine al Giorno*
> *per cui, cercato, a lo stranier ti addita.*[52]

But he knew very well that none of them gave a damn, at all, and that the novel, bound to real characters and a real environment, was stupid as those characters and that environment were. Fat chance! There were other things to do and to think of, in Maradagàl and in all of South America in times like these. And above all he was sure, or almost, that he was to be considered a fool.

A novel! With female characters! With all that experience that Christ had made him have, so he wouldn't become dull, experience of the human psyche! The psyche! And also of his own.

The others barely saw him. He hastily shut the door again: from the steps, cursing, he started to go out on the terrace. The chickens flapped away, maddened. Little feathers floated down. Clouds passed over, from the mountain, in that sky, so serene and broad that it seemed infinite. They crossed over the distant ridges. They advanced, patient caravans: like the generations of man toward the future. The terrace, of cement blocks and therefore porous, worn, was dry and warm, caravaned by that endless scratching of the ants. And from the thicket, perhaps, of the ivy, there, or there, where a corymb swayed, Puck, perhaps: or the lightning-lizard meditating its dart. The son leaned, bending (given the height of his person), on the wooden railing. And he looked; perhaps, he listened. There before him, from the meadow, were the almond trees, branches erect in the sky, which the peon had ferociously beaten (at night, however), almost without leaves now; a pale blue drupe, instead, with rime, extended by the bold pollens of the plumtrees: the butter-pears, espaliered, were surely harder than the hardest rock of the Serruchón. But San Carlo had taken care of everything. The son looked, looked, as if forever. And surely, too, he listened.

At intervals, suspended beyond any resolution, two notes came from the silence, as if from abstract space and time, long notes and deep, like the knowledge of grief: immanent in the earth, when lights and shadows migrated there. And, softly, coming to him from the remote source of the countryside, the desperate sob died away.

The indecent invasion of the crowd . . . The clogs, the feet, in the house that should have been his . . . The horse-shit-colored heels, the toes, divisible by ten, with the nails . . . And the piss of the cowardly dog, flea-ridden, its right eye full of jam, where splat splot the quadruped soles of those clogs slopped. An enormous belch, futility, the years seemed to him, after the idiocies with which his elders had stuffed themselves. . . .

The nose surely, now, was worth more than the soul.

The olfactory perceptions had befouled the years, the autumns, the months of school . . . The community; the others; the masculine plural . . . The interminable procession toward the piss . . . From the conduits clogged with croconsuelo crusts it poured over the steps of black-ish beola. "Beola, beola!" he shouted from the terrace, toward the fields. The foremen, the practical men, had beolized the simplician city, the industrious and hard-working Pastrufazio.[53]

The older marquess, lovingly, every morning, prepared the son's lunch himself: in the half-empty basket, which was the aereated and still parallellopiped delight of hygienists and of the parents of the period. A slice of boiled beef, known as mannso in Spanish style—that is, a mansuete creature, stringy like a rope of fraying hemp losing its strands, with, over it, a pinch of kitchen salt: Serruchonese and Pastrufazian salt: a roll. Never fruit or a sweet, since the senior marquess was concerned at any possibility of his son's indigestion, even if only imagined. And the little bottle of watered wine. With the cork. Woe to the boy if he should misplace the cork. Hours of anguish on certain sad days, spent in the recovery of the cork: on the lost stopper the hissing severity of the schoolmistress, who entered then with frowning brows, in a state of sadistic tension, inwardly drooling. Pastrufazian pedagogy admitted no replies. The child's implorations proved to be vain. Woe to him if the cork had rolled under the last bench of the last row after having traveled, ever so lightly, through the whole classroom amid the odor and the trampling of eighty-two feet. "I am thy cork and thou shalt have no cork before me . . ."

His educators had been great and above all perspicacious and sensitive, like all educators. Sparta: also known as Lacedaemon: Sparta and, at the same time, a certain modern and Pastrufazian breadth of views. Even the little bottle of watered wine, even the cork, for the Young Master. While many poor creatures wandered alone, or in packs, in the meadows, tattered, merry, with their bottoms sticking out of their trousers, without little bottle, without cork . . . And they shot stones with slingshots, wham, at the sparrows, in the park. And they left, under the bridges, almonded turds, and on the ruins of the Spanish forts crumbling like dry nougats, soaked like babas . . . The policeman chases them; with what results! the Authoritative. . . .

And, for the future, pears: espaliered trees, which bring forth, with San Carlo's help, butter-pears. The spittle of the most chattering magpies and lively and loquacious crows of Pastrufazio, invited to supper, will exert themselves on the buttery pulp of the pear, and so they will keep quiet for five minutes, or at least one hopes so. What buttery mush, the pears, on the croconsuelo-tongue of the old crows, adorned with three nouns,[54] among three teeth. The omnibus-substantive is a patented heritage of the Serruchonese race. An Elysium of butter-pears was, according to the marquess, the future . . . Humanity, beyond doubt, under the golden rays of autumn was tending toward pears. . . .

The son, from the terrace, saw those years again; the people; trees and hills, bells upturned to shake the tower of glory. Whence holy waves in the timpana, like holy water according to the poetic opinion of Abbot Zanella;[55] and it seemed impossible to him that his life had become covered with the film of such nonsense. It seemed impossible that the narcissistic energies of his progenitors had been resolved in pears, in the Josés, in the Lukones belltower, when they had two children, in the serrated Serruchón. "So that there is no one who, on first seeing it, providing he faces it, for example from the walls of Pastrufazio. . . ."

Oh! don't swell with pride: it's the Serruchón, of course. And the walls were the corbeled bastions in the modern century of green horse chestnuts over the jerseys of the cyclists speeding past, with a rain of white flowers in the nocturnal hair of the disheveled women . . . Ding, ding. And the roundabouts and the threadbare magic of the Spanish bastions, at carnival, were discomfort and shame amid the insults of the crowd, in the vulgar cloud of confetti. A discomfort, an anguish, reduced the frightened child to nervous collapse, after the hoped-for and then vanished sweets of the futile San Giuseppe . . . Too dear for the marquesses of Lukones, engaged in the battle of the pears, were the sweets of San Giuseppe.

The child beseeched God to put an end to the merriment. Handfuls of chalk-flour in his eyes; if that was what merriment had to be, he rejected it.

Stupefied horses circled, swaying, in a ring, horns grasped by women riders with legs spread, with torn drawers, he couldn't tell whether they were rents or lace, pieces of skin surely . . . A faint nasal music came forth from the pivot of the great machine, centuries of music and the musical tradition had to be honored, as if Wretchedness had caught a cold. Later in the years that celestial music came back to him with the clearest gouts of moonlight and it was *Norma*. But then, from the carousel, it seemed to him the music of raggedness, of runny nose, of revolt, of nougat, of jostling and fritters, of roast peanuts which precipitate the bellyache into shit.

The hoped-for poem with a pink maiden aloft on the trapeze, who blows kisses, also to the child, to him, to him, was wrecked in the smell of rotting almond paste in the gluey whites of egg . . . ah! how disgusting. The spun sugar, in the brute's huge hands, terrified him. The rogue had hung the pitchy skein of his sugar from a hook the color of colophony, and he shouted: he shouted from his swollen neck: everyone stopped, to hear curses in dialect: and he pulled it, that sticky sugar, and spun it and twisted it, and then he kneaded it into a braid and shaped it into a figure-eight, the sugar, with his hands: and even that skein, subject to constant metamorphosis and stress, to the child seemed guilty, lying: an accomplice of the obscenity: and the man spat on his hands one after the other, to grease them, so that they would slip more easily in that task, the pig. . . .

Melancholy magic, hangings of cheap cotton, faded stockings and jerseys, fringe, the horrible serpent on the shoulders of the dancing girl, floured thighs. The clown who made no one laugh, not for a moment, with his red nose, his foolish face, floured, full of wretchedness . . . A horrid orangutan had kidnapped Cleopatra, nude,

211

waxy: and the woman's hand was encircled by an asp to which she proffered her breast.

She was nude and white, as women must be when they come out of the tub, after a good lathering. . . .

But nothing could be salvaged from the stink, from the horrible dialect, from the braggadocio . . . from the confetti, from the peanut shells and roast chestnut hulls, from the naranja rinds, called also skins. Pink almond sweets, chewy, and girls became foul, in the child's eyes, in the disappearance of all gentility. . . .

What the child suffered was not the festival of a people, but the screeching of a horde of devils, crazed, filthy, in a futile, bestial, devilishness. . . . His was surely, the son now thought, a sick childhood. The man tried to recover himself from that delirium. He agreed to consider himself retarded in his development, morbid, an abnormal sensitivity: he decided he had been a sick child and he was a fool. Only in this way could he establish a relationship between himself and his fellow citizens.

And besides, in the light of psychiatry these phobias of the youth concerning the plurality of bodies and of impulses, are, today, wholly declared. But, then, other crowds arrived from every street: they burst out into the clamor, the savage riot; they pressed from every side, they screamed: they surrounded him. He wasn't a child, he wasn't even war-deaf. He dreamed then, in the futility of that sunlight, as the ants patiently crossed the Ogaden,[56] heroic caravans . . . He dreamed, standing, in the sun. He could do nothing else.

He climbed up to the attic. From a chest, draped with greasy cobwebs, he prized off the lid. Then, he lifted out, in packs, the whole run of *Maradagàl Literario*, as much as the rats had left, one pack after another, to the bottom. . . . His knees became dusty, his nose . . . At the

212

bottom, at the bottom, buried under literature and dust, there ought to be also. . . . The little automatic, the one he had brought back from the trenches. . . . It should be there, it should be there, if the rats hadn't eaten that too. . . . There it was! He took from the holster the light gun, he tested the mechanism, unloaded. . . . Everything was shiny, as it had been then, every cog was greased, every catch as then . . . the vaseline seemed to have been swabbed on it yesterday. There was the loader and the spring: were they in working order? Oh! were they indeed! Snap, the spring! The catch. As on the shoulder of the mountain. The loaders were shiny, with sharp tips, like combs, as when the reddish earth was marked by them, on the breastwork of Faiti; or in the noonday without trenches, ready, in the stink, among the scales of rock, five minutes after the reply.

He went down: the steps of his house. He went down. The room was full of louts. He took up his position then on the terrace, erect, legs apart on the terrace of his house, with the machine pistol, as if he were holding a lovely mandoline, to scratch it! to scratch that mandoline good and proper. *Click-clack:* the spring, the pin, the catch. A shining loader, a comb. The barrel of the mandoline stuck into the room. Oh! what a lovely song, what a mandoline, what a *sole mio*, in the house, freed! disinfected!

The mother appeared before him, bent, serene, looking at him. Her face, with its swollen sockets, the sagging skin, almost yellow, was no longer able to express her inner tenderness: as if the inexorable had already driven from her any possibility of expression: but her love was manifested by the attempt at a smile, by the tension in the eyes, which age had made farsighted.

"Would you like coffee?" she asked him sweetly.

213

He looked at her without answering, then said, grim, "Why all these pigs in the house?"

The mother then was terrified. She had believed him calm.

"They came . . . for a moment . . . ," she stammered. "To bring me some mushrooms . . . poor things . . . ," and she started to go away as if she meant to enter and take the basket from the table, to show it to him. In reality, she attempted to flee, in terror.

He restrained her by the arm, with violence: "I don't want . . . I don't want pigs in the house . . . ," he shouted, fiercely holding his face close to his mother's.

The mother withdrew her head slightly, shut her eyes, she couldn't clasp her hands over her lap as she usually did, because he was holding one of her arms upraised: the arm ended in a high, dried-up hand, now without strength: in a hand incapable of imploring. He let go of her at once and then the arm fell alongside her body. But she didn't dare raise her eyelids again.

The upper part of the head, the brow, high, and the temples, above the arcs of the eyes, closed, seemed the face of one who is meditating in the silent and deep richness of one's being, so as not to know the hatred: of those who are so loved!

So Suetonius reports of Caesar, who raised his toga to his head, before the sudden gleam of the blades.

A desperate sorrow filled the son's spirit: the weary September sweetness seemed unreality to him, the fugitive image of things lost, impossible. He would have liked to kneel and say: "Forgive me, forgive me! Mama, it's I!" He said: "If I find you again in that pack of pigs, I'll cut your throat and theirs too." These words had no meaning, but he really uttered them (thus, at times, the boat, on approaching the dock, overshoots it).

He crossed the terrace and the room, he flung to the

floor the basket with all its mushrooms; he threw out of the plate the yellow sliminess of the animal, without touching it.

He went up to his room, where, opened to the page, the book was awaiting him. He grasped instead the valise, filled it confusedly with what was necessary, poor object, went down all the stairs again, and left the house from below. The lares, unable to follow him, said to him from the bedroom, "Farewell! Farewell!"

The mother saw him going off, descending the path of the fields from the terrace where she had remained. She said good-bye to him in her mind, calling him, calling him, with the name she had given him, distant sweetness of the years. When, more vigorous and green, the horse chestnuts grew thick, along the paths of the Spanish bastions.

Then the smoke rose from the farmhouses, at the edge of the distant west. Half an hour later the train whistled, rolling along the peatbog: as over a deaf, lost world, already licked by tongues of darkness.

II

*T*he two cousins, enrolled for the night by Captain Trabatta, as guards of the castle, where it was enough for them to stay and sleep, and nothing else, and if they snored, then they could snore as much as they liked, had presented themselves as two exceptionally sturdy young men. Sturdy and massive and solid, they were, and of hardened skin, or to put it more clearly, scorched, even compared to those who are already so on their own, or because of their profession. They had also a toilet and a washstand at their disposal, with running water and a flushing system which, strangely enough, actually worked, with cataracts of water over the turds in flight.

One of the two, Bruno Olocati, had also managed to present a maternal uncle of his with a knife-stab in a thigh, a bit too close, perhaps, the stab to the femoral artery. Nobody knows why. It seems, at least according to rumors, that the uncle did his best, moneyed as he was, the old man, and a shopkeeper as well, to steal from him, in his leisure hours, or on Sunday, a certain tall girl, variously identified, according to one group or another.

To make ends meet, also, they had then made good use of their legs, both of them. Along black gorges and cliffs of the Renesquetera, over the howling depths, against the cold of the sleet and the wind, fiercely perforating the fear and the night, they had ferried in this direction more rucksacks of coffee, the two of them, and of tobacco and sugar, from paradisiacal Parapagàl, than the notorious Guitierrez and his whole band of muchachos perdidos: perhaps because the muchachos of Guitierrez, already officially inscribed in myth, took it a bit too easily with too high surcharges added to the real cost of the sacks. So the two cousins in the end performed a double labor and ran a double risk: avoiding the police and avoiding the official smugglers who dubbed them scabs and had already promised to do them in one of these days. The official smugglers were more to be feared than the police. *"C'est de la concurrence."*

As for Captain Trabatta, as has already been indicated, he was one who had an eye for situations and for men and, though a financier, he was not lacking a certain humanity. In 1932, all of a sudden, overnight, the changed rapport of prices and valutas and the unforeseen fiscal provisions decided upon by the Parapagàl government, had permitted all the smugglers of the Renesquetera to stretch their legs in the sweet season of repose, however unforeseen. Some, the more restless and the younger, sitting beside the barmaid in a tobacconist's, or after having tightened their belts month after month, talked of joining up (before being drafted) in the Corps of Republican Guards of the frontier; and, among their number, were in fact the two unemployed cousins, namely Olocati Bruno and Gomez Ermenegildo; when finally, thank God, like manna from Heaven arrived the romance of the robbery of the eleven thousand lire from the left-hand drawer, the second from the top, with a lock, of the desk in the ground-floor study of the castle, with portraits on the floor of the poor Señora Teresa, rendered unrecognizable under the feet of the thieves. Who had then escaped through the window.

Private guards, therefore, for the moment in the service of Trabatta, the two young men were accustomed every evening to take a turn in the park, before being reduced to the slate and the lamp of their briscola game, in the little room on the ground floor, next to the entrance, that the Caballero had put at the disposal of their slumber, flavorsome yes, but at the same time subject to prompt interruption and armed wakening in defense of the sacred private locked-up property: they slept in their drawers, like firemen in American films, ready to spring into action: and to frustrate the snares of the darkness.

The park, toward the west, in its lowest and flattest part, which was planted with fruit trees, and where the famous pears were, with the little pots and the San Pellegrino magnesia bottles filled with water and honey to catch the wasps, and with also, from time to time, a few real pears, though hard as rocks, was circumscribed, the park, by a wall of little account, which ran along the hill and separated it from a small field of banzavóis: beyond those leaves, of the shiny banzavóis, under high and very remote stars, you could glimpse a gently sloping roof, the house of the mother and the son; silent and meek, and as if abandoned in the night, which was silence punctuated by lost sapphires atrociously distant. A little path cuts across that field and leads to the already-described civic road, which flanks the already-described wall of the plumtrees: this civic institution, designated on the registry maps as "civic road on the hill," where it grazes the wall of the espaliered plums is a kind of cataract of rubble and pebbles as big as bowls,

218

and some indeed big as watermelons, but much harder, with crescents of broken dishes and bottoms of glasses and bottles, very sharp, a few empty cans, various turds of various color and consistency, and one or two thread-bare toothbrushes, abandoned to the destiny of thread-bare things, naturally.

Nobody ever went by there at night, because the awful road, which in the end, after many turns and rocks and darting lizards from the brambles, descends to Lu-kones, does not connect in a direct way with any built-up areas. It serves only a few fields of scrawny banzavóis and the Swiss-haughty villas, occupied by gentlemen and ladies, widows and widowers for the most part: Captain Trabatta, Commendador Ponzoni, Tolommei; Señora Carpioni and the various Pia Sapias[57] by whom those very lovely hills had been so dearly gentilified around 1890–1900. The latter, not only widows and sometimes deaf ones, were also rather disheveled, on the pretext that "in the country you can do as you like, with this fine air here!" And the other, even better, excuse that "we don't have to stand on ceremony, among ourselves." These ladies, to train the local working population in good works and to distract them from idleness, commis-sioned stools, rustic consoles, from time to time, and other gadgets and little jobs from Poronga, who, having taken the orders, filled them in a few months and for a few dozen lire the item; elements of a domestic bazaar more and more foolish and senseless as the years passed, though, along with the fine air, it constituted the delight of those crazy old women. To satisfy them all, he worked up to eighteen hours a week, our artisan: with big pencil and saw, with plane and hammer, before Saturday came!: and he painted too; with a paint that meant trouble, afterwards, if you happened to pick up the stool. When autumn came, after the Madonna of September,

219

when the swallows had vanished or were close to vanishing and the various Sapias were about to exchange the
fine air for the other air slightly more musty of printer's
ink of Bottonuto or of Pasquirolo,[58] with great utilitarian bunches of overblown roses and utilitarian rosemary
on tram number twenty-eight, then Poronga delivered the
stool or the console, one evening when they had forgotten all about it: and he found them in the kitchen, half-
blind in the infernal shadows and smoke, with a big
blacksmith's apron stained and sticky, licking their fingers, first all ten and immediately thereafter the big
wooden spoon, with which they stirred some shadowy
and spattering gruel of theirs in a big pot in the fireplace, weeping into it at the sting of that smoke, tomato
sauce or plum jam: which they are accustomed to cook
"over a slow fire," so they say, that is with two or three
mean and wet sticks under the kettle, and then they gloriously ladle it up, smoky and acid, and very sour, because of the sugar economized on: because they are
miserly and foolish like almost all the lady-cooks of
Maradagàl. (There, in fact, the sugar-producing com-
panies are exempted from half the sugar tax, to sweeten
their jam: and they can therefore beat, without difficulty, any lady-cook, even the most stupid.)

Then Poronga appeared all of a sudden, as if the
twilight had produced him at the kitchen door. He looked
like a stray dog, with his coat ruffled, with heavy, naked
bangles: which, however, doesn't bite, and indeed re-
leases an air of self-confidence and the good smell of
life: though rather filthy. He brought in person, in shirt
sleeves somewhat humid at the armpits, the elaborated
and painted stool, sticky, which there was no receiving
from his hands, along with the spectacle of the endangered trousers, ahi, ahi, but restrained however by a
belt, at least for a few minutes more, yes, yes, in an

amphibious probability between yes and no: from which, moreover, healthy artisan effluvia were released, from the better provinces of his person. Paid, after long arguments and sometimes after a glass of wine, from the maidservant's flask, he cordially said good-bye and went off.

One of these mad Sapias, a Lombard immigrant, was also a poetess and charitable toward the poor: she educated pears, plums, and cherries: she made jams of medlars, insipid; she was beneficent toward the mad of San Giuseppe, as far as possible: she rhymed Ambrogio with orologio and mogio mogio: she deceased amid general mourning, in the provincial psychiatric hospital of Pastrufazio on September 22, 1926; that is to say, several years before the autumn season in which the events which we have set out to record took place.

No one, then, passed along that road in the silent hours of the night: or perhaps, at times, with a bicycle which had no headlight, Palumbo came, who had to stick his little slip of paper in some point of the gates, every other villa.

One night, at the moment of playing his trump, a seven, over a black ace, in the moment of suspense and of silence with the card in the still air, preceding the smack on the table, he thought, Bruno did, and then Ermenegildo, or they dreamed, they heard footsteps, down, down, on the gravel of a path; which seemed to be following in the park the path taken some nights before by the thieves, when they had come and gone again, with the eleven thousand lire, along the Iglesia Road.

The two looked at each other, each holding his last card of the hand; they listened. The footsteps seemed to go down, or it was a hallucination, toward the most distant and lowest part of the park, where the arbors with the pears were.

They stared at each other again, they rose, they dropped their cards.

"You stay here," Bruno said. "If I need you, I'll whistle for you . . .": he took the revolver, the light, and he rushed into the hall, then ran outside, into the darkness, without bothering to shut the door after himself. Captain Trabatta, that night, was away; he was in Pastrufazio, because those were seismic days, in the Stock Market, for all of Maradagàl.

The other cousin couldn't restrain himself; he ran up, taking the steps four at a time, to waken Battista; he wakened the women, who immediately began to scream. Then he flung himself down the stairs again, armed himself as well, and ran out after the other, with a light and a revolver, too.

He overtook him, panting, when they had almost reached the arbors, perhaps because the other had lingered, to peer about. He called, "Bruno, Bruno," almost in a whisper, as if they had the police on their heels, in the gorges and among the howls of the Renesquetera. Together in the darkness and in the wind and in the clamor of the valleys. Bruno had crouched down near a limetree: "I'm here, don't shoot, mocoso . . . why didn't you stay where I told you?"

"I woke up Battista . . ." In a sense he had mobilized the reserves, for the defense of the bases.

"They heard you . . . All's quiet now. Mocoso!" Even in the darkness, the harsh, pitiless instinct of the youth could be felt, raging: even in the darkness, one would have said a dog pointing, electrified by a rustle in the underbrush.

"Be careful," said Gildo, whose courage was of a calmer kind; he often obeyed his cousin.

With rapid, instantaneous ignitions of the two lights, they fell to searching, rummaging almost, but where? in the foliage of the shrubbery, amid the populace of old trees, laden with sleep and with shadow or perhaps with ancient peace. They seemed two fireflies seeking each other, in June. The iron bars of the arbor, in that abandon of the lifeless night, supported pears, (among the curving leaves) extracted suddenly from the shadows, by the jet of the light, hard as rocks, shiny. With a bit of bluish rime, on some pears, some leaves, of copper sulphate. In the syrupy water of the pots, wasps and flies, a rotten ragout of wasps and flies. No body. "What'll we do? . . . I tell you we dreamed it all," Gildo said. They were about to go back to the castle.

They had, however, an idea that someone, having gone along the path, had climbed the wall there nearby. And the Iglesia Road, deserted, funereal, took shape again in their minds, accustomed to the night and to the muffled footsteps that travel there over black cliffs. A car, they imagined on the road, waiting for the booty, and the unharmed freebooters. Of course. Its headlights off. But to get there! Or perhaps the shadow, black and mute, which had appeared on the terrace: no telling who it was; it passed the fields and the walls like an image. But they had heard the footsteps, by God! That was no shadow!

Their master's villa had been sacked a month before. Now, for sure, it was somebody else's turn. One of the nonsubscribers, of course. This was the idea that led them from their unconscious, and which later they couldn't recall, or still less, put into words.

At that moment, in their spirits generously turned against fear and uncertainty, and endured to risk under the weight and the sweat of the rucksacks, there was only the laudable determination to go where was most necessary, to be useful at least to someone, to earn their wages, which it had seemed to them, in those first days

223

of loosening of their belts, they were collecting for nothing.

With a leap apiece, the two youths were over the wall. They came out from the path on to the little road, they walked softly, lifting their feet. Each took care to be as silent as possible. At times they turned on their lights, enlivening the stones. A door slammed inside, they heard distinctly, in the house of the mother and of the son, perhaps because a breath of wind came, at intervals, from the boreal gorge of the Seegrün. Then the walnut trees and the almonds and the locusts uttered a whisper as of regret and caress and shudder, which arrived from afar, communicated to them by the rustling of the pines, the lindens: and it was the reconnaissance of the night, the patrol beneath distant stars of the wind. The door slammed again: it was the brief reply of the house toward the hill: the sound came from a little window over the steps: they knew, more or less, the internal arrangement of the house, like everyone in Lukones, from having been inside it at times: to take a basket, to deliver a message, to drink a glass of wine, which the Señora would offer to anyone who came along (to Gildo as a child, the Señora had given a jersey and a few pennies). Reaching the little iron gate, they tried it: it was locked. They hadn't foreseen this, they thought they would surely find it open. Now what do we do? they said to each other. Captain Trabatta, on engaging them, had poured into their brains a few juridical ideas, and had also opportunely remarked *pro domo sua:* entering, breaking and entering, et cetera. It was not right to climb over a neighbor's gate, they thought, still less at that hour.

So they hesitated for some time, flashlights peering sharply, watching; like children at the fair without any money. The house seemed calm, as if it were the house

224

of the dead, under silent stars: which a hand had hung very high in the glacial illumination of eternity. The little wooden door which corresponded to the gate seemed closed, they cast, through the gate's bars, the two luminous circles of their flashlights; the brass of the handles gleamed. It was in order: the shutters at the windows were all closed. No light shone through them. What was to be done? Wake the peon? Call out? But why, for what reason, they said to each other, because of an idea that had occurred to them, just like that. The fear of ridicule determined the succession of their actions: it is very strong in the Celts of Keltiké, it intimidates them far more than danger. They decided to go on; descending toward Lukones, no longer concerned with walking unheard. The heavy pebbles of the road shifted as they passed, they almost avalanched, beneath their shoes. Were the cousins thinking perhaps (though afterwards they could not justify their decision) to reach Lukones and to return along the Iglesia Road, to come, revolvers drawn, upon the supposed automobile? But in that case they could reach it from the park, from the other side of the park. No, no, because now they were at the Señora's house, in quite a different place. Did they consider their duty fulfilled, perhaps, or were they thinking to follow the presumed wayfarer of the night, or to reach the village and waken the people? In war, too, many times, in the darkness, patrols don't know which road to take. The exchange of sounds, between the walls of the villas and the hill, when the wind is silent, are singularly circumscribed. They were not yet very far from the villa when they thought they heard a key slipped into a lock, a heavy key which produced the sound of iron against iron: it was the iron lock of the gate, of that damned gate. Then they stopped. They had both reacted with a start because the key turned with a sinister sound, scraping in the dry, rusted lock: the gate creaked rapidly, on the rodés hinges; then there was silence; but it creaked again and shut, the key rattled again, relocking. Of all this they were quite sure. A footstep, and of this they weren't certain, seemed to move off in the darkness, but all was silent at once.

Then they ran back up again, the gate was locked, damn it! Well? What else could it be, since the key had worked. Nobody there. What to do? It was a house, inhabited. Private property . . . Captain Trabatta had warned them on this score, as if he were warning, instead of them, the thieves . . . Exhaling, taking off his pince-nez, which he had carefully polished with his handkerchief. Private property.

They shouted, "José! José!" It was the name of the peon; nobody answered. They thought then that it had been the peon, going out, though the thing, at that hour, would be unusual. Then they thought to go away, really, this time; but from the western side of the house, where there is the terrace at ground level (which they didn't see, since the gate opens in the long side, the northern one), they heard a leaf of the French window slam, as if the patrolling wind, slipping into the house, had oddly lingered there.

The French window to the steps: the one, to be precise, through which the son, that afternoon, had come out on the terrace.

On with it then! They climbed the wall, they ran to the terrace. They called again, in dialect: "José! José!" from the railing of the terrace. Nothing; no one. They approached the French window, they cast the light-circles of their flashlights on it. One of the two sliding shutters allowed passage. After the shutters, the glass door, the left leaf, ajar, also allowed passage: who had come out there? they asked each other. Since the glass panes seemed intact. They opened the door all the way, which proved splintered at the level of the brass knob and the hook, they cast their lights inside the house. Shadows occupied the corridor: in the bookcases, the books. No one! But on the landing of the steps, just inside the door, by the table, there was on the ground an incredible jumble: a little grass brush, a basket, two brooms, some stools, a watering can, some pages of newspaper. Why? They looked at that interior with amazed curiosity, like two boys observing, through the surgical aperture, the mysterious interior of an organism. Bruno remembered then the Señora's precautions and in another moment he would have laughed: they were the talk of the people. That woman, who wasn't afraid to sleep alone in an isolated country house, still barricaded herself in the house every evening, with an inconceivable anguish. She placed behind the French windows of the terrace, behind the barred shutters and then behind the various doors of the rooms, the most varied and unimaginable furnishings: little armchairs, tables, benches—although a kick would send them flying—stools, brooms, brushes, the empty green watering can, the bottle of pickled peppers, when with a shove, and not even, everything could be flung open anyway, despite those encumbrances. In the dining room, she made José push up against the barred shutters the fairly heavy cargo of the sewing machine (which, as a sewing machine, however, didn't work), and, over it, a little wicker chair, and over this, tottering a bit, an old spinning wheel. "In that way, if they come, at least I'll hear them," she said, not convinced that she was deaf. She believed with great faith in that evening ceremony of shutting and bolting every door, with which she tried to exorcize the imminent shadows and anguish; and in the last few years she had José help her, lacking now sufficient strength to do it herself. It was more a

227

liturgy than a precaution, a magic ritual more than a technical practice. Then finally the peon went off through the little kitchen door and the wooden entrance door, spitting in his flight half-pints of liquid, chocolate-colored saliva; and then put the chain across the wooden door, and behind the kitchen door placed two more chairs, one per leaf of the door, to barricade that one well, too, and behind the chairs, two copper buckets, and finally the glass pot, the smallest, the pickled cucumbers. Sometimes, in the extreme rear-guard, a flatiron.

They called: "Señora!" then "José!" All was silent. The furniture. They didn't dare say anything further: no one, nothing.

The wind, in brief gusts, with intervals of a slow and distant rustling, stirred the poor branches of the almond trees (beaten already, at night), skeletal, fasting arms. It blew through the olea, the plums, the locusts: in the single laurel, the single olive. And it went off, the wind. No one, nothing. The two cousins dared no more. They were in another's house, at night: no one had called them. All was darkness. Fear gripped them, if they were to be found there like that. Something could "happen," even if they didn't want it to. They raised their eyes to the windows of the second floor, all shut. The phrase private property seemed very difficult, it commanded respect, now.

They thought, uncertain, of the outside wall, to go off, to flee. They could climb over it easily, there, at once, more easily than they had come in: right there, at the point which is about two yards distant from the northwestern corner of the house, at the junction of the long side facing north, and the short side of the terrace, to the west. It is the lowest point of the wall, which in September the ragamuffins scramble up, with slight skinning of knees, given the absence of bottle fragments, and with

228

slight wear on the behind. The lowest point, which, on the other hand, corresponded, outside, with the highest curbstone. They looked at it uncertainly, now, in the darkness. Bruno in fact remembered well that morning, a year before, when he had been able to go to the Señora with a basket of mushrooms, and was waiting on the terrace for the money, with the glass-into-the-bargain in his hand, of white wine. The sacristan's yellow, glabrous face had appeared to him suddenly, looking inside, like a sinister apparition of the moor, on the ridge of the wall, among the erect whips of the plum-shoots, as if the moor might abort such spies. All wrinkles under the freckles and the ragged hat, the little face. And in that gnome's face, the mouth had opened: and the gnome, in amazement, had allowed to hang over his lip, as usual, about half of his idiot's tongue.

But now it was dark, all dark: and night. And nobody could spy on them. But the terror of being caught gripped them. The gate was locked. They were locked in. "Let's go! let's go," they said to each other. They scrambled up the wall, one after the other. Swelling drupes, from the suckers of the plum trees, lashed their faces, they jumped, they fell on the ridge, bounced, and rolled forward in the rockiness and the dark. They had sprung on the road, oh! thank God, free to be there. They twisted no ankles, on the stones.

It was only then that they said to each other, "What'll we do?" and decided to sound the alarm in Lukones or in the nearby villas: and that night has not been forgotten. For after an hour or two there were robes and slippers, as of uncombed ghosts, in all the villas, with the lights burning everywhere.

With explicit authorization from the alcade, an hour later, or perhaps more, they entered the garden of the house in a sizeable body, including Peppa, who,

229

summoned from the street, had dressed in a rush and quite summarily, as if she were instead Beppina, the fish-peddler. They entered the garden from below, through the great wooden gate which had no lock but a great bolt on the inside, slipped through two rings, which Peppa knew about. They circled the house, went up the outside steps; they called again, "José, José," and in fact, as they went past, they knocked loudly and a number of times on the private door of his dwelling. Locked. They tried also the little door to the main house. Also locked. Then they came to the terrace. They hesitated, in fear of ridicule; they didn't want to disturb. But, after all, the French window was open, on to the terrace: and no one answered. Where the devil had the peon, José, got to? No one answered. The wind, a brief gust, stirred the branches of the plums, the olea, the arms of the almonds, skeletal, which could barely be glimpsed in the night. A door slammed, inside the house. The wind sneaked off, like a thief. They had various lanterns among them, the kind with glass boxes, square, with a wick inside, which hang, swaying, from a wire hook: they raised them every now and then; weak triangles of a yellow light stirred on the walls, on the terrace: they had weapons, one even had a shotgun, the alcade's cousin a pistol, like the two young men.

They called the mother, the son, by name, shouting, toward the windows of the floor above, putting the appelatives Señora, Señor, before the names . . . but Peppa guaranteed that the son had left that same evening, he couldn't be there. . . . She guaranteed in fact that she had seen him go . . . with a little valise . . . the mother had waved to him from the terrace, saying, "Good-bye! . . . don't be upset."

Then they proceeded resolutely to the landing of the stairway, but they stumbled over something, from the

230

half-opened French window. They pushed the sliding half-shutter into its embrasure. They all went inside, with the lanterns, Bruno with the flashlight: Gildo was going about the other villas with a man from Lukones. They stumbled over some brooms, stools, and even a watering can that Peppa promptly recognized (and explained to the others, gutturalizing excitedly, but in a low voice) as the elements of the evening barricade with which the Señora thought to confirm the closed-idea expressed by the locks; which a thief had fabricated. Behind the two bolted French windows, the Señora piled up tables, stools, brooms, to arrest the furtive footsteps of the night.

The house seemed deserted. Peppa, Bruno, and others were immediately in the kitchen, then in the dining room; and Peppa, after a cursory examination, found the room as she had left it, in the late afternoon.

Then they turned on the electric lights, went up to the floor above, men first, they knocked at the son's bedroom; they called him, "Señor . . . Señor . . ."; they received no answer; they entered: Peppa turned on the electric light; no one. The bed untouched. The great table cleared. On the table an open book, a photograph of his brother, a smiling-faced boy, after all these years!: with one hand on the butt of a machine gun: you could see, in part, the structure of the plane. One of the intruders lingered to look at the photograph, and read then some lines in the open book. "But the laws of the perfect city must . . ."

Some set down their lanterns. They held, in the corridor of the upper floor, a brief council, uneasy. They decided to look first into all the other bedrooms. Two went down again to call the peon and went to the little door of his dwelling; and they rapped and shouted again. The others were there between the corridor and

231

the stairs, puzzled; they didn't dare knock at the Señora's room. Then somebody recalled that the peon, at the tobacconist's, and also in the tavern, had said he wanted to find a new place, since that dog, the son, had discharged him . . . or threatened to discharge him . . . and would have to go to Cabeza, beyond Prado, yes, no, beyond Cabeza, where there was, perhaps, a possible offer.

But others insisted he had postponed the trip, that at half-past six he was still about the house, that the Señora had prepared supper for him: it was her custom in fact to cook supper and serve it personally to her servants. . . .

At the little iron gate, in the meanwhile, another two or three or more arrived from Lukones, other lanterns and voices and even one with a torch; and they started calling from the locked gate and they mingled their Celtic shouts with the Longobard calls of the two who were rapping at the peon's door. And they recognized one another by their voices, like animals in the dark, so that new racket was born, shouts, explanations; urgent incitement directed, from those two inside, to the others, to pluck up their nerve and climb over the gate, and, in the agilulfo-Celtic uproar, though shrouded by the night, warning that they could be stuck like chickens on the tips of those spikes of the gate, poke holes in their belly, twist their tripes on the tips, they should watch out! and then in fact the word trip, "büsekka," plural: "büsekk." And then quips and ironic amazement at the torch, what's happened and protests and new gutturalizing from the cavemen, routed by that alarm from the moonless lairs of their sleep. A bustle of voices, monosyllabic for the most part, epigastric, jolting, shouting, or at most bisyllabic, but oxytone in that case, in spurts and shots. . . . An oxytone-throated crowd barked and grew enormously in the night, with endangered trou-

232

sers, quadruped clogs, crunch crunch, clogs . . . clogs, *zòkur,* triangles of light, smoke, the waxy drip of lanterns and newspapers on the ground, thrown there by the onrush of a gale. From the closest park of Captain Trabatta, instead, the pines, the lindens were animated from time to time, in unison, by their elegant whisper. To every passage of the wind the distant rustle of the night had been a prelude: to every breath of the wind that the almond trees here, by the house, tried in vain to caress, as if to attenuate, to rearrange their stolid tresses, with their rare fronds, like combs.

Orangs clogged about the house, or behind the house, or along the plum-tree path; others on the terrace, in the hesitation of shyness and in the libidinousness of curiosity, asked for news: "What is it, what is it?" In the house, where the electric light had been turned on, among the chairs and the stools that were constantly under foot, the brooms, the watering can, at knee-level the lanterns went on smoking, with the smell of roast paint, the wicks dropped great drops of liquefied wax on to the waste paper, like molten lead, on the newspapers that had been scattered over the floor, from the table in the corridor, and everyone walked over them. The head of the collective serpent was represented by those six or seven, among them Bruno, Peppa, the alcade's cousin, who had gone over the house, above, to the bathrooms and were now confabulating in the corridor outside the door of the bedroom where the Señora was sleeping. They mustered up courage, since no one answered. They knocked at the Señora's room, gently at first, then harder and calling her, each in turn. No answer. But the Señora perhaps was deaf, with age. The door opened: then the second door, too. One of the men stuck his head forward, said, "May I come in," then introduced the lantern; then they entered. The lanterns halved, cut the shadows of the great room that was over the dining room. They turned on the light, they said, already aghast, "Señora, Señora!" addressing the bed.

In the great nuptial bed one place seemed occupied, under the covers. A blanket of very good wool, fringed, colored in checks, salt and pepper, of the sort the English call "rugs" and used when they traveled, in the time of Dickens, concealed almost completely the pillow and the head of the sleeper. She was, Peppa thought, rather susceptible to cold, and perhaps she had shielded her head in that way. But that drapery seemed to all of them to be concealing death.

The trampling of the six or seven people on the bedroom's wooden floor finally came to a stop. Those who had come closest to the bed, to the occupied part, including the woman, called again, almost in a whisper, out of respect, "Señora, Señora," bending over. And Olocati uncovered her. The Señora's eyes, open, did not look at them; they looked at nothingness. A horrible clot of blood had coagulated, still vivid on the gray hair, loose, two threads of blood ran from her nostrils, descended to her half-open mouth. Her eyes were open, the right cheek swollen, the skin torn, also under the socket, horrible. The two poor hands raised, skeletal, seemed stretched out toward "the others" as if in defense or in an extreme imploration. They seemed scratched then, too: stains and drops of blood were on the pillow and on the hem of the sheet.

They realized she was breathing, only the hands were like that, almost cold: slow, weak, the pulse was still beating. Then the doctor was sent for at once; it was Bruno who ran off. In the village they had already wakened him, as if in presage.

He finally arrived, passing through the great wooden gates and the outside staircase: about thirty

234

people had been set outside the door by the cousin of the alcade, who had also arrived, and they stood on the terrace, confabulating, shuddering. No one could find the key of the little iron gate. In the house Peppa had remained, with Beppina, the woman from the cemetery, authorized to make themselves useful as best they could: and some men, those "entitled."

The old doctor from Lukones in that sad situation made himself very useful. He had a four-day beard on his sagging cheeks, not yet totally white, and he was without a tie, wearing a starched collar, frayed and a bit "foedra de salamm,"[59] his eyes reddened as if by a blepharitis, tired, swollen, and narrowed by fatigue and by sleepiness: under the two little sockets the bags were swollen, crescents; they looked like a pair of hammocks or of waterskins. He had brought the predictable with him in his black and greasy bag that all knew, packed instinctively, as over long years his hard, omnibus experience had prompted, then gradually corrected its suggestions with the more and more perfected inventions of first aid. He set it on the little table in a corner. Other encumbrances and bandages he had entrusted to Bruno, who also set them down. The doctor approached the bed, looked at that immobile and so terribly outraged being: "Is this how you found her?" he said, took the hand and stretched out as if with some effort the skeletal arm that the nightgown's laces, falling, had allowed to emerge in imploration and defense, both vain. He touched the right wrist while the other hand he rearranged, placing it against the body, the other arm of the poor helpless woman. He bent to listen to the heart, and again, with the stethoscope.

Then, saying nothing, he took what was required from his bag and set everything on the little table; the peasants were silent, watching; Peppa repeatedly, energetically, made the Sign of the Cross; he asked her to climb on to the bed, on her knees, from the other, empty side and gently lift her mistress, then, bending, he made in the thigh, one after another, three injections, of camphorated oil, of strophanthin, and the third of yet another heart stimulant, perhaps adrenalin, which in fact revived the pulse. The Señora, however, showed no sign of having to resume facial movement, the lid of the right eye, swollen, could not even have opened; nor, gently interrogated by those present, by the doctor, did she answer anything. The whole right cheek was horribly swollen. She breathed now with difficulty, her tongue seemed to have sunk into her palate, a rattling came from it, with her breath. The bloodied and slightly parted lips allowed the doctor to glimpse it, down there, flabby, in the back of the mouth, which it was clogging up. The doctor, with two fingers, tried then to pull it out and restore it to its normal position. The lid of the left eye, with a slight pressure of the fingers, was closed by him. The men lamented: "Poor Señora, poor Señora!"; the women wept and prayed softly, then softly blew their noses, save the viriloid Peppa, who only, from time to time, made the Sign of the Cross.

Then the head, all blood, was gently cleansed, without moving it, without tearing a hair from it, with absorbent cotton soaked in alcohol and then, as if that weren't enough, with gasoline and cologne, found in a little bottle on the table: and that with extreme precaution; all the room was soon aromatic with alcohol, gasoline, cologne, which overpowered the Christian garments of those present. But, to cleanse required patience and time, of the doctor, while the onlookers were horrified. The head, then, revealed two wounds, apparently not serious, at the right parietal and the right temple, and

236

other minor lacerations and abrasions: and that horrible bruise on the right cheek, which was so frightfully swollen, up to below the eye. The hemorrhaging had bloodied the head, the face, the lips; the coagulation had clotted and stagnated in the hair, in the right ear, on the face, below the nose; also from the nose had come a great deal of blood: the edge of the sheet, the pillow, were atrociously red with it.

It was understood by all, at seeing the traces of blood on the edge of the night table, toward the bed, that the wounded head must have struck against it violently; perhaps someone had gripped her with both hands, by the neck, and slammed her head against the edge of the table, to terrify her, or with intent to kill her. For all, the sight of that outraged face was terrible and so remained, when they had known it noble and good even in the decay of old age.

Now swollen, wounded. Debased by a wicked cause operating in the absurdity of the night; with the Señora's trust and her very goodness as accomplices. This chain of causes led the sweet and lofty system of life back to the horror of the subordinate systems, nature, blood, matter: solitude of viscera and of countenances without thought. Abandonment.

"Let's leave her in peace," the doctor said. "Go, go out."

In the unassisted weariness where the poor countenance had to collect itself, swollen, as if in an extreme recovery of its dignity, it seemed to all that they could read the terrible word of death and the supreme awareness of the impossibility of saying: I.

The aid of medical art, soothing, bandages, dissimulated in part the horror. They heard the rest of water and alcohol from the wrung cloths fall dripping

237

in a basin. And at the slats of the shutters already the dawn. The cock, suddenly, roused it from the distant mountains, peremptory and unaware, as always. He invited it to proceed and to number the mulberry trees, in the solitude of the countryside, disclosed.

NOTES

1. *Porta Tosa.* One of the gates of Milan. On March 22, 1848, during the famous "five days," the insurgent Italians drove the Austrians from the city through this gate.

2. *Carlo Dossi.* Pen name of Alberto Pisani Dossi (1849–1910), eccentric Lombard writer, indicated by some critics as a literary ancestor of Gadda.

3. *descend gently.* A quotation from Manzoni's *I promessi sposi.*

4. *Fagnano-Olona.* A local railway in Lombardy. Giuseppe Sommaruga and Alessio Coppedé were much admired architects around the turn of the century; their work was highly eclectic in style.

5. *Upon that same horse until Sunday,*
giving us the war cry "Return!"
As in the times when the gringo, frightened,
left this land in blood, and turned his back.

6. *battle of wheat.* A reference to Mussolini's "battaglia del grano" campaign, designed to increase Italian wheat production.

7. *a bough over the tables.* In some Italian regions, especially around Rome, a green bough, usually over the door, is the sign of a wine shop or tavern.

8. *crawling over stony ground.* A reference to Gadda's World War I experiences at the front, in the infantry.

9. *Babylon.* Gadda refers, of course, to Rome.

10. (Author's note) "The *Mirabilia* of this good Padre Lopez, who in his travels came to know those curious customs, seem to wish to confirm a kind of morality, or ethic, however remote from the usual

239

and perennial controversy of philosophers about predestination and free will and they describe the inner mechanism, proper to the life of every individual. His last chapter, on the approach of death, asserts that it is a separation or extinction of every combination of indulged possibilities: so that it comes tacitly, as if it were walking behind your back."

(Translator's note) The meaning of this passage and of some subsequent passages will be clearer to the English-language reader if he bears in mind that the Italian word *male* can mean both "sickness" or "illness" and "evil" or "bad." Gadda, naturally, uses the word in its fullest sense, which can—inevitably—be translated only partially.

11. *a distant rumbling.* The "Alp without return" refers to the death of Gadda's brother, who was in the Italian Air Force and was killed in action during World War I.

12. *The Song of Legnano.* In Giosuè Carducci's famous poem "La canzone di Legnano," the last verses read: "the sun/laughed, setting behind Resegone." This is a geographical impossibility, much enjoyed by Italian schoolteachers and by Gadda.

13. (Author's note) *Olea fragrans.* In Italian, the botanical name is also the ordinary name.

14. (Author's note) The honorarium of a house visit, according to the fees in the Serruchón, established by the Council of Physicians.

(Translator's note) In the subsequent dialogue, the author plays on the fact that Pájaro (bird), while an imaginary denomination of currency in Maradagàl, in Spanish is vulgarly used to signify the male member (like its Italian equivalent, *uccello*).

15. *the volcano Akatapulqui.* Gadda refers to Mussolini.

16. (Author's note) In reality, of the west.

17. (Author's note) The word must be interpreted in its broadest meaning.

18. *cry of grief.* A reference to the speech of Victor Emmanuel II, on January 10, 1859, in which he spoke of the *grido di dolore* from all parts of still-divided Italy. The speech was virtually the beginning of the second Italian war of independence against Austria in 1859.

19. (Author's note) The chocolates of the Perugina factory are highly prized in South America, and so are the Tuscan half-cigars of the Italian State Monopoly, which are exported in cylindrical tins of fifty or of one hundred, hermetically sealed.

As for the Hospital Visitors of San Juan, they are an association or sodality of the most distinguished ladies of Pastrufazio, who have hearts open to all the poor and the wretched, who languish in hospitals; and also to soldiers who are ill or, in any case, pest-ridden, to whom they bear, means permitting, beneficial gifts.

20. *generous Incassi.* In his poem "Il mattino," the poet Giuseppe Parini (1729–1799) calls the Incas "generosi Incassi"; Gadda makes an untranslatable pun, since *incassi,* in Italian, more normally means "cash receipts."

21. Melchoirre Gioia (1769–1829), Italian priest, political writer, and statistician.

22. *terraces and loggias.* A quotation from Leopardi's poem "The Calm after the Storm."

23. The abbot-poet is Parini (see above, note 20). The painter-disciple is the Lombard Marco d'Oggiono, a follower of Leonardo.

24. Alvise Ca' da Mosto (1432–1488) and Antoniotto Usodimare (1415–1461), two Italian navigators in the service of the Portuguese.

25. (Author's note) Modetia was settled in 1695 at the foot of the last morainic undulations of the Serruchón by some immigrants from Monza, who gave to the newly found city the Latin name of the city they had lost.

26. (Author's note) Descartes opined that the hypophysis gland (Latin: *pituita*) was the "seat of the soul"—the point of encounter, in any case, of the movements of the soul with those of the corporeal system.

27. (Author's note) The good woman of Corfù, weeping with emotion, had let them go at a price, in reality, somewhat high; because of the need in which she had come to find herself, with the passing years. Double, perhaps, of what they would have cost new. "You've finally succeeded, eh!" Gonzalo had sneered, then a youth of nineteen, "in letting her palm these off on you, too." He was more in need of resoling his shoes than of twisted forks; to him she, his Mama, had lied about the amount, telling him a smaller sum: to be able to obey, without the rudeness of that wretched son, the great commandment of charity.

28. (Author's note) In biological reasoning (*species*), we must consider contemporary, forming a reciprocal limitation (Spinoza's "mode"), impetus and necessity of struggle, impetus and genetic necessity. The Greeks, as usual, saw and expressed these phenomena in wondrous symbols. So war and peace in Hellenic mythology achieved states of equilibrium, among the opposing powers of the opposing Ascensions (*Numina*).

29. (Author's note) An anachronistic transposition from the seventeenth century. Of Martin Guerre even Leibnitz spoke in his *Nou-*

veaux Essais. An Italian Martin *redivivus* was Canella-Bruneri, whose long-disputed identity was the subject of thousands of columns of print and millions of lire (press, lawyers, appeals, etc., etc.). Justice, with its rightful scruples, does not heed expense.

30. (Author's note) *"In foribus pugnam ex auro solidoque elephanto . . ."* (Virgil, *Georgics* III, opening verse).

31. *Liebig.* A European firm long famous for its canned meat and its bouillon cubes.

32. (Author's note) With short legs. "Skelic index," in anthropology, is the relationship between the length of the legs and the height of the body.

33. (Author's note) That is, of the Southern Hemisphere. The Pampero is the wind of the Pampas.

34. (Author's note) An unjustified Gallicism for the *Arachi hypogaea* or American peanut.

35. (Author's note) The Liceo Presidente Uguirre, situated in the northeastern quarter of the city.

(Translator's note) The Uguirre is, actually, the Liceo Parini, a celebrated Milanese school, where Gadda studied.

36. *Brusuglio.* A small town in Lombardy. Gadda probably uses it to signify the humble, boorish origins of these Pastrufazian citizens.

37. *pure and hidden joy. (pura gioia ascosa)*, a quotation from Manzoni's hymn, "Pentecost."

38. (Author's note) A pun on the word Marchese (Marquess) and Marchionn, a character of the poet Porta. The author imagines that the hormones of the customer, delighted by the obsequiousness, run the risk of new and marvelous chemical combinations (spells). Dextrogyrate, laevogyrate: terms of structural chemistry, of geometry, and of crystallography: they are used also, in general, to describe two symmetrical molecular structures, that is to say metrically equal but not superimposable (left screw and right screw).

39. *Meazza, Boffi.* Two famous Italian football players of the thirties.

40. *"From the Apennines to the Andes."* Celebrated, lachrymose story in the volume *Cuore* by Edmondo De Amicis (1846–1908).

41. "How I would like, you know, Señor Gonzalo . . . to sit down and take a little glass of liqueur . . . in the afternoon, at a table . . . that one . . . at the Café Donisetti . . . seeing the pretty girls strolling all along the street . . . the gentlemen . . . the automobiles . . . you know, that Benedictine . . . I suppose that you . . . every day . . . can allow yourself this luxury . . . Allow me, Señor Ingeniero . . . You know? Like that ad we see everywhere. A great artist made it, don't you agree? . . . with that raised hand . . . and the little glass in front of him . . . and the cigarette—would you like some Magnesia?—burning."

42. The quotation is from Dante (*Inferno*, XXIV, 7): "the peasant, whose fodder fails." Gadda, willfully misreading *robba* for *roba* (stuff) and then, Gallicizing it, for *robe*, makes a complex and untranslatable play on words.

43. *aberrant violence* "of that wretch, we still would like to open our spirit to the shadow of a doubt; and this charitable residue lies in the concept and, who knows, in the uneasiness that such a profound sickness might somewhere find its origin, however recondite and obscure . . ."

44. Camillo Sbarbaro (1888–1967), Ligurian poet.

45. (Author's note) *Ficulne*—of fig wood. A Latinism. "*Olim truncus eram ficulnus, inutile lignum*" (Horace, *Satires* I, VIII, 1).

46. (Author's note) There is no ready explanation why, in Néa Keltiké, the diminutive "Beppina" should exist, when it is well known that the Keltikese in question knows only Peppinas, Peppinos, Peppes, and Pepps, Pinas, Pinos, Pinins, and Giusepps, all—in both genders—with the hard labial *p*, as well as, of course, the Peppatencia, who is none other than the Queen of Spades. This example is no doubt a misunderstanding, or the result of inadequate philological preparation on the part of the author. Another very curious circumstance, which philological criticism and perhaps even history and aesthetics will be called upon to illuminate is the fact that in South America there are no mushrooms—neither the edible Boletus, nor the soporific variety, nor the various, dread species of Mycetes.

47. An oblique reference to the *crepuscolari*, a school of Italian poets at the end of the last century and in the first years of this century, including Sergio Corazzini (1887–1907) and Guido Gozzano (1884–1916).

48. Another reference to the poet Carducci and his *Canzone di Legnano*.

49. Donna Paola Travasa is described in a little poem by the Milanese dialect poet Carlo Porta (1775–1821) (see Note 38, above).

50. (Author's note) This sentence must be interpreted as meaning that the head of the Pastrufazio School of Engineering was named Colombo and that he had granted the fallen son an honorary degree.

51. Horace, *Odes,* Book II, XX, 21–22.

52. A quotation from Parini (see Note 20, above). In his poem "La caduta," he refers to his yet-unfinished long work, *The Day* (which he never completed). "And, vexatious [the fatherland] urges you to complete *The Day* for which, when sought, you are pointed out to the foreigner."

53. *beola.* A kind of cheap stone, much used in Lombardy and much deplored by Gadda.

54. (Author's note) The three omnibus-nouns, for those who don't know them, are *roba* (plur. *roppp*) ; *mestèe; de fà de polin.* Through careful combination, by using only these three words, the Pastrufazian woman manages to express any of her twenty-two ideas. Naturally this great need is made lighter by the fact that, of those twenty-two ideas, eighteen are fixed. The remaining four are marvelously articulated.

(Translator's note) The three expressions are, of course, Milanese. *Roba* can be translated as "stuff" or "goods." *Mestèe* means, generically, "work" or "job." *De fà de polin* is, literally, "to act the turkey," or, in the Army expression, to "gold-brick."

55. Abate Giacomo Zanella (1820–1888), poet-patriot of Vicenza.

56. *Ogaden.* Region of East Africa, in Ethiopia and Somalia.

57. Pia and Sapia are, originally, in Dante's *Purgatorio.* Pia de'Tolomei (V, 133) and Sapia dei Saracini (XIII, 109), both from Siena.

58. Via Bottonuto and Via Pasquirolo are streets in Milan.

59. *foedra de salamm.* A Milanese expression (literally, "salami case"), meaning "greasy." From Porta's poem "La nomina del Capelaan," mentioned in Note 49.